BRITAIN BY TRAIN

Patrick Goldring is a freelance journalist who has contributed to a wide variety of newspapers and magazines. He lives with his wife in a cottage in Norfolk.

GW00695816

BRITAIN BY TRAIN

Patrick Goldring

ARROW BOOKS

Arrow Books Limited
62–65 Chandos Place, London WC2N 4NW

An imprint of Century Hutchinson Ltd

London Melbourne Sydney Auckland
Johannesburg and agencies throughout
the world

First published by Hamlyn Paperbacks 1982
Reprinted 1983, 1984

Arrow edition 1986

© Patrick Goldring 1982, 1986

Cover photographs and maps supplied by
Central Advertising Services,
British Railways Board

Photoset by Rowland Phototypesetting Ltd
Bury St Edmunds, Suffolk
Printed and bound in Great Britain by
Anchor Brendon Limited, Tiptree, Essex

ISBN 0 09 948390 4

To Joan
who keeps me from going off the rails
with love

Contents

Acknowledgements

In preparing this book I have had much generous help and co-operation. I acknowledge most gratefully the assistance of British Rail's headquarters and regional staff; the national tourist boards of England, Scotland and Wales and the English regional tourist boards; Best Western Hotels; Prestige Hotels; Embassy Hotels; Thistle Hotels; Ravenglass and Eskdale Railway; North York Moors Railway; Festiniog Railway; Steamtown Railway Museum; National Railway Museum; Scottish Transport Group (Caledonian Macbrayne); the managers of the hotels mentioned in the text; and Michael Oakley for many helpful corrections.

Foreword

Gazing out of a train window has been a universally popular pastime for as long as railways have existed. It is only perhaps more recently, in the quickened pace of life in this last quarter of the twentieth century, that we have begun to lose sight of the view. Getting there, however, can still be fun.

Patrick Goldring gives us an enlivening and timely reminder that a world exists outside the train window, and even at 125 mph, the passing scene has much to interest the discerning traveller.

Britain By Train recalls the chunky guidebooks produced by our Victorian predecessors in public transport – guidebooks which combined enthusiasm for rail travel with a lively appetite for the sights and sounds on offer at the end of the line. It is a fascinating mix of basic information about tickets and timetables with tempting descriptions of town and countryside. So tempting, that it would be a man or woman with soul so dead who, on reading the book, did not wish themselves aboard the train and beginning a new journey of discovery.

Mr Goldring has bridged a gap in the travel guide market with skill and originality, and with delight. *Britain By Train* will enhance the rail travel of the regular and the occasional passenger alike.

Sir Peter Parker, MVO
Chairman
British Railways Board, 1976 to 1983

Preface to the Second Edition

Since this book first appeared there have been many changes on the railways and many more are in prospect. The gains far outweigh the losses and the indications are that Britain's railways may be at the start of a renaissance.

Among the losses to passengers have been the lines from March to Spalding and from Tunbridge Wells to Eridge. The much-loved Settle and Carlisle line is threatened, as I write, with imminent closure caused by the bad state of repair of one of its viaducts.

Against the losses there are substantial gains. Electrification has come to the Norwich main line from London and is due to be completed on the East Coast main line from King's Cross to Edinburgh in 1991. A number of stations previously closed have been reopened with the support of the communities they serve. New stations, and the complete refurbishment of old ones, as exemplified by Milton Keynes and Crewe, testify to a new willingness to invest in the railways' future.

New services have been introduced, including the imaginative Nightrider overnight trains between London and Scotland, providing first-class comfort at rock-bottom prices. Catering both on trains and at stations has been much improved and diversified, with a wider choice at the main stations, gourmet meals on some business trains and freelance refreshment trolley services on trains which had nothing of the sort before.

The new proliferation of colours in coaches and locomotives reflects the new spirit of local initiative that is now spreading through Britain's railways. Not only are the main line InterCity trains turning from their former staid blue and white to a more thrusting black and white with a smart red central line but local variations are burgeoning all over; the gaudiest of these is possibly the Sealink boat train between Glasgow and Stranraer. Strathclyde local trains add their own colours, and British Rail north of the border has become Scotrail – with a Scottish blue line replacing the English red. At the other end of the country BR has become Cornish Railways for the purposes of publicity and special offers, though they seem not to have blossomed out in different colours yet. The impression given everywhere is of local managements and staffs doing their own thing with pride and panache. BR is all the better for this diversity.

There is more enterprise too – national and local – in the organization of excursions. The pre-war luxury of the Orient Express is now available for a variety of excursion runs and there are now a great number of day-out and overnight excursions by train on offer, as well as many more tickets for round trips on scenic routes.

The first edition of this book was published during a week between two railway strikes. If setbacks of this sort can be eliminated, then the railways of Britain seem poised for progress which will give great pleasure to all who travel by train.

Patrick Goldring
Norfolk, 1986

1
Enjoying the Railways

Train journeys can be among the major pleasures of life for people of all ages. You can sit comfortably by a window while some of the world's most beautiful scenery unrolls before you – not too fast for you to take in, not so slowly as to bore you. Over viaducts and embankments, following sparkling rivers down wooded valleys, climbing among majestic mountains, the train introduces you to the beauties of Britain in a way no other form of transport can. It shows you the great cities without embroiling you in traffic jams, provides the only enjoyable way of travelling through the great industrial areas, takes you deep into the remote recesses of unspoilt countryside.

All this it does without scarring the country, the railway's graceful stone viaducts and sturdy bridges often enhancing the rural scene and becoming an integral part of it. The train is perhaps the most civilized form of transport yet invented. For holidays, weekend breaks or day trips it is not just a way to get somewhere but an important part of the enjoyment.

The basic pleasure of watching the passing scene in all its variety leads to many other pleasures of train travel. There is the pleasure of speculation, giving your imagination free play with the intriguing sights the train reveals. What on earth do they make in that works with all those steaming pipes? Your guess is almost certainly more entertaining than the facts.

There is the pleasure of meditation. Only in a train, with the passing scene occupying the front of your mind but with no other distractions for perhaps a couple of hours, can your inner mind get down to serious thoughts about life, death, ambition, love and similar matters of great moment.

The pleasures of eating and drinking must rank high on any train journey but the very shortest. Whether you do it in style in the restaurant car on a long-distance express, have a sandwich and a beer in the buffet car or bring your own picnic, there's something about train travel that gives food and drink an extra flavour and the travelling consumer an enhanced sense of well-being.

There's the pleasure of arriving at a place new to you – hearing different accents on the platform, getting the feel of the place as you set out into its streets. And arriving may sometimes bring you the very great pleasure of being met at a railway station, the only location in which this ceremony can be conducted properly. The passenger getting off the train can be fallen on, hugged, kissed, held at arm's length, have his or her hand wrung, baggage seized, arm taken, healthy look admired – all in a place where there's plenty of room for everyone to get into the act and no danger of holding up traffic. If you're not lucky enough to have it happen to you, or to be one of the welcoming party, the next best thing is to see a large family do it properly.

A valuable pleasure of the train is being able to enjoy company to the full. When you travel with a companion you can both enjoy the trip – nobody has to keep an eye on the road.

Touring by train is an enjoyable way of absorbing some of the basic facts of British geography and history. It demonstrates the relationship between the hills and river valleys, highlands and lowlands. It shows how concentrations of major industries close to coalfields have left large areas of the country completely rural. You discover how a move from one county to the next can mean a change of building materials, different styles of building, different forms of farming, different modes of speech, different food and drink; and you learn to love the boundless variety of Britain.

You may learn, too, something of how much violent struggle has gone into the making of the country as it is today. Nearly every castle has a tale to tell of how Edward I tried to subdue the Scots, how Robert the Bruce's men swept down into Yorkshire, how rebellions were raised here and put down there, how the Romans, the Saxons, the Vikings, the Normans, the Plantagenets, the Tudors, the Stuarts, the Roundheads all fought to impose their rule and left their marks on our cities, their castles on our hills.

Just a word about the plan of this book. I start with some journeys that sample the pleasures of long-distance travel. Journeys thereafter are grouped in five sections roughly corresponding with the five British Rail regions but overlapping them here and there where a continuing journey takes me from one region to another. In order to get in some interesting long cross-country journeys I had to tack back and forth from one area to another instead of working steadily through one area before going on to the next. Consequently each section consists of descriptions of separate journeys made, or places visited; some follow in sequence but by no means all. Each journey is a trip in itself and should be read as such.

For the purpose of this book I have travelled over the greater part of the British Rail system, covering thousands of miles. I found this wholly enjoyable and I have tried to convey something of that enjoyment in the pages that follow. But I can only indicate what interested me and caught my eye. The pleasures of exploration and discovery by train are different for each individual. Though particular services may be changed or withdrawn the railways are there and the trains are running for all of us to enjoy in our own ways.

2
Practical Matters

Train travel can be easy, pleasant and not too expensive if you know how to go about it. Here are some practical hints for the inexperienced rail traveller.

Tickets

For most journeys a variety of tickets is available, and although there has been some simplification it is still sensible to ask the station ticket clerk or travel agency assistant what is the cheapest way of making your journey. In general it is cheaper to set out at off-peak times of day, avoiding Fridays (and summer Saturdays). Tickets for such quiet-time journeys are called Savers. They are valid for return journeys for up to a month on any except peak-time trains. On Fridays and summer Saturdays they cost more. They are not available for first-class travel, but at weekends they can sometimes be upgraded to first class on payment of a small supplement. Inquire when you buy your ticket if you want this.

For short trips, and longer ones in the London and South-east area, second-class cheap day returns are available.

If you want to travel at peak times or go first class the more expensive Standard single or return is needed.

These are the tickets to buy if you need to travel to a particular destination.

You get a one-third discount off the cost of a Saver or a Standard ticket if you hold a Railcard, which you can buy if you are over 60, under 24, a student, severely disabled or travelling as a family. Railcards are very good value and can sometimes pay for themselves in one trip.

If you would like to take a train trip but have an open mind about where to go and when, check your local paper and nearest main railway station or travel agency for news of any special offers that may be available. There are many of these, changing frequently and differing from place to place. One-day excursions by special or regular trains, round trips to take in scenic lines or attractive cities and resorts, special bargain fares and much else can be found by browsing through the racks of leaflets on display.

Rover, ranger or runabout tickets are of special interest to tourists and holidaymakers. The names vary but they all offer periods of unlimited travel in a particular area or over the whole system (see page 25 if you are visiting Britain from abroad). In Scotland and Wales you can get runabout tickets combining train travel with ferry or bus. In some areas there are runabouts on a daily basis. Golden Rail offers holidays and short breaks by train to many resorts, with a wide choice of accommodation. Railcard holders get discounts on many of these.

Reservations may be necessary on some summer trains to the West Country and to ferry ports and may be desirable on main-line trains at busy times. First-class travel is worth having if you can afford it. You pay about 50 per cent more than the Standard second-class fare, get more comfort, more space – three seats across the train in a saloon instead of four – and usually a less crowded coach. Some local and cross-country trains do not have first class (the timetables tell you which).

Eating and drinking

On the main-line long-distance expresses there are restaurant and buffet cars, the former for full meals, the latter for snacks and drinks. The lavish restaurant car breakfast is one of the traditional pleasures of train travel. Lunch or dinner is a four-course meal, excellent value though usually limited in choice. Buffets vary, the bigger ones offering hot dishes. Even the smallest can manage sandwiches, tea or coffee and canned beer. Railway sandwiches are perfectly palatable.

Trolleys serving tea and sandwiches, operated by private enterprise, sometimes appear on trains which do not have buffets, but are not always notified in the timetable.

For a day's outing there is absolutely no reason why you should not take your own picnic. Beer and sandwiches or a gourmet feast with a bottle of wine, it's entirely up to you.

There are no licensing hours on trains. You can drink whenever you like and buy drink whenever the buffet is open. Sometimes the buffet closes before the train reaches its destination, but you are usually given warning of this.

Catering at stations has been much improved over recent years. Elaborate meals are still available at the big station hotels and restaurants but the recent trend has been towards informal bistros serving good meals at reasonable prices. I have had an excellent lunch at the Europa Bistro at King's Cross, London and other major stations now offer a variety of restaurants, fast-food eateries and take-away kiosks. At Glasgow Central I was able to buy an excellent bacon-and-egg hot breakfast to eat on the train – at about a third of the price of a restaurant car breakfast. Otherwise there are station buffets varying from elaborate to basic according to the importance of the station. Buffets normally include bars, open during pub hours, but at major stations you will find separate pubs with more of a traditional atmosphere than the ordinary buffet bars can provide.

Accommodation

Accommodation in small hotels, pubs and bed-and-breakfast houses is available near the station in most towns and many quite small villages. The traveller keen to save money can use most of these with confidence. Experience has led me to prefer the private house bed-and-breakfast to the small commercial hotel. Sometimes the pub across the road can be a dubious proposition but if so this is usually obvious from the outside: many are excellent. As a rule, cheaper accommodation is better and more plentiful when the station is on the edge of town than when it is in the centre.

If you are not committed to saving every possible penny, station hotels are nearly always excellent propositions, particularly if you take advantage of the special deals they sometimes offer. In those that once belonged to the old railway companies wonders have been accomplished in lightening and freshening the great Victorian piles, making them into comfortable and friendly places, with space and old-world grandeur – and handiness to the station – as agreeable extras.

When the station is some way from the action a hotel in the centre is often a better bet. At seaside resorts, of course, you'll want to be by the sea. On my travels I looked for hotels within walking distance of the station and found a wide choice, both in cities and resorts. Regional Tourist Boards publish useful accommodation guides.

You miss the sights if you travel by night but if time is short and you want a few days in the Highlands, for instance, a sleeper to Fort William or Inverness could be a good way to save time. There are sleepers between London and Scotland, the north of England, Wales and the West Country and between the South-west, the Midlands and Scotland. In some cases, when the train arrives early in the morning, you can sleep aboard until 07.30 or 08.00. Sleepers are cheaper than a hotel and quite comfortable. Even cheaper night trains are the Nightriders from London to Scotland. You pay no more than the price of a Saver ticket to travel in a reserved first-class seat in a special overnight train with late buffet and even, for insomniacs, a video lounge with free film shows.

Trains

The best trains, on the main routes, are comfortable, well-equipped, clean and fast. The InterCity 125 trains, with their wedge-shaped power units at each end, are the fastest diesel trains in the world. The figure 125 refers to their top operating speed. They serve most of the main-line routes which have not yet been electrified and provide some of the major cross-country trains between the north of England and points to the South and west. Trains on the main line out of Euston are hauled by high-speed electric locomotives and electrification is being extended to the East Coast main line from King's Cross and the Norwich line from Liverpool Street. In the Southern Region most of the lines are electric, with motor units built into the coaches.

On all the main-line trains, whatever the mode of traction, the coaches are comfortable and modern. Most now are open saloons with automatic doors but on some trains six-seat compartments are still found. Most seats in the saloons are arranged at tables but the 125s have some seats without tables and with restricted vision. On these trains the best view is obtainable from seats in the middle of the coach.

Trains on some secondary lines, and many specials and excursions, use older but still comfortable coaches retired from main-line service. Other secondary and most country lines are served by diesel multiple units with the diesel motors incorporated in the coaches. These units include guards' compartments, with space for bicycles and prams, and lavatories. Most suburban trains have coaches with more doors and no lavatories. On some country routes old diesel units are being replaced by trains built on bus bodies. They are lighter, having seating like that of buses, lack lavatories and bicycle space and give a noisier, rather rougher ride.

Stations

These vary from major stations in London and the big cities, which have every amenity, to wayside halts which have none but a platform and a primitive shelter. Major termini, big city stations and important junctions will have places to eat and drink, general and ladies' waiting rooms, loos, left luggage offices or lockers, bookstalls, information offices, plenty of covered space. Cleanliness varies according to local circumstances. The best stations, often in resorts, are well-kept, clean, welcoming with flowers. The worst, in some depressed urban areas, reflect the depression that surrounds them.

Staff

Whether on trains, in ticket offices, on station platforms or over the phone, railway staff are normally friendly and helpful. They are patient in answering questions and will try to help when you have a problem. If you are not sure where to get your train, ask. If your train is running late and you risk missing an important connection, consult the guard or ticket collector. He may be able to help or advise. Porters are thin on the ground almost everywhere, extinct at many stations. Use the free trolleys to push your luggage between station entrance and train. There are special facilities for the disabled: ask if you need them, preferably before you set out.

Information

The more information you have before you start, the easier your journey will be. Information about train times can be obtained by phone (number in the phone book under British Rail) or at the station, where free local timetables can be obtained together with leaflets and brochures about BR services and special offers.

For touring the country it's best to buy the complete BR Passenger Timetable, giving information about BR services, timetables for the whole BR system and some private lines, and a map. If you can't buy it at your nearest main station, consult it in your local reference library.

When you show your ticket you are usually told which platform your train leaves from. At nearly every station there are posters headed *Departures*, listing in order of time all the trains leaving during the day and the platforms from which they start. Many stations also have public address systems or information screens similar to those at airports.

Timetables

These are not nearly as difficult to understand as people sometimes like to pretend but they do have to be read with care. The figures against the name of each station are the times the trains arrive and depart, using the 24-hour clock system in which afternoon hours run from 13 to 24 (the system used in this book). If there is no figure against a station name the train doesn't go there or doesn't stop there. A column of figures in bold type represents a through train. Figures in lighter type indicate departure or arrival times when you have to change trains during a journey. If the arrival time is in light type you have to change trains at the last station showing an arrival in bold type. If a section of station names is marked off it is a branch line and the main route continues after the marked-off section. In some timetables, for instance King's Cross to Edinburgh and Aberdeen, a station name may appear twice (e.g. Leeds). When this happens it is important to make sure whether you are looking at the arrival or departure entry.

When your final destination is not shown on the timetable, consult the route map to see what other timetable you need. Remember to leave time for changing trains; at least a quarter of an hour is desirable.

Train times in timetables are often set about with signs, symbols and letters large and small. These refer to footnotes and the golden rule in reading a timetable is always to look up the footnote whenever you see a sign or letter. It could contain vital information, such as 'does not run on Fridays' or 'Saturdays only after Sept. 30th'. Trains carrying restaurant or buffet cars are indicated by symbols. Make sure you are looking at the right timetable. There is sometimes a different one for Saturdays, nearly always a different one for Sundays. They change every year and are amended from time to time.

Timetables in poster form at stations may be set out on the same principle as in the timetable volume or in the simpler but not always so detailed form of an alphabetical list of destinations served from the station, with a list of train departures and arrival times for each place. Free pocket timetables give details of particular services. Their layout varies in clarity from region to region – some have to be read across instead of following the more usual column layout. Read them carefully and check again to be sure you've got the right times.

It's quite a good idea to use the full timetable to plan your journey and then check with the nearest BR main station before setting out on a trip involving cross-country connections. Station staff can often reel off the answer instantly, may have a locally produced timetable setting out your trip in simple terms and can certainly read the timetable accurately for you.

Bicycles

These are carried free on most trains but there are sometimes restrictions, so check before you take your bike. When you do take it, put it in the guards' compartment and collect it at your destination, or whenever you have to change trains. This is a wonderful facility for touring in the country and increases the traveller's range considerably.

Children

The train is the only mode of land transport which allows children to move about freely when they get restless, lets them go to the loo whenever they feel the need, makes it easy to give them food and drink on the way, provides them with something to watch continually and offers facilities for them to read, play Scrabble, solve crosswords or do jigsaws when they are tired of watching. Train-travelling children don't need special games to distract them because they can take cards or their own favourite games, puzzles or toys with them.

Encourage the kids to join BR's own Rail Riders' Club. It gives all the usual children's club essentials – badge, news magazine and so on – helps them to get more interest out of railway journeys and gives them cheap travel.

Children get cheap travel in other ways too, of course: free under five, half-price for under-sixteens, much less if they accompany parents with a Family Railcard or annual season ticket holder's Railcard, or grandparents with a Senior Citizen Railcard.

Planning a trip

Whether it's a day out or a fortnight's tour, it's best to plan ahead. Work out the trains from the timetable and make a note of them, check for possible special fares, get tickets in advance where necessary or convenient, lay in food and drink. Get a map and take it with you. Read about the places you are going to.

If you are spending a day in town decide beforehand what you are going to do – you can't do everything in a day. If you are going for more than a day, check for possible hotel deals. Tourist offices can be helpful, with information about places to visit and with ideas for outings.

Britrail Pass

For overseas visitors on holiday in Britain the best train travel bargain is the Britrail Pass. You buy this in your own country before your visit, through your local travel agent. It is also available from American or Canadian offices of Britrail Travel International Inc. Further advice can be obtained from British Tourist Authority overseas offices, listed on pages 235–6.

The Britrail Pass provides unlimited train travel in Britain for whatever period of time you choose. You don't have to decide the starting date until you have the card validated, which is done in Britain at a British Rail station or travel centre.

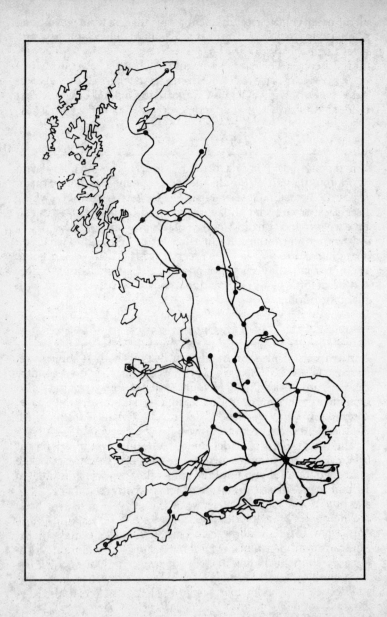

3

The Length and Breadth
of Britain

Britain has many faces and so has British Rail, as I found on these long-distance trips. High speed on the main lines to Scotland or leisurely progress on cross-country routes – each train journey has a character all its own.

Royal Scot to Glasgow

Every two hours, about five and a half hours
Euston is the proper place to start touring Britain by train. Even without the great Doric arch which once proclaimed the triumph of the railways it is impressive as perhaps Britain's most important station in terms of destinations. It was the terminus of Britain's first trunk trailway, the London and Birmingham, which began carrying passengers in 1838. Today it is the station from which to set out from London for most of Scotland, Ireland and Wales. From the capital it serves Britain's four greatest centres of population, Birmingham, Glasgow, Liverpool and Manchester. The electrified main line from Euston to Glasgow Central constitutes the backbone of Britain's rail services.

The modern station, rebuilt in the sixties, proclaims its importance in the sheer size and spaciousness of its concourse, a huge airy box in which passengers take on the elegance of figures in an architect's drawing. It is designed for standing and walking in and only a few seats are allowed to cluster round its cental pillars. There are waiting rooms, several bars, a pub, a restaurant and a range of shops including a small supermarket. Out-of-town influence is marked. Scotland provides knots of travellers in tweeds and deerstalkers and a contingent of whisky drinkers in the bar; the train announcer's voice is unmistakably Irish.

Our first train-ride must be the 401 miles to Glasgow. We could go comfortably overnight and get to Glasgow for an early breakfast but this time we want to see the view, so we take the 9.45 Royal Scot, conveniently timed and the fastest train of the day, taking five hours 4 minutes with stops at Preston and Carlisle.

From Euston's elegant concourse, from which no trains are visible, it's something of an anti-climax to find the ramp for platform 4 and descend into a train shed with a utilitarian low roof. The soaring roofs of the other great termini were built in the days when steam locomotives blew clouds of smoke into the air. No need for them in a station served by electric traction but you miss them all the same. They give a sense of occasion.

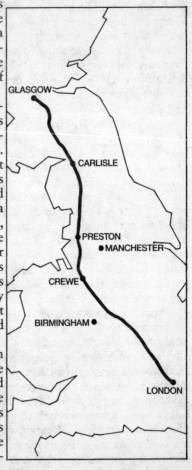

The train we join has air-conditioned InterCity coaches hauled by an electric locomotive, the *Sir Walter Scott*. The seats are comfortable, set out on an open plan with tables between; inner doors open and close automatically. There is a restaurant car and a buffet, coffee brought to our seats; the guard announces the stops over a public address system; all is clean and comfortable. This is British Rail travel at its very considerable best, a most civilized blend of speed and comfort.

We slide out of the station silently and on time. There are two main lines to Scotland from London. This one, the Euston–Glasgow line, runs west of the Pennines, England's mountain backbone. The other, King's Cross–Edinburgh, is eight miles shorter and runs up the eastern side of England over mostly flat country. In the last century competing railways companies raced to Scotland and the rivalry continued right up until the last war, with the London, Midland and Scottish Company's *Royal Scot* fighting it out with the London and North Eastern's *Flying Scotsman*. The LNER had the advantage of flat ground and its streamlined locomotive *Mallard* created a world record, still unbroken, of 126 mph under steam. The LMS had to develop more powerful locomotives to haul its trains over the two great summits of Shap and Beattock.

The competition never had an outright winner. It simply established what each line did best. Today, trains from Euston serve Glasgow and the Highlands, the East Coast line from King's Cross serving Edinburgh, Dundee and Aberdeen, with a train also to Inverness.

We pull briskly out through the tunnels under Camden Town and Primrose Hill and pick up speed through the north-west London suburbs. The bulk of Wembley Stadium, scene of modern battles between the English and the Scots, slides past on our right. Harrow on the Hill, where Churchill went to school, stands up out of a sea of semis on the left and we're away into Hertfordshire. Watford Junction, about 15 minutes from Euston, is the end of the suburban line. Time now for coffee in the dining car, where a party of four is already into a round of gins: no doubt a business conference. You can drink all the way to Scotland if you like and some do.

Now we've raced out through the Home Counties, getting an impression of neat towns of commuter houses, clean, light industry and modest prosperity. Whatever terrible things are happening to the country's economy are having least effect here.

We climb out through the Chiltern Hills between Tring and Aldbury and now we're into flat country which hardly begins to lift until we're in Staffordshire. There is a spanking new station at Milton Keynes, where a new town is knitting together several small places into a town the size of Southampton. It's still a bit far-flung and all we can see are a few distant factories.

We're now getting into the Midlands and here is red-brick Rugby with extensive sidings to prove that we're out of the effete south into those places where real work is done. Rugby is famous for its public school and its form of football, of course, but we see cement works, streets of small terrace houses and the great aerial of the Government radio station, draped over a small forest of masts.

It's one of the features of the line to Glasgow that it doesn't actually pass through any of the great conurbations on the way. It slips between Liverpool and Manchester. Trains for Coventry and Birmingham branch off to the left after Rugby and we see Coventry's tower blocks and cathedral spire as we pass. No sign of Birmingham, but we pass through the edge of its small, gracious neighbour, the city of Lichfield, Dr Johnson's birthplace.

Now comes the first lifting of the hills to show we're leaving the Midlands plain to go through Staffordshire and we're faintly surprised to find the county town alive with engineering industry. The potteries for which the county is famous are around Stoke-on-Trent, on the line which branches off to Manchester.

We're now beginning to appreciate the characteristic landmarks of this country, the clumps of huge cooling towers giving off clouds of white smoke from steel works or power stations, and the winding gear, topped by large wheels, which indicates coal mines.

Crewe, through which we now slip smoothly, is the most famous of all railway towns. Before the railways came there was nothing here but a few cottages. It grew to importance as the site of the big locomotive works and as the railway crossroads of the North-west. It's a changing point for Manchester, Liverpool, North Wales, Hereford and South Wales. Passengers for Ireland are switched west to Holyhead while those for Scotland go on through Warrington and Wigan.

It was in Crewe, in the days of Victorian music hall, that the young lady who wanted to go to Birmingham found herself stranded and sang: 'Oh, Mr Porter, what shall I do?' Touring theatrical companies of the time, doomed to move always on Sundays, traditionally spent long hours on its platforms.

Here's Preston, just over halfway to Glasgow, first stop after two hours 42 minutes. Its reputation is for being proud, perhaps because it is on a hill, perhaps because it stands well clear of the shapeless conurbation that embraces Greater Manchester and Merseyside. Preston is indisputably Lancashire and has the mills to prove it.

These mill buildings, another prominent feature of the scene in the North, are no mere factories. They stand four-square like fortresses of industry, great brick castles with tall chimneys sentinel beside them. In their heyday they would be proudly flying the firm's house flag from a tower. Now, all too many are empty and seeking tenants.

Time now for lunch in the dining car as we pull out of Preston. The menu says roast beef or fillet of plaice, but the chief steward has some trout and this is now served, perfectly grilled, to be washed down with a good chilled white wine costing less than you'd pay in a restaurant. The meal, miraculously cooked and served at high speed, is certainly as good as in many a pricier restaurant which is not going anywhere and has no view. Whereas by the time we've finished our cheese and coffee we've had the whole of the Lake District mountains paraded past the window on our left.

After the train passes Oxenholme, where the Windermere line branches off, we're given a panoramic view of majestic hills which include the Old Man of Coniston, Scafell Pike, at 3210 feet the highest mountain in England, Bow Fell, Great Gable and Langdale Pikes. Later, from Penrith, there's a view of Helvellyn. Lovely country, all this. We take in the general picture as we whisk through. We can see it in more detail at our leisure.

Now we're climbing the famous Shap gradient, one in 75 for four miles and steep in railway terms. Steam locomotives used to puff and grunt a bit on this but we hardly notice except for the pick-up of extra speed when we're over the summit, 916 feet above sea level, and have started the run down to Penrith and Carlisle.

Carlisle, near the western end of Hadrian's Wall, was a border stronghold against the Scots, as a suitably forbidding piece of fortified wall and castle looming over the line reminds us. The train now moves off again across the marshland at the end of the Solway Firth, which can be seen on the left. Soon after crossing the River Esk we're over the border into Scotland.

The border village is Gretna Green, where runaway couples used to be married without banns by the blacksmith under Scots law. It didn't have to be the blacksmith – several local characters were in the marriage business – and it was a lucrative trade until a change in the law put a stop to it.

Like so many romantic affairs, it had its sordid side. Many of the elopers were adventurers abducting heiresses to get their hands on the loot. They had to get the girl across the border and married, before her guardians caught up. Nowadays any railway runaways would have to carry on to Lockerbie, the first station in Scotland on the main line.

Beattock is desolate moorland but soon the train is over into the Upper Clyde valley, following this pretty, sparkling stream down between the Lowther and Tweedsmuir hills through the southern uplands and into the industrial spread of the Glasgow area that begins at Motherwell.

We meet the Clyde again as an urban waterway when our train rolls over a bridge and clatters across points to its platform under the glass and steel canopy of Glasgow Central station. Voices, faces, clothes, the feel of the place tell us we're in a different country and the train has shown us some of the variety of life – the contentment, the striving, the ugliness, the beauty, the grandeur and the oddity – that joins England to Scotland.

Glasgow/Edinburgh to King's Cross

Trains every hour taking under five hours

Sunday is never the best day to travel long distances by train. It's the day for track maintenance, when delays and diversions can be expected. And because there are fewer trains, those that do run can be crowded. So a journey from Glasgow to London on a Sunday can be tricky. A study of the timetable shows that you can have a reasonably fast journey if you're prepared to start in the late afternoon.

If you want to arrive in the afternoon you are advised to travel by way of Edinburgh; a 125 runs from Queen Street to King's Cross via Edinburgh at 10.15. Wanting an earlier arrival, I chose instead an 8.00 start from Queen Street to Edinburgh to join the London 125. In the normal way this would go by way of Lenzie and Falkirk High but this Sunday we started out to Cowlairs Junction, then reversed on to a line through Cumbernauld and Falkirk Grahamston. This is heavily populated country with both whisky and steel among the industries along the way. At Falkirk there was a glimpse of the Firth of Forth to remind us that we were crossing Scotland's narrow waist from the Clyde to the Forth, with the Kilsyth hills to the north.

At Linlithgow the train gave a chance to see the ruins of the great fortified palace that stands beside the small loch there. It has had a rich history since King James I of Scotland planned it in the early fifteenth century. Mary Queen of Scots was born here,

Charles I stayed here. Cromwell was here, Bonnie Prince Charlie looked in.

It took just over an hour (it's 45 minutes on weekdays) to cross between Scotland's two great cities and slide through the cutting between Princes Street and the Castle into Waverley Station, hiding discreetly in its cutting. Waverley is so discreet, in fact, that you might easily miss its one flamboyant gesture, the concourse under a glass dome, replete with cherubs and swags in the overblown grand classical manner of the Nineties. Though a little faded, it still creates a sense of occasion that helps to give train travel its own special character.

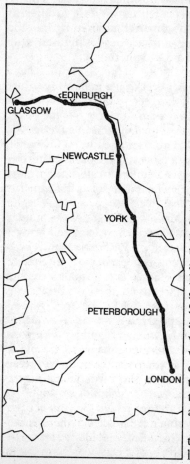

I found the London train already filling fast. We pulled out punctually for what was timed to be a fairly leisurely ride by 125 standards. We ran out eastwards with brief views of the Firth of Forth, reached the North Sea coast at Dunbar and then ran over a corner of Lammermuir, back to the coast and out of Scotland. Dunbar, now a popular resort, has a castle on the harbour which figured often in Scotland's history. Edward II, on the run after defeat at Bannockburn by Robert the Bruce, escaped by ship from here. Mary Queen of Scots was here with Darnley, and after Darnley's murder with her next husband, Bothwell. Cromwell completed the destruction of the castle, so there is little left to prompt the traveller's historical imagination.

Berwick-upon-Tweed, over the border into Northumberland, is quite another matter.

After leaving the station the train swept around the town giving magnificent views across the River Tweed of the old town perched on its hill with defensive walls on the river side. The railway enhances the scene, in fact, for as the line curves south and east travellers can see the great stone viaduct of Robert Stephenson's Royal Border Bridge, built in 1849, which carries the line over the river. Berwick was once a Scottish Royal Burgh and changed hands many times in battles between the Scots and English. Robert the Bruce captured and recaptured it and for a time it was declared neutral territory, but now the border runs some miles to the north.

Our train then ran down the coast with glimpses of Holy Island and later of the attractive little seaside village of Alnmouth, with yachts in the river. There is still a station here.

There was the delightful wooded valley of the River Coquet and a view of Coquet Island with its lighthouse and monastery before we got to Morpeth and plunged into the industrial and mining area of the North-east. Not far away to the west is some of the wildest and most beautiful country in England but we moved quickly between the mines and factories to run into Newcastle, coming in through a forest of tower blocks. It's not a beautiful city but even the passing traveller gets a feeling of its strength and individual character, a place for any explorer of Britain to stop and get to know.

On this trip, though, we had only a quick sight of the Sunday market in progress on the quay and of the road and rail bridges over the Tyne as we rolled into the station. We crossed the Tyne at a high level. Its bridges are among the city's most impressive features and if the main road bridge looks like a smaller copy of the Sydney Harbour Bridge, don't be misled: the Tyne Bridge was built first.

No sign so far of the 125's top speed but it was not yet time for that. First, we had to skirt the ancient city of Durham. We went round on a curving embankment and got a magnificent view of the massive cathedral and castle towering over a huddle of small houses. The old Bishops of Durham were princes wielding great secular power and it shows in the way these buildings dominate the city.

Our train now went wandering off down a side line not normally used for passenger services at all, let alone the lordly mainliners. Instead of a scheduled stop at Darlington we found ourselves at the other end of that father of all passenger railways, the Stockton and Darlington. When it was opened in 1825 the inaugural train carried a band as well as about 800 people and was greeted at Stockton with a salute of guns before all the official guests went off to a banquet.

Today Stockton was far from *en fête*. This had been a decent red-brick station but now the roof had gone and there was an air of dereliction which seemed to be shared by the town. Many of the small houses in the streets we passed were boarded up. We stopped here to take up the Darlington passengers and hurried on through Eaglescliff, not as handsome as its name, to rejoin the main line at Northallerton. We were out of the industrial Northeast and into the spaciousness of Yorkshire, with the Hambleton and Cleveland hills on the left and the country of the Dales away to the west.

Now the 125 was able to show what it could do as we raced down the straight line to York. Although the train must now have been doing its designed operating speed of 125 mph there was no sway or shake and miraculously little noise. The ride was as smooth as it had been when we were creeping round diversions.

It was soon after passing through Thirsk that I saw the white horse, away to the left on the side of a hill, a splendid animal cut into the chalk. For something like ten miles or more it stayed in sight as I looked back. Then it was time to look forward again and soon the three great towers of York Minster came into view, distant at first but then quite close as we slowed down to stop at the station.

After the Minster we had done with the great sights of the route. There would be nothing from now on to match Berwick, Newcastle, Durham and York.

During the week trains on this line offer a lunch service very similar to that of the West Coast line. Had I come by the Flying Scotsman I could have had a meal rivalling the Royal Scot's in every way. At weekends, however, the most you can expect from the buffet car in the way of a hot meal is a hamburger. Otherwise the usual snacks and drinks are available.

We made our last stop at Doncaster, junction for Sheffield, Grimsby and Lincoln, and then romped down the line, well clear of the industrial Midlands, through the minor junctions of Newark and Grantham and the more important one of Peterborough towards the Home Counties.

Peterborough station is organized so that non-stop trains can swish through at high speed, while stopping trains find platforms away from the main line. There was just time to look back for a quick glimpse of the city's squat, low-lying cathedral, its low towers having a sawn-off look. Then we were off through the edge of Fenland, racing down the flat lands towards the New Town country north of London.

Letchworth, the oldest of the Garden Cities, we skirted in favour of Hitchin, its close neighbour, then Stevenage, earliest of the post-war New Towns. Angry old residents not wanting to be New renamed it Silkingrad, the inoffensive Lewis Silkin being the Planning Minister responsible for New Towns. Not much sign today of either offensive newness or political rancour: from the train it looked as neat and conventional as any other commuter community.

Welwyn Garden City and Hatfield were both designated New Towns but both were already too well established for it to show much, Welwyn with its charming neo-Georgian terraces, redolent of early town planning and vegetarianism, Hatfield secure in possession of Hatfield House, Jacobean home of the Salisburys, where Queen Elizabeth I grew up.

And so past Potter's Bar, traditionally where the wild North begins in Londoners' view, and into built-up London. Sad to see, as we slowed down through Wood Green, the burnt-out shell of Alexandra Palace – the Ally Pally to generations of Londoners – on its hill to our right. The great Victorian leisure centre gave pleasure to millions in its day. Now we were through Finsbury Park and Holloway and into fine, airy King's Cross, with clean biscuit-coloured walls supporting a high pair of curved glass and iron roofs, Cubitt's simple, functional and most satisfying station.

In spite of diversions it had been a smooth and comfortable ride down the east of England, and we had arrived on time. Six hours is a bit leisurely for the trip but it *was* Sunday. If we had really wanted a fast ride we would have waited for the week-day Flying Scotsman, which does the 393 miles with one stop at Newcastle in four hours 35 minutes.

North-east to South-west

Four trains a day Newcastle to Plymouth and beyond

One of the things train travel does well is take you from one part of the country to somewhere completely different fast enough for you to appreciate the contrast. I decided to go in a day from the harsh industrial North-east to the most famous holiday haunt of the gentle South-west, from Hartlepool to St Ives.

The distance was 495 miles and it would take ten hours, mostly by 125 with a buffet car. The most difficult part was getting up early enough to catch the 6.36 from Hartlepool to make the four-minute connection with the 125 from Newcastle to Plymouth, due to leave Darlington at 7.31. The weather was sharply cold for July and threatening rain.

The local train to Darlington goes through the heart of the Teesside industrial area.

Darlington has a spacious, airy station befitting the town where railway travel began. The buffet, naturally called *The Locomotion* after Stephenson's engine which ran from here to Stockton, has a pleasing wall decoration celebrating those heroic days.

But where was the splendid engine itself? Had it not once stood on the platform here to remind us of Darlington's railway glory? The answer was that, yes, it had. But while Darlington is the town, this is not the station where it all started. The

Stockton and Darlington Railway terminus was at what is now Darlington North Road, on a short branch line to Bishop Auckland. The original station building is now a museum, where you can see *Locomotion*, the later mineral engine *Derwent* and much else relating to early railways in the area. Pity in a way: *Locomotion* deserved her place of honour on the main line.

However, the branch line is worth a ride. Further on is Shildon, where the S & DR had its workshop and the train terminates at Bishop Auckland, a mining town but still the princely seat of the Bishop of Durham, who lives in the splendour of Auckland Castle.

The train from Newcastle was on time, not over-full for a Friday at this stage – it would fill up later and on Saturdays reservation would be required. First leg of the journey was the run up the main line through York to Doncaster. Here we left the King's Cross route and set off to the south-west up the Don valley through Conisbrough, where there is a fine Norman castle, Mexborough, and through the steel town of Rotherham into adjoining Sheffield. There had been some open country at first but in these parts farming was clearly just something you did with bits of land that were not being mined.

The iron-working town of Rotherham looked much cleaner than might have been expected. Even today, when most places have cleaned away the grime of the black smoke era, one somehow expects heavy industry to look filthy. Updating one's preconceptions doesn't always work that way, however. On previous visits to Sheffield I had seen what a handsome city was tucked into its hills. From the train, I simply wondered why an area of corrugated iron sheds and rusting metal should be called Brightside.

We came into Chesterfield on a high embankment giving an excellent view of the town's chief distinction, the church's high spire (228 feet) twisted eight feet out of the perpendicular. It looks very odd indeed and has been the subject of many legends. The truth is that the timbers were warped.

After Chesterfield there were some signs that we were on the edge of the Derbyshire Peak District. East Moor and Matlock were not too far away to the right and the hills of the Peak District made themselves felt as we hurried through Clay Cross and Belper, both mining districts.

Derby is the home of British Rail's locomotive works and is thus popular as the destination for many railway enthusiasts' excursions. It was the headquarters of the old Midland Railway and is the home of Rolls-Royce.

After leaving the edges of the Peak District we were now in the central Midland plain. Burton-on-Trent offered us maltings, an old grain warehouse, yards piled high with beer kegs, large modern breweries. One sign proclaimed it to be the home of Double Diamond. It is also the home of Bass and several other breweries; there's even a museum of brewing.

And then very soon we could see in the distance ahead the triple spires of Lichfield cathedral. Lichfield was directly down the line but that was for freight only. Our route lay through Tamworth, where we crossed the main Euston–Scotland line, and so into Birmingham, joined by the line from Peterborough.

Birmingham is the centre and main changing point for trains from Scotland, the North-west and North-east, Wales, the South and South-west. There is at least one through train a day from each area to the others but if the through train does not suit, you can usually do almost as well by taking any train to Birmingham and changing there.

As soon as the train pulled out of Birmingham, now well filled with holiday-makers, it was clear that we were in different country. From the North-east to Birmingham, with only a few breaks between Darlington and York and south of Chesterfield, we had been running through an industrial or mining landscape of greater or lesser density. Now we were into the lusher, more rural West Country, where modest cities and towns, properly spaced out, were surrounded by real country. It seemed time for a beer and sandwich in the buffet.

After Cheltenham Spa – no elegance in sight from the railway – the railway map shows the Bristol line bypassing Gloucester. It doesn't do that but merely bypasses the station, going through the city so that we could see the cathedral. Then down the Severn valley with the Cotswolds showing nicely to our left to join the main line into Bristol Temple Meads, gateway to the South-west.

After leaving Temple Meads and passing through Parson Street station the line emerges from a cutting to give fine views to the north of the Clifton suspension bridge perched breathtakingly over the Avon Gorge and the principal buildings of the city spread out.

The line now runs down behind the Bristol Channel shore with the Mendip Hills on the left and Cheddar Gorge somewhere among them. A loop runs off to Weston-super-Mare station but we skirted the back of the town – a popular resort, with sandy beaches and donkey rides – and carried on through Bridgwater to Taunton, where we joined the main line from Paddington.

This is also the connecting point for the West Somerset Railway. Buses from here run to Bishop's Lydeard for the 20-mile preserved railway to Minehead, whose Blue Anchor Bay inspired Coleridge's 'The Ancient Mariner'. Taunton is also, of course, a centre of cider-making, as wagon-loads of the stuff reminded us.

The rolling country of the Blackdown Hills takes the line out of Somerset into Devon's hills and pastures, with a river valley to run down into Exeter. The main station, St David's, is the point where, before the days of British Rail, the Great Western and the Southern systems used to meet and overlap. The Southern's Atlantic Coast Express from Waterloo used to run down through Salisbury and come into St David's on an up platform. Then it would pull out towards Barnstaple, dropping coaches for various branch lines serving north Cornwall.

We were on the old Great Western line, which skirts the city centre – giving a good view of the cathedral – and runs down the west side of the Exe estuary. This stretch of line was the scene of Brunel's short-lived experiment, the Atmospheric railway, on which trains were worked by atmospheric pressure. This moved a piston attached to the train along a trough closed with a leather flap. It worked up to a point but the leather rotted and the air pressure fell and so the idea died. But at Starcross one of the pumping stations can still be seen and a pub, the Atmospheric, recalls the venture.

We reached the Channel coast at Dawlish Warren and from Dawlish to Teignmouth the train ran along the foot of towering red cliffs, one of the most celebrated stretches of railway in the world. Trains dive in and out of short tunnels under headlands and in winter waves can break over the embankment. There is a footpath alongside the track and this is a great favourite for railway photographers. The line runs across the sea front at Dawlish but is a bit kinder to Teignmouth, cutting off behind the front to run inland beside the Teign estuary.

Teignmouth is a pretty little Victorian resort with Italianate stucco in a characteristic West Country style that gives it some elegance. Behind a spit of land which guards the narrow river outlet there's anchorage for yachts and a small port for coasters. Across the river, the village of Shaldon on a hillside completes a very attractive scene.

The train runs up the beautiful Teign estuary, shelved on a steep hillside, until it reaches Newton Abbot at the head of the estuary. This is the junction for the Torbay line to Torquay and Paignton. From Paignton the Torbay and Dartmouth Railway runs steam trains for seven miles through lovely country to Kingswear on the Dart estuary opposite Dartmouth, which can be reached by ferry. This is an attractive little port sheltering under a high hill. In summer you can take a trip up the river to Totnes, where you can rejoin the main line or take another seven-mile trip with the Dart Valley Railway to Buckfastleigh. Torquay and Paignton are now integrated into the holiday conurbation of Torbay, which stretches right round the bay.

From Newton Abbot the main line goes to Totnes, a little hill town with a castle on a mound, and then along the southern edge of Dartmoor, with its dramatic granite tors and half-wild ponies, the brooding length of which can be seen to the north, and on into Plymouth, swooping into the town over viaducts and down steep gradients. I changed here onto a train from Paddington. Both trains had been dropping off passengers from Exeter onwards and there was now plenty of room.

The ride out of Plymouth into Cornwall is spectacular. First, a glimpse of warships in the naval dockyard, with more anchored out in the estuary. Then the train crosses the Tamar into Cornwall on the Royal Albert Bridge at Saltash. This is one of Brunel's masterpieces, bearing at each entrance in huge letters the legend: I. K. Brunel, Engineer, 1859.

After crossing the bridge the line turns sharply to follow the riverside, giving a view of the fine bridge itself and down the estuary to the port in the distance. Of all the great railway views in Britain this must be one of the best. Further up the river the line crosses the River Tiddy by St Germans and there's another superb view from a high level over the village, the water and the steep wooded hills beyond.

Our train now turned inland and climbed to Liskeard, a junction for the branch line that runs down to the charming little rivermouth resort of Looe. There followed a winding course through the wooded gorges of the Fowey valley with Bodmin Moor not far away to the north. The strange circular Restormel Castle can be seen on the right approaching Lostwithiel. The Royalists captured it during the Civil War.

Par, next stop, is the junction for Newquay on the north Cornwall coast, a popular resort for surfers. The port has a ghostly white look from the china clay that is shipped from here. St Austell, a little further on, is the capital of the china clay industry. The pits and refuse tips create a white lunar landscape with sometimes pools of intensely blue water in the pits.

At Truro the line curves round to give a fine view of the cathedral with its three spires standing high above the surrounding low buildings. The city is on the Truro river, which flows into the Fal and the big Falmouth harbour.

After leaving Truro the train ran down into the heart of the tin-mining area. Only one or two mines are being operated now, but the landscape is dotted with the engine-houses and chimneys, now abandoned, which once served them. Some can be seen from the train. We were now on the bony stone foot of England, a long way from the lushness of Devon. The twin towns of Redruth and Camborne were once an important mining centre.

At St Erth, a few miles short of Penzance, I changed to the last branch line on the system for the few miles to St Ives, past the saltings of the Hayle estuary and along the shore of Carbis Bay to a terminus under the cliff at St Ives, just a short walk from the picturesque harbour. St Ives is a cramped little town – that's part of its charm – and a car is a liability in its narrow streets. The railway branch does good business by running a park-and-ride service into St Ives from Lelant Saltings, where motorists can leave their cars.

In St Ives the sun was shining, as it had been for most of the afternoon. It was much warmer and would remain so late into the night. There was a relaxing softness in the air. Life was more leisurely down here, with no great concentrations of major industry this side of Bristol. From the North-east to the South-west through the heart of England I had seen something of how England is put together, how her parts relate and how wide are the contrasts to be found in a single day's train ride.

Yarmouth to Barmouth

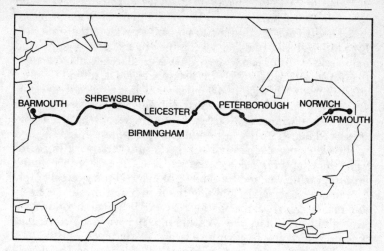

One through connection

Travelling on InterCity lines out of London at high speed with food and drink readily available is one form of train-ride pleasure. Journeying across the grain of the railway system gives pleasure of a different kind. It's not for the impatient but it can impart a satisfying sense of individual achievement and discovery. I tackled the challenge of Great Yarmouth to Barmouth in the spirit of a climber tackling Everest – because it was there. Not only does it sound poetically right but it is somewhere near the longest true east–west coast-to-coast journey you can make in Britain, the two resorts being very close to the same latitude.

It takes at least five different trains and ten hours 39 minutes to cover the 326 miles from Yarmouth to Barmouth, crossing England and Wales by way of Norwich, Peterborough, Leicester, Birmingham, Wolverhampton and Shrewsbury. It requires some stamina and forethought. Your reward is that you see a cross-section of Britain from the North Sea to the Irish Sea and get a sense of the variety of scene and society that makes up the country. So let's set off one weekday morning from Yarmouth on the 6.50 two-coach diesel train to Norwich via Acle.

Great Yarmouth, a port on the North Sea, is a popular family resort with a long sandy beach, a lot of entertainment and a modern leisure centre. It figures in Dickens's *David Copperfield* and one of its pubs, Shadingfield Lodge, was once a weekend retreat where King Edward VII, when Prince of Wales, used to take lady friends. Behind the town, and seen from the station, is Breydon Water, a tidal lake where three rivers come together and many estuary birds can be seen. This is the flat marshland area of the Norfolk Broads, alive with pleasure boats in summer.

The run to Norwich of 18 miles takes just over half an hour, first crossing a flat Dutch landscape of which the most prominent features are windmills — the tall one away on the left is the preserved Berney Arms mill — and the wind-pumps formerly used to lift water out of the drainage dykes into the rivers. In recent years there has been a fight by preservationists to save this unique area of grazing wetland from being ploughed up for cereal crops. The line runs straight alongside the marshland through Acle to join the River Yare at the boating centre of Brundall. It follows the Yare and its tributary the Wensum into Norwich, a historic and well-preserved city of great beauty and character.

At Norwich there was 16 minutes before joining the diesel-hauled train of rather aged coaches for the next leg of the journey, the 176 miles to Birmingham, taking four and a quarter hours.

The first part of this journey is through the fairly flat but pleasant farmland of west Norfolk and then into the extensive forests and heaths of Breckland. Brandon, passed soon after a stop at Thetford, is famous for flint-knapping, the craft of splitting flints so as to expose a flat, shiny surface. These surfaces are used to face walls and can be seen to great decorative effect on the churches and Guildhall in Norwich.

The train passes then into the flat fenland, drained in the seventeenth century and now farmland of fertile black earth crossed by long, straight drainage rivers. Its capital is Ely, standing on a mound above the surrounding levels and said to have got its name from the great number of eels caught in the area. Ely was one of the last strongholds of the Saxons against the conquering Normans. Its cathedral, begun in 1083, is one of the largest in England and has a distinctive octagonal lantern tower.

It is this and the great nave, a dreamy white shape in the morning mist, that we see as the train takes the loop line that enables it to avoid going into Ely station to reverse.

Off now across the fens again and through the small town of

March. Brickworks, with kilns and tall chimneys, and other industrial sites mark the approach to Peterborough and the end of the journey across East Anglia and Fenland.

Peterborough has some old buildings but it has been expanding fast. It is the first main railway junction out of King's Cross on the East Coast main line and many passengers from our train change here to catch expresses going North.

The line now takes off on a series of wide curves to Leicester. No more flat country now; we're into the rolling land of the hunting shires. Once past Stamford, coaching stop on the Great North Road, and sixteenth century Burghley House (its turrets just visible in Capability Brown's park) we're ready to sweep through what used to be Rutlandshire (Britain's smallest county, now absorbed by Leicestershire), past Rutland Water and Oakham and through Melton Mowbray to Leicester. This is beautiful country of green hills and lush fields. Melton, through which we hurry without stopping, is a centre for high-class hunting – the Quorn, the Belvoir and the Cottesmore all chase foxes round here. More to the taste of some, it's also noted for pork pies and stilton cheese.

The rich country of the shires ends at Leicester and we've come into another part of Britain, the industrial East Midlands. Leicester made its name as a centre for hosiery and knitwear but has a wide spread of light engineering as well. It's 99 miles from London on the main line to Sheffield and is very nearly the centre of England.

This is a busy station with lots of serious-looking people getting on and off. For the first time since leaving Yarmouth we're conscious of tower blocks looming with vague menace. We're now in the more densely populated part of the country – Leicester is comfortably bigger than Norwich and Peterborough put together – and out of the quiet agricultural east.

The line stops wandering about after leaving Leicester and makes purposefully for Hinckley, Nuneaton and Birmingham. Now the landscape is industrial, with coal mines, power stations, cooling towers, lines of coal wagons, factories, canals. Nuneaton, with a surprisingly ornate station building, is on the main electric line from Euston to the North. Our train offers a connection here to Holyhead and the ferry to Ireland.

Now we're approaching Birmingham, heart of the Midlands, Britain's second city with a population of over a million. There are

supposed to be more than 1500 different trades carried on here
and this is easy to believe as the train moves steadily through an
increasingly complicated factory landscape, with canals, roads on
concrete stilts and railway viaducts writhing away in every direction. Our line comes into the city on a viaduct giving an impressive
panorama of what makes a city great – its thrusting office blocks,
factories, high-rise flats, shops and warehouses all in self-
confident, assertive profusion. It is not picturesque and far from
beautiful but the total picture is one of power. It shows us at a
glance what a modern industrial civilization means.

Leicester may be close to the centre of England but Birmingham
can claim to be the railway centre of Britain, New Street station
having through trains to more destinations than any other single
station in Britain.

Our train slides exhausted into the big low-level station, on
time at 11.50 even if it hasn't been any great feat of speedy
running. New Street, in a cutting with the concourse above, is
not a beautiful station to come into. Its twelve platforms are
utilitarian; modernization has left none of the endearing excesses of Victorian architecture which give interest to other
stations. But this is no doubt how practical Birmingham folk
prefer it.

At Birmingham a choice presents itself – to wait an hour and a
half here and then take the through train from Euston to Shrewsbury or to take the next train to Wolverhampton with an hour and
20 minutes for lunch there before joining the Shrewsbury train. I
opt for Wolverhampton, noting that the through train must in any
case wait for nine minutes at Wolverhampton while the electric
locomotive is replaced by a diesel. After a brief whirl on a fast
train I alight at Wolverhampton and make for the buffet for a
leisurely lunch. This establishment makes no pretence of bidding
for the gourmet trade but it's clean, the service is cheerful and
you're glad to see it when you've come half across Britain since
breakfast.

Known to most of us largely for its footballing Wanderers,
Wolverhampton is a smaller and – at a casual glance from the
buffet window – less aggressively modernized version of big
brother Brum. The Victorian office buildings have not yet sunk
completely out of sight but look well cared for. This is the capital
of the Black Country, so called from the mines and iron works in
the area.

I study my fellow passengers and refreshment-takers; several comfortable stout parties, a large man who looks as if he has supped some ale in his time, and why not? And two or three cheerful and confident-looking young mothers with small children, the mothers relaxed, the children not whining. Wolverhampton can't be too bad a place.

Now on to Shrewsbury by the train from London, still going west. The industrial build-up which started in Leicester and seemed as if it would never end now falls away quite quickly. We're in the country again and over there to the left is a long hill that must be Wenlock Edge. Beyond that, quite soon, those distant mountains must surely be Wales. We go through the New Town of Telford and are soon in Wellington with the Wrekin on our left. It looks a decent, sober place and so it should be. The Iron Duke took his title from the town and it has a public school. (Not Wellington School, in Somerset, nor Wellington College, in Berkshire, but Wrekin College).

Shrewsbury, next changing point, is a city of spires and towers in a loop of the Severn, and a key junction point, with lines going to Crewe, Chester, Llanelli and Hereford as well as mid-Wales. As the train enters the station there's a view of the castle and the cathedral. The station itself is in a prime position with the River Severn flowing under its platforms. The old Great Western Railway evidently felt that the site called for something rather special so they put up a Gothic extravaganza which holds its own with the rest of the town and has become one of the city sights. With its central Gothic tower, pepperpot embellishments and tall, ornamental chimneys, it's a far cry from the concrete austerity of Birmingham New Street. Clive of India lived in Shrewsbury and his fine Georgian house is a museum. There are also some well-preserved half-timbered houses.

Now the train is in for the final stages of the cross-Britain journey. It's a six-coach diesel local train and our 86½ mile ride to Barmouth, including a change of trains at Machynlleth, is scheduled to take two and threequarter hours, going up the Severn valley, through the Cambrian mountains and round the coast beneath the majestic Cader Idris mountain to Barmouth. Our line is a single track, not built for speed.

As soon as we leave Shrewsbury we can see the Welsh hills ahead but we're not actually into the Principality until we pass Middletown. Before that we run through agricultural Shropshire and through a gap between the Long Mountain range of hills on the left and the Breidden hills on the right. There are wild roses on the embankment.

Through the hills and into the Severn valley again and we're in Wales. At Welshpool, the first station over the border, and thereafter, the signs give the names in Welsh and English. We can hear Welsh spoken by some of the women passengers on the train and realize that we are in another country, very different from the flat land we crossed during the morning.

Welshpool shows the railway traveller a huge heap of scrap metal of a determinedly unromantic nature. But those who alight here find an ancient market town of character, with Powis Castle nearby and a little steam railway to Llanfair.

We push up the narrowing Severn valley through mist-topped brooding hills to Newtown, where Robert Owen, the pioneer of factory reform and co-operation, is buried. There's a climb into the heart of the Cambrian mountains, with the train toiling up to the summit at Talerddig. Then it's downhill all the way, steeply at first, until the line enters the Dovey valley and runs down between the hills to Machynlleth. This is the heart and soul of the line, an exhilarating run through some lovely country, the mountains on either side getting ever higher and the mist, on this occasion, deepening into rain.

Machynlleth, where there's a short wait for the Pwllheli train, is a charming town with an oversized clock tower and memories of Owen Glyndwr, who summoned a parliament here to govern Wales. The river broadens and soon we're at Dovey Junction, where the lines to Aberystwyth and Pwllheli divide. A junction, in fact, is all there is – there's not even a road there, let alone a village.

The Pwllheli train turns north and crosses the river, then runs alongside river and sea for the rest of the journey to Barmouth. And here, running along the shore beside the Dovey estuary, we find again the same species of estuary birds we saw on Breydon Water on the other side of Britain, curlews and other waders delicately foraging the wide sandbanks exposed by the ebbing tide.

Aberdovey looks south over the sandbanks and is a yachting centre. The train fights its way north up the coast clinging to the side of the cliffs or running along the beach on only a low ledge above sea level. Tywyn is the terminus of the Talyllyn Railway, one of the famous narrow-gauge steam lines. By now there are views across Tremadog Bay to the Lleyn Peninsula.

After running around the headland at Friog the line turns to cross the Mawddach estuary on a long wooden viaduct, with Cader Idris towering behind us. The train creeps across, giving time to appreciate the noble mountain-ringed estuary.

This viaduct was found to be weakened by marine creatures and had to be closed for a time. When it re-opened the first train that crossed it to reach Barmouth met a civic welcome with brass band and choir, for the railway is an important line of communication on this coast, not just a scenic ride.

The train gets into Barmouth more or less on time. It's a small, quiet resort in Cardigan Bay, a long way in atmosphere as well as miles from its rumbustious North Sea counterpart. But what it lacks in size and entertainment resources it makes up in the natural beauty of the country around and the hospitality of its people.

The journey wasn't really necessary. There is beauty, friendliness and charm on either side of Britain. But going across the middle of Britain from coast to coast in a leisurely day shows us the variety of the regions of Britain, how they differ in character and feel, and how they are all parts of a whole.

4
Scotland

Scotland provides some of the finest train travel experience to be found in Europe, a marvellous combination of mountain and moorland scenery, big city spectaculars, heroic engineering and a pervading sense of living history.

The Freedom of Scotland ticket covers the whole of Scotland and over the border to Carlisle and Berwick. Good day trip centres are Glasgow, Edinburgh, Inverness and Perth.

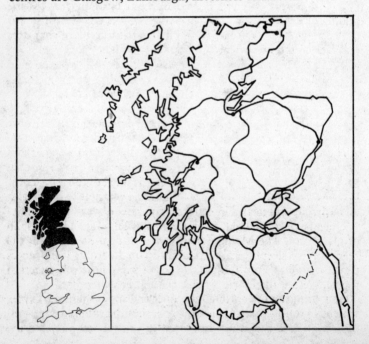

Glasgow to Mallaig

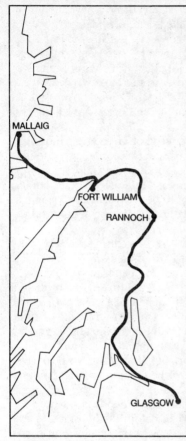

Three trains a day each to Oban and Mallaig

On any tour of Scotland by train the West Highland line to Fort William and Mallaig is a must. From Glasgow it runs by lochs and moors through some of the most magnificent scenery in the world, with a branch to the charming port and seaside resort of Oban.

The leisurely way to tackle the Mallaig line is to take the 9.50 train from Glasgow Queen Street, reaching Fort William for a late lunch, stay overnight and go on by the 10.05 train next morning. It's also possible to do the trip on a steam-hauled excursion. I decided to take it at one gulp and to go on from Mallaig by boat to Kyle of Lochalsh.

This meant catching the 5.50 train from Queen Street, only to be contemplated when staying at the station hotel. From the comfortable North British, a handsome building in George Square, I was able to be up with an early cup of tea and into the station next door in good time.

Queen Street is a light, uncluttered station under a single span of glass roof. The Mallaig train was waiting with buffet at the rear and two sleeping-cars from Euston on the front. The sleepers travel as far as Fort William. Most of my fellow passengers, I found, were walkers with rucksacks and heavy boots.

Our train ran out through a tunnel and soon found the Clyde, which we followed through industrial suburbs, stopping at Dumbarton, where the River Leven from Loch Lomond joins the

Clyde. We left the electric suburban line just before Craigendoran to take the single-track West Highland line.

Gare Loch is the first loch to be seen on the journey. It was from Faslane, below us as we approached Garelochhead Station, that Winston Churchill sailed for North Africa during the last war.

From Garelochhead we went alongside Loch Long, the railway line high above the water with fine views of the mountains on either side, to Arrochar and Tarbet in the narrow neck of low-lying land between Loch Long and Loch Lomond. Across Loch Lomond loomed the stately height of Ben Lomond, 3192 feet but quite easy to walk up.

For centuries this area was the scene of Highland feuding and clan battles. Chieftains from the Isles, it is recorded, used to have their war galleys hauled over the neck of land from Loch Long, a sea loch, to strike terror with them on landlocked Loch Lomond. But this morning, with not a boat to be seen, scarcely a ripple on its surface and its mountains wreathed in mist, Loch Lomond was a picture of peace.

At the top of Loch Lomond the line climbs Glen Falloch crossing the tributary of the River Falloch on a high viaduct. High time for some breakfast as we climbed deeper into the circle of mountains at Crianlarich. Poached egg and tea or coffee in a buffet car may not be the ultimate height of British Rail's great British breakfast but it's just what's needed on a train full of hikers trundling through the early morning mists in the Highlands.

From Crianlarich we were still climbing steeply. The Oban line goes off to the left here, to the south of Fillan Water, while the Fort William line takes the northern bank. Tyndrum has a station on each line. Here I noticed how neat and well-kept these Highland stations are. Tyndrum Upper had a rhododendron bush, lots of whitewash and the station name in coloured chippings. A previous station had had a great show of irises. It was clear, too, that this line was a vital communications link for the small communities it served. At each stop mail and newspapers were unloaded on to waiting trolleys. At one station three small girls got on to attend school three stops up the line.

The glens through which we had come had been green with forests, the hillsides brown with heather. Now we were climbing high on the hillside above Loch Tulla and on to wild Rannoch Moor, where 20 miles of treacherous peat bogs had to be crossed. For most of this way there are no roads or houses to be seen, only the ruins of Achallader Castle at the edge of the moor. The railway line was floated across the bog on a raft of tree trunks, branches and masses of earth and ashes.

Building this railway a century ago must have been quite a feat. There is a memorial to Sir William McAlpine, the contractor, at Rannoch station on the far side of the wilderness.

Rannoch seemed desolate enough but it has a road back eastwards along Loch Rannoch to Pitlochry. Our train continued to climb through even more remote wilderness to Corrour station, the highest on the British Rail system at 1327 feet above sea level. Rough tracks lead to shooting lodges and there are paths for walkers but the railway is the only practical link with the outside world here.

The situation is so wild that just before reaching Corrour the train passes through Britain's only snow shed, built to keep the cutting free from snowdrifts which would otherwise block it every winter. This is an all-the-year-round line and it offers an even more exciting ride when the high ground is covered with snow.

Our train continued along a mountain ledge 400 feet above lonely Loch Treig, hemmed in between steeply rising mountain-sides. But now we were going down a steep one-in-67 gradient to Tulloch. Here we turned west to run down Glen Spean to Fort William, southern end of the Caledonian Canal which links lochs through the Great Glen to Inverness and enables boats to sail through the middle of the Highlands from Scotland's west to east coast.

Though high peaks still crowded round and Ben Nevis, Britain's highest mountain, now loomed majestically to the south, we had left the almost uninhabited desolation of the moors and were following the tumbling River Spean down through villages served by roads, with farmhouses dotted here and there, horses cantering in the fields and sheep grazing. For the first time since leaving Tyndrum we saw a human figure unconnected with the railway, a man out walking with his dog. At Roy Bridge station a postwoman in smart grey trouser-suit uniform collected the mails and newspapers.

At Spean Bridge there is a bus service to Fort Augustus at the southern end of Loch Ness and a number of walkers left us here. A monument on the hill beyond the station reminded us that this was a training ground for commandos in the last war. Soon we had run down through a broadening valley under the great bulk of

Ben Nevis to the terminus at Fort William at the head of Loch Linnhe, an arm of the sea. The 123 miles had taken just four hours from Glasgow and every minute of it was absorbing.

Fort William is a popular resort for walkers and climbers and for those who just want to get away from it all in the solitude of the Highlands. Ben Nevis, for all its height, requires no special climbing skills. The West Highland museum here has many natural history exhibits and Jacobite relics.

Our train now shed its two sleeping cars and picked up two more day coaches in their place. We were now hauled back by another locomotive to curve away to the left for the run to Mallaig. As we crossed the southern end of the Caledonian Canal we could see above us to the right the set of linked locks called Neptune's Staircase. We ran along the side of Loch Eil, linked to the sea through Loch Linnhe, and caught the last view of Ben Nevis behind us.

We were soon in the mountains again and shortly came upon one of the major sights of the trip, first a view of the impressive 100-foot-high Glenfinnan viaduct curving ahead of us, then, as we crossed it, a spectacular view down the almost straight Loch Shiel. In 1745 Bonnie Prince Charlie was rowed up the loch after sailing to the mainland from the Outer Hebrides. He raised the Stuart banner at the head of the loch before going on to Edinburgh. A monument marks the spot where Jacobite hopes once seemed so bright.

And so we ran westward through the mountains, beside Loch Eilt and on to the sea at Arisaig, with the islands of Rhum and Eigg before us. Now clear of the mountains, the line turned north and we ran the last few miles to the little port of Mallaig with the great Cuillin hills of Skye rising in a huge blue line across the water. The 165 miles from Glasgow had taken us five hours and 45 minutes but we had been given a sense of the wildness and the splendour of the Highlands that had made the impression of a lifetime.

Mallaig to Kyle of Lochalsh

Mallaig is a pleasant little fishing and ferry port, with shops and guest houses, friendly folk and tremendous views. The sensible thing is to stop a couple of nights and spend a day – if it's Monday, Wednesday or Saturday – sailing with the little ferry steamer around the islands of Eigg, Rhum and Canna (on Wednesdays

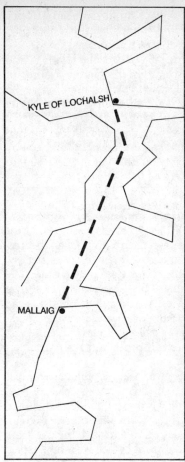

KYLE OF LOCHALSH

MALLAIG

they throw in Muck as well). It starts at 12.30 and the round trip takes seven hours.

But this was Tuesday, the day the little ferry steamer *Lochmor* sails up the Sound of Sleat between the island of Skye and the mainland to Kyle of Lochalsh, the main ferry point for Skye. The ship does not sell alcoholic drinks on this trip but sandwiches, tea and coffee are available in the buffet lounge.

The two-hour trip up to Kyle of Lochalsh on a cold June day was fascinating. On our left, or to port since we were now at sea, the green tree-clad hills of the island of Skye lay bathed in sunshine. On the mainland the steeper and higher hills were brown and bare under cloud, their summits swathed in mist.

The hills on both sides closed in as we made for the narrow passage from Glenelg Bay into Loch Alsh. Though we were at sea we seemed to be sailing always in a landlocked lake. The trip was a continuous delight but the most spectacular views were saved for the last. As the *Lochmor* turned west in Loch Alsh we could look astern and see a great double file of blue, rounded mountains receding into the distance. Up there at the entrance to Loch Duich was Eilean Donan Castle, dating back to 1220. Jacobite troops occupied it in 1719 and it was blown up by an English man of war. Now it is restored and open to the public.

From the railway pier at Kyle of Lochalsh, where *Lochmor* now tied up, there was a magnificent view across the Inner Sound to the blue mountains of Skye. I came ashore at Kyle of Lochalsh feeling much refreshed in body and spirit. The rain had kept off, the air sparkled and the world looked marvellous.

From Kyle of Lochalsh there is a five minute car ferry across the water to Kyleakin on Skye. Buses make the trip to Portree, the island capital and a most enjoyable and friendly place.

Kyle of Lochalsh itself has a hotel, the Loch Alsh, facing Skye across the sound with magnificent views. This area of great beauty is one to linger in and explore on foot or by boat or bus. The indefatigable little *Lochmor* cruises to Portree and to Loch Duich.

Kyle to Inverness

Three trains a day, two hours 40 minutes

Even a short time in the Highlands impresses on you one of history's ironies. Of the people I met on my travels around the Highlands many looked fierce enough, with great black beards, but all were notably gentle in manner, soft-spoken and friendly. Not only to me, a stranger, I noticed, but also to each other. Yet their ancestors had spilled each other's blood in endless feuds over the centuries as well as fighting off the invading English, who justified their incursions on the grounds that these were savage and uncivilized tribes. Today the once bloodthirsty Highlands are probably among the safest places in Britain and offer strangers courtesy second to none.

The next stage of my journey was the 82 miles across the country to Inverness, from the Atlantic waters of Scotland's west coast to the North Sea inlets of the Cromarty and Moray Firths. Not quite the expedition through the wilds that the West Highland line provided but a gentler, easier ride through the glens and straths of Wester and Easter Ross, during which we might expect to see seals in Loch Carron and roe deer on the hillsides. Easier for the passengers, that is: the Dingwall and Skye Railway Company, which built the line, had to use prodigious amounts of explosive to get through the solid rock which forms the Kyle peninsula. But get through they did, urged on by the thought that the West Highland line was stealing the Skye passengers from them, so here we were at the simple wooden station standing on its own pier at Kyle of Lochalsh. The seven-coach train was standing at the platform and would depart at 17.10.

The train, on inspection, proved refreshingly different. Tacked

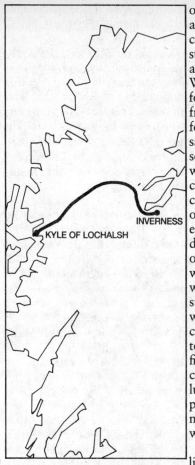

KYLE OF LOCHALSH

INVERNESS

on the end of the serviceable and familiar second-class coaches, with buffet car, was a strange coach in the chocolate and cream livery of the Great Western Railway, one of the four big private companies from which British Rail was formed. Inside it had two saloons divided by a kitchen section, each saloon set about with armchairs – tatty but comfortable – and even a couple of settees. This was an old parlour coach used for entertaining VIPs in pre-war days, built in 1931 and now owned by the Steamtown Railway Museum at Carnforth, which keeps a collection of such treasures. Its purpose here was to provide an observation car. For a small supplement on top of the second-class fare the first 26 travellers who applied could travel the line in pre-war luxury while a young lady pointed out the sights and narrated legends associated with the route.

A locomotive came down the line with a few coal wagons, shunted these and was then ready for us. We started out by the side of Loch Carron, still able to see the islands of Raasay, Scalpay and the Crowlins as well as Skye across the Inner Sound. No seals were on view but sometimes they appeared in the loch, our knowledgeable guide assured us. There were boat trips from Kyleakin to see them. She told us also about Castle Moil, near Kyleakin, over on Skye, at a point where the kyle is very narrow. Its owner at one time had been a Norwegian princess who caused a chain to be stretched from her castle to the mainland and levied a toll on passing ships.

Over the rocky coastline which gave the original contractors so much trouble we cut across the base of a small peninsula and emerged by the side of a bay surrounded by hills. Across the bay we saw the white cottages of the pretty village of Plockton. Now a yachting centre with a notable regatta, it was once a trading port from which schooners sailed for the Baltic.

Along the loch side again to Stromeferry, terminus of the railway for years, then on beside the loch and a steep climb out of the glen at the other side. There were hills on either side with some noble rock ridges but this was not really wild country. Crofters' cottages dotted the hillsides, sheep grazed, goats were in attendance. Rivers ran down the glens to feed the loch.

Only memories evoke more stirring times. Attadale, beside the loch, is where Norsemen used to fight duels and hold sporting events. Across the water Lochcarron (formerly Jeantown) and Slumbay used to be busy herring and salmon fishing ports until the industry failed more than a century ago.

We went up through beautiful forest country with mountains in the background. Loch Scavan had its own monster, the kelpie, which lived at the bottom of the loch and ate any unwary passer-by it could catch – all except the victim's lungs, which floated to the surface and gave the water the name of Loch of the Lungs.

That took us up into the wild moorland of the summit, some 646 feet above sea level, where by rights there ought to have been red deer and their calves. No sign of these: we had to be content with numerous rabbits as representatives of Highland wildlife.

This was not only wildlife country but also the habitat of that other Highland phenomenon, hydroelectricity. Water is trapped in high level lochs or reservoirs and led down the hillsides through pipes to operate hydroelectic turbines. We passed one such power station at which a salmon ladder had been provided to allow salmon to leap their way up beside the pipes to their spawning waters.

Now it was downhill most of the way, past Achnasheen, the half-way point where Queen Victoria once stayed. The old Queen was an enthusiastic sightseer and was frequently conducted by canny hosts to lookout points which thereafter could be marketed as Royal Views. Achnasheen means 'the field of rain' and often lives up to its name, but this afternoon there were only a few clouds and we could watch the play of shadows alternating with sunshine on the dark blue hills.

After two more lochs the hills opened out into wider pastures. Near Garve our guide pointed out the modest red-roofed croft which was the birthplace of Ramsay MacDonald, the first Labour Prime Minister. Soon we could see across a valley to Strathpeffer, once a well-known spa, where there are still two very large hotels. Local landowners prevented the railway going through the place as originally planned and an expensive detour had to be made. Later the spa achieved a branch line but this was closed.

Coming out now into gentle countryside we could see the Fodderty churchyard, said to be haunted by a young girl looking for her lover, and above it a hill, Knockfarril, on the slopes of which the Macdonalds and the Mackenzies staged one of the bloodiest clan battles of all time in 1429.

And so into Dingwall to join the line to the far north. Dingwall is at the head of the Cromarty Firth, so we had completed the crossing from the Atlantic to the North Sea. Macbeth was born and Robert the Bruce's wife imprisoned here and if you planned to take the train north, as I did, this would be a rational place to stay overnight. But Inverness called, capital of the Highlands and now only half an hour away, so I settled back in my GWR armchair.

We now crossed flat, unexciting country and ran through Muir of Ord, where cattle were auctioned which had been driven down from the glens we had passed through. Now we skirted Black Isle, the peninsula topped by high hills which separates the Cromarty and Moray Firths. This fertile, green land was famous for witches, who were supposed to go about disguised as hares. We came down to Beauly and turned east along the southern shore of Beauly Firth, which extends west from Moray Firth and is a popular stop of migrating birds. The place was named by Mary Queen of Scots, who stayed here and thought it a beautiful place. Mary Queen of Scots got around Scotland even more indefatigably than Queen Victoria.

We slowed to walking pace to cross a swing bridge over the Caledonian Canal, which comes out here into the Beauly Firth to complete the navigable link through Loch Ness with the Atlantic coast at Fort William. There used to be considerable traffic through the canal of small cargo steamers called puffers but now it is used mostly by pleasure craft. Over a handsome stone viaduct crossing the River Ness, next, and into the simple but clean and cheerful Inverness station.

As we left the train there was a great blast of bagpipe music from an office in the station. Was this the Inverness way of greeting the arrival of train-loads of tourists? As it turned out, no: it was the railway club band beginning its practice. But the impression was not entirely false. Inverness, as chief city of the Highlands, never forgets that the clans and their traditions are an important part of the tourist industry. A piper in full fig plays every evening on the castle terrace in the season and as I stood on the castle hill later I could see a full pipe band in uniform skirling its way along a road beside the river below.

The Station Hotel has other virtues beside the not inconsiderable one for the railway traveller of being beside the station. It had the good fortune to be built in the 1850s when hotel architects' legitimate desire to create a stately and imposing effect had not yet toppled over into vulgarities and excesses of a later period. It's a pleasant stone building with a fine staircase mounting from an airy foyer. The wide staircase with its floral iron banisters is a favourite background for bridal photographs. The dining room is spacious and elegant, the food well above the average.

Inverness is a very good centre for exploring Scotland by railway. It is also the starting place for Monster-hunting boat trips down the Caledonian Canal to Loch Ness. Needless to say, Mary Queen of Scots was here, staying at the castle, and there were numerous bloody clan battles around the place. The castle – actually law courts and a museum – is modern but is built on the site of the old one. There's plenty of summer entertainment in the form of singing, dancing and piping 'Scottish evenings' and the citizens are much addicted to open-air music-making. On the morning I left a 40-strong school band from Norway in smart red uniforms was filling the High Street with cheerful sound.

The Far North

Three trains a day, four hours
The line from Inverness to Wick and Thurso represents the Far North of British Rail. Wick is a fine, historic town, a busy centre with air services to Orkney and Shetland. It is as far as you can get from Penzance, the other extreme at the toe of Cornwall – about 925 rail miles and a 24-hour journey, though it can be done more

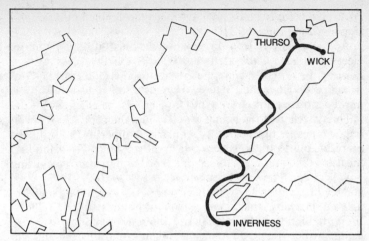

slowly with only two changes of train, at Edinburgh and Inverness. Thurso is the farthest north and was my choice. There are three trains a day from Inverness and I chose the 11.35 taking about four hours for the 154 miles. There was a buffet car for the first two hours.

I was in good time for the train, so there was time to admire the cast-iron coat of arms of the old Highland Railway, supported by wild-looking characters dressed in a few green leaves and carrying clubs – presumably not typical rail travellers.

Fellow passengers in June included the usual contingent of rucksacked young people, many from abroad, but this was not by any means only a tourist train. One of the six coaches in the all-second-class train was reserved for a party of schoolchildren on an outing from Dingwall to Tain, a pleasant little resort on the southern shore of the Dornoch Firth of which I had heard good reports. And there were numerous local people returning north after forays into the urban delights of Inverness. The line is not in fact promoted as a tourist attraction in the way the West Highland and Kyle of Lochalsh lines are and does not offer quite the same amount of visual drama. Yet it has a great deal of interest in a quieter way and some surprises.

The line goes first to Dingwall, where the Kyle of Lochalsh line goes off to the west, then follows the shore of Cromarty Firth and Nigg Bay, with hills rising to the left. An early stop is at the industrial town of Invergordon, remembered as the scene of the great naval mutiny of 1931, when units of the Atlantic Fleet, assembled in Cromarty Firth for fleet exercises, refused duty as a protest against pay cuts. Even without that drama the Atlantic Fleet must have made a stirring sight at anchor in the Firth – *Repulse, Valiant, Warspite, Nelson, Hood, Rodney* were all great warships which would figure a few years later in momentous naval actions and then pass into the mists of history.

Today we could see no naval craft. At the entrance to the firth huge cranes were wrestling over the construction of an oil exploration platform, North Sea oil being the new source of employment for the area.

We crossed flat land to the southern shore of the Dornoch Firth and let the children and their teachers off at Tain. Running inland now up the side of the firth we found the country gentler than the West Highlands, but also colder. Ardgay is the station for Bonar Bridge, which has a youth hostel and is a centre for walking, and we took aboard more young walkers at Lairg, the furthest point inland here, at the bottom of Loch Shin.

We lost our buffet service at Rogart, a halt in the middle of forest and cattle pasture.

Back on the coast at Golspie we caught a glimpse of the lodge and tree-lined avenue leading to Dunrobin Castle, stronghold of the Dukes of Sutherland for centuries. The castle, mostly rebuilt during the last century, used to have its own private station, a neat little half-timbered building, now restored.

Now the line ran through neat farmland between the sea and heather-covered hills. We could see sheep grazing, haymaking in progress, a mare and foal cantering, rabbits everywhere, a picture of ordered prosperity reinforced at Helmsdale by the girls to be seen – tall, pretty, with elegant bearing.

We turned inland to climb the Strath of Kildonan, up a broad valley with white farmhouses into the purple hills. As we climbed, the country became more bare. At Kinbrace there was very little but reservoirs and conifer forest. Further up at Forsinard, where the railway left the company of the road and turned north-east across wild moorland, there was nothing at all except a hotel and a handful of houses. At the summit, reached soon after, 708 feet above sea level, we were in an empty landscape of moorland dotted with small lakes, with mountain peaks looming like battleships on the horizon.

We ran out of the wilderness into smiling farmland again. We had found the valley of the River Thurso and were back among neat white houses and grazing cattle and sheep. Very soon we were at Georgemas Junction, the parting of the ways. Our locomotive hauled off the first two coaches to Wick. Another, which had been waiting up the branch line, hitched up the remaining four coaches and pulled them backwards up the branch to the neat little station at Thurso. We were as far north as the railway went and only a few miles south of mainland Britain's most northerly point at Dunnet Head.

I had vaguely expected Thurso to feel remote, especially after the wilderness we had come through, but quite the contrary. We had come through cold, overcast weather with occasional rain, but out on the plain the weather had cleared, the sun had come out and the whole place sparkled. Far from looking remote, Thurso presented a street of grey stone houses with immaculate suburban front lawns leading down to a shopping centre with a Woolworths, a good bookshop and much the same consumer durables as you'd find in any other small town.

Thurso has a couple of ruined castles, as what self-respecting Scots town has not. A bus goes to nearby Scrabster, which has a ferry service to Stromness on the mainland of Orkney and in summer one to the Faroes. Also meeting our train was a rather elderly coach offering a free service to John o' Groats, whence a competing ferry would take foot passengers to South Ronaldsay in the Orkneys.

The walk from the station down through the town to the sea-shore of Thurso Bay takes about fifteen minutes. From here you can see the Orkney island of Hoy, a high wall of rock. Look due north slightly to the left of Hoy and you are staring at the North Pole – at least, there's nothing between you and it except a lot of cold water and ice. No wonder it feels a bit chilly up here even in June with the sun shining.

The last train of the day starts back to Inverness at 18.02 getting in at 22.21. The buffet car comes on soon after eight, but it seemed sensible to be on the safe side and stock up with food and drink for the return. Return journeys lack the thrill of new discovery but I found this one quite rewarding. I spotted a herd of deer on the moor near Forsinard and appreciated more fully the beauty of the Strath of Kildonan.

This evening train was the main mail train for the area and at every stop a postman was waiting with his bags. At one I spotted a red estate car grandly lettered *Royal Mail Bus*, a reminder of the sensible procedure of carrying passengers with the mail in remote areas.

At Lairg a man was waiting with a wheelbarrow filled with large fish encased in basketwork covers, a consignment of salmon for Aberdeen. 'Sometimes there'll be fifty boxes of salmon,' the guard said, 'that's a fair pennyworth.'

At some of the stations on this line the platforms are lower than usual and a series of footstools is placed ready for passengers to step out. Train travel is a personal service here. Some of the stops are by request only— you tell the guard where you want to get off and he makes sure you sit in the right coach.

Well provisioned or not, it was cheering when the buffet car opened up, this time with a sociable steward in full red and blue uniform. Buffets vary and this one doesn't do hot dishes but there are always sandwiches, tea and coffee, beer and whisky.

By the time I got back to Inverness I felt I'd had more of an expedition than a mere day out. In spite of the Woolworths it was difficult not to think of Thurso as a rare travelling experience in hitherto undiscovered territory. There aren't so many places where you travel four hours *south* to get to Inverness.

Inverness to Aberdeen

Seven trains a day, about two and a half hours

Inverness and Aberdeen are both important InterCity termini receiving top-class trains from Edinburgh, Glasgow and London. Between them runs a minor line of 108 miles offering seven trains a day of second-class coaches, most with the bonus of a buffet car. The journey takes about two and a half hours and offers the stimulus of a change of scene after a tour of the Highlands. I caught the 10.25 and arrived in Aberdeen in nice time for lunch.

Almost all of Scotland has memories of battles, massacres, hangings, castle burnings and power struggles of a gory kind. This north-east corner of the country is richly endowed with all of these. One of the bloodiest was Culloden, the last battle to be fought on British soil, when the Duke of Cumberland's forces crushed the Highland army led by Bonnie Prince Charlie in 1746, ended the Jacobite rising and extinguished all hopes of the Stuarts regaining the throne. The Inverness–Aberdeen line passed the moor, on the right shortly after the train leaves Inverness. The

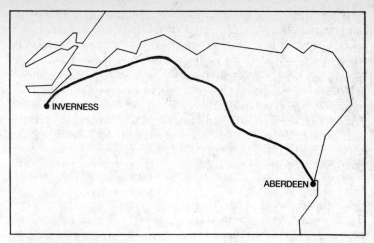

INVERNESS

ABERDEEN

main line from Perth to Inverness passes across the moor very close to the battlefield.

The weather was appropriately gloomy and wet as my train ran out of Inverness, with the top of Black Isle's hill obscured by mist in the Moray Firth. This was plainly industrious, well-kept farming country, not at all conducive to thoughts of massacred Highlanders.

Nairn, which we soon reached, is reckoned to be the gateway to the Highlands and it was along this coastal plain that Cumberland marched on Inverness. The night before Culloden he slept at Nairn while Bonnie Prince Charlie was staying overnight at Kilravock Castle, near Cawdor, some miles south of our line. Nairn, seen from the train, seemed not at all portentous. I saw a panorama of a neat town and I knew it from a past visit as a cheerful little seaside resort.

If I wasn't to brood over the '45 and the sadness of all that, the next stop, Forres, reminded me that this was Macbeth country, where he might well have murdered Duncan if he didn't do so at Cawdor Castle a few miles away or back in Inverness – theories differ. At any rate, Macbeth's meeting with the three witches is placed somewhere near here. When he and Banquo come to the blasted heath Banquo asks, 'How far is't called to Forres?' Unfortunately nobody tells him, so the place cannot be precisely pinpointed. Macbeth is too preoccupied with the greetings that name him Thane of Cawdor and king hereafter.

'When shall we three meet again, in thunder, lightning or in rain?' the witches wonder. The thought that it might be a fine day doesn't occur to them, but the weather here is not as bad as all that and it brightened for me as soon as the train was clear of Elgin, the next stop. This was the scene of a good deal of burning and butchery, notably by a character called the Wolf of Badenoch aided by a large cast of wild Highlandmen. Its most notable feature is a ruined cathedral.

After crossing the River Spey, which had run down Strath Spey past many distilleries, we were passing more cheering, if less historic, sights: great square warehouses full of whisky and at Keith a railway tank wagon transporting Chivas Regal from its birthplace near here.

We turned south and ran up beside the River Deveron to Huntly, where there is a castle from which the Gordons held sway in these parts. On the hills of Strath Bogie, through which we now passed, is the most extensive of the Forestry Commission's plantations, and Huntly is a popular stop for walkers.

On a conical hill to the left before the line reached Insch is the site of an Iron Age hill fort. After Insch, on the same side, comes Pitcaple Castle with two round towers. Now we were out of hills and into rolling, well-populated farmland again. From Inverurie, an ancient royal burgh, we followed the River Don. Industry began near Dyce airport and we were soon running through a series of cuttings into Aberdeen.

Aberdeen station has a bus terminus in the front yard, which is as it always should be, and a Station Hotel stands ready to receive those sensible enough to stop over for a day or two. The Granite City, with a population of more than 200,000, was an important place before it received the additional boost of becoming a centre of the North Sea oil industry. Union Street, the main shopping street, is one of the most gracious in Europe, a long, gentle slope of stone buildings closed at top and bottom by towers. It's one of those streets which are exciting just to walk in.

The tower at the bottom end of the street looks dignified and forbidding enough to have been captured by Robert the Bruce or to have accommodated Mary Queen of Scots. It is, in fact, the Salvation Army Citadel but it closes the vista none the less effectively for that. Up the street a little way, past another fortress that turns out to be the Town Hall, a classical Ionic screen fronts the graveyard of the parish church. Here the wealth and solidity of the city are marked by marble tombstones on which are inscribed the occupations – merchant, deputy chief constable, advocate – as well as the names of the departed.

This solid city on its hills overlooking an extensive harbour appears exciting but hard-working, and somehow quite foreign. A walk away to the north is the old city, clustered round the university, and between Union Street and the docks, behind the castles of commerce, stand some forbidding tenements. I crept down the sinisterly named Correction Wynd to find lunch at a pub near the market.

In the lounge of the Market Inn the menu offered Stovies, new to me. They turned out to be a large helping of meat and potato hash, the meat providing the flavour and the potato the substance. Tasty and nourishing, but probably not for slimmers.

For the interest of its old quarter, its docks, its beach and for many interesting day trips Aberdeen is well worth a stop.

Down the East Coast

Good service, at least one train an hour
The Flying Scotsman, covering the 524 miles from King's Cross to Aberdeen in just seven hours, takes two hours 20 minutes over the last 130 miles, not bad when you consider that there are two spectacular bridges to be negotiated. The other two named expresses, the Aberdonian and the Talisman, take only six minutes longer on this stretch. I started my journey from Aberdeen to the Scottish capital at 14.00 in the Talisman but by stopping off to look at Montrose I gave up much of this speed and comfort.

Montrose was an arbitrary choice. Stonehaven, the first stop out of Aberdeen, is a lively holiday resort with an old fishing town around the harbour. Arbroath, next stop down the coast after Montrose, is also a resort and fishing port and the place where in 1320 the Arbroath Declaration was signed proclaiming Scotland's independence under King Robert the Bruce. The room in which the declaration was signed can be seen in the abbey building.

Montrose, too, has its share of antiquity and historial associations. There was a castle here which Wallace destroyed in 1297. And the heart of Robert the Bruce is said to have been taken from here by ship to the Holy Land. Most of its notable buildings, however, are of more recent date. A few minutes' walk takes you

into the wide High Street, with
an eighteenth-century Old
Town Hall, several notable
stone buildings of a later period
and statues of David Hume, the
philosopher, and Sir Robert
Peel. At one time it had a vogue
as a spa and the buildings show
the influence of the town's
trade with the Netherlands.

To the right of the station as
you come in from Aberdeen is a
large tidal basin of the River
Esk, where many estuary birds
can usually be seen. The town
has a popular beach some way
from the town centre. The
harbour in the river is a busy
one and is now one of the ports
supplying the oil platforms.

Later, I caught a train to
Dundee, 31 miles down the line
past Arbroath, Carnoustie
(notable mainly for its championship golf courses), and
Broughty Ferry at the head of
the Firth of Tay. Broughty
Castle, standing tall and square
by the sea, was built in the
fifteenth century, occupied by
the English in 1547 and recaptured by French troops on the Scots'
side in 1550.

Dundee is an ancient city which has become a flourishing port
and commercial centre with many modern buildings. It occupies a
magnificent hillside site looking south over the Firth of Tay and
looks altogether a much more attractive place than is suggested by
its rather dour former reputation as the home of the three Js – jute,
jam and journalism (Bonnie Dundee was Viscount Dundee, a
soldier, not the city). This is the junction for the line to Perth,
Stirling and Glasgow and here I left the comfortable Glasgow
train for a crowded local service to Edinburgh.

This quickly provided one of the most dramatic experiences of train travel in Britain, when it drew out of the station and shortly afterwards turned to carry us across the two-mile-wide Firth of Tay on the Tay Bridge, BR's longest. Before the train turns on to the bridge the length and beauty of it can be seen, the line being carried on the top of the girders supported by piers. In the middle section the lattice-work of girders stands up above the others and the line is carried on the lower level, in this way creating higher clearance for ships in the channel below. As the train enters the curve of the bridge and goes across at a height of 92 feet above the water there are superb views up and down the firth – the towers and spires of Dundee on its hillside and the elegant road bridge two miles downstream.

One slightly chilly note is struck by the stubs of old piers to be seen beside those that carry the railway bridge. These are the remains of the ill-fated first Tay Bridge, which collapsed in a storm during the winter of 1879. A train crossing at the time plunged into the Tay and all the passengers were killed. William McGonagall, Dundee's celebrated poet and tragedian, had written an ode beginning 'Beautiful Railway Bridge of the Silvery Tay!/With your numerous arches and pillars in so grand array,/And your central girders, which seem to the eye/To be almost towering to the sky'.

After the disaster he wrote another ode telling how 'the cry rang out all o'er the town,/Good heavens! The Tay Bridge is blown down', adding that 'your central girders would not have given way . . . had they been supported on each side with buttresses'. However, he was eventually able to write a third poem addressed to 'the beautiful new railway bridge o' the Silvery Tay', noting that 'Thy structure to my eye seems strong and grand,/And the workmanship most skilfully planned', adding the hope that Queen Victoria would visit it very soon.

But now we were over the bridge and away from the Silvery Tay into the old Kingdom of Fife, the self-contained region between the Tay and the Forth. In this area farming, mining and manufacture manage to exist side by side; considering how much is going on the country looks remarkably unspoiled, though the evidence of industry became more marked as we crossed the peninsula. We stopped at Leuchars, where there is an RAF base, the old town of Cupar and the industrial town of Kirkcaldy on the shore of the Firth of Forth. From here as the train made its way along

the north bank of the Forth we could see the dark mass of
Edinburgh over the water and then the massive girders of the
Forth Bridge.

This mighty bridge with its three great cantilever towers,
completed in 1890, gives an impression of tremendous strength
and the train-ride over its more than a mile and a half length,
passing close to the huge dark red steel tubes, is a thrilling
experience. A tanker lying at anchor in the river 158 feet below
looks quite small. There are views down the Forth to the sea and
upriver where the road suspension bridge provides a study in
contrasting elegance.

The train now rattled through Edinburgh's industrial outskirts,
stopped at Haymarket on the west side of the city and ran on into
Waverley station.

Coming up the ramp from Waverley and looking around is a
stunning experience. No other railway station exit in the world
offers so much visual drama so close. The traveller emerges right
into the middle of the action. The castle on its rock and the
buildings of the city's Royal Mile tower on one side, the imposing
line of Princes Street rears on the other, the North British Hotel
with its big clock tower looms above you.

Edinburgh never lets you forget that it is a capital city and one
of the most exciting places in Europe. The riches it offers in the
ordinary way – never mind the Festival – are almost infinite and
any holiday-maker with the time could explore it happily for a
month. For a day or a weekend it is a memorable experience.
There are two convenient hotels: the North British, built by the
railway company, is the station hotel for Waverley Station and
can be entered from it. The Caledonian, built by the railway of
that ilk, was the hotel for a station now closed, and is a ten-minute
walk from Waverley. To make up for this it plays a very active
part in the life of the city and the Cally is the venue of many social
events and entertainments. While the building is grand in the
turn-of-the-century manner, the atmosphere is relaxed and informal.

On this visit I stayed at the Roxburgh, near the Cally but in
Charlotte Square, one of the fine squares in the eighteenth-century
New Town area behind Princes Street. Charlotte Square was
designed by Robert Adam and the quietly elegant Roxburgh suits
its style to its surroundings; a meal and a stay overnight there are
an experience of Edinburgh living up to its traditions.

Edinburgh–Perth–Aviemore–Perth–Glasgow

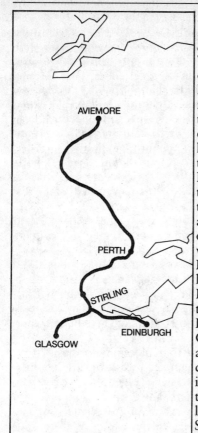

Edinburgh or Glasgow to Inverness, seven trains a day, about four hours

The journey from Edinburgh or Glasgow through Perth to Inverness takes the classic route to the Highlands through the Grampian mountains. It is one of the most scenic and historically interesting of all train rides in Scotland. From Perth, once the Scottish capital, the line runs up Strath Tay – the valley of the River Tay – and Glen Garry, over the Pass of Drumochter, where the railway reaches its highest point in Britain at 1484 feet above sea level, then down beside the River Spey to Aviemore before turning north over the hills to Inverness, passing the scene of Culloden. With its mountain and moorland views, its vistas down the length of quiet lochs, its castles and battlefields and tumbling salmon rivers, the line takes in the essence of Scotland.

I caught the 9.23 from Edinburgh and decided to go as far as Aviemore for lunch, taking an afternoon train down the line again to Stirling and Glasgow. I caught a final glimpse of Edinburgh Castle as the train moved out and the route led first back to Falkirk before turning north to Stirling and Perth.

At Stirling we were able to see another of the great railway sights of Britain: Stirling Castle, high on its rock with the historic town spread over the hillside below. It's easy to see why the town and its castle have been so important in Scottish history – the fortress stands guard over the River Forth at a point where, joined by Allan Water, it flows through a gap in the hills into the Firth of Forth. The castle is in view on the left from the train for some time. From the station, mercifully not covered, the impressive stone castle, the church of the Holy Rude and other historic buildings can be seen.

The castle's history is much older than the mainly fifteenth and sixteenth century buildings on view. It is thought that King Arthur held it for a time. Edward I captured it after a tremendous siege, since even the most impregnable castle could be starved out, but the Scots won it back after Bannockburn, again by siege. Mary Queen of Scots was crowned here and Bonnie Prince Charlie unsuccessfully besieged it in 1746. Bannockburn itself, where in 1314 Robert the Bruce with 30,000 Scots crushed an English army of 100,000, lies three miles to the south-east.

From Stirling the train went on to Dunblane, then up Strath-allan to Gleneagles, the station for the famous golf courses giving nothing away in a deep cutting, and so to Perth.

Perth is one of the major railway crossroads of Scotland, well placed as a rail touring centre. It is an ancient capital of the country. John Knox preached here to such effect that the city's monasteries were destroyed. The city was occupied by Montrose in 1644, captured by Cromwell in 1651, taken by Bonnie Dundee in 1689, and occupied by Jacobites in 1715 and 1745.

In the park here in 1396 there took place a notorious battle in which two clans fielded thirty champions a side to settle a point of honour. Most of the contestants were killed. Sir Walter Scott describes it in *The Fair Maid of Perth* and the Fair Maid's House is one of the city sights. Scone Palace and Huntingtower Castle are not far away.

For all its weight of bloodthirsty history Perth is a fine city with pleasant riverside walks and panoramic views towards the Firth of Tay from the top of Kinnoull Hill.

From Perth we began a gentle climb into hill and forest country, past towering crags. The train had filled up and I was joined by two young mothers with their five children off for a day out at Pitlochry.

Just before Dunkeld, the first stop after Perth, we passed through Birnam, the movement of whose wood to Dunsinane boded no good for Macbeth. Dunkeld has a ruined cathedral and is the site of a battle in which the Highlanders victorious at Killiecrankie were defeated in their turn by the burning down of the town.

We went on up the river and into the forest, the mountain scenery increasingly wild and beautiful in sparkling sunshine. We were following the road made by General Wade after 1715, part of a network designed to make it easier for the Hanoverians to keep the Highlands in order.

Pitlochry, the next stop, is a favourite centre for walkers and for excursions. Crowds from our train got off here, many of them transferring to coaches for trips to the Pass of Killiecrankie, to the Queen's View on Loch Tummel, a beauty spot much enjoyed by Queen Victoria, or for a scenic drive along Loch Tay. Pitlochry is said to be the centre of Scotland. It is certainly the centre of a great deal of beautiful country – mountains, lochs and forests all being readily accessible from here. It has a summer theatre festival and weekly Highland nights.

Shortly after leaving Pitlochry the train passes Loch Faskally and then goes through the Pass of Killiecrankie, a narrow gorge where in 1689 Highlanders commanded by Bonnie Dundee (Bloody Clavers to his enemies) roared down to overwhelm the troops of King William III.

Up beside the River Garry we climbed to Blair Atholl. Blair Castle, among the trees above the village, was the last castle in Britain to be besieged – by Lord George Murray just before Culloden. The Duke of Atholl, who owns it, is the only British subject allowed a private army. The castle is open to the public and has many Jacobite relics. Our train stopped here for 20 minutes, delayed by a breakdown further up the line.

As we went up Glen Garry we could see the river running down the way we had come. We passed the small Loch Garry at the top of the glen and crossed an area of bog, rocks and heather. The hills closed in on either side as we reached the summit of the Pass of Drumochter. After a while we were joined by another stream, running the way we were going. This was the River Truim and we were soon running down with it to join the Spey. More wild country at first, with the 15 miles of Loch Ericht offering a vista of solitude as we came into Dalwhinnie station, still nearly 1200 feet above sea level. Nothing but desolation here; a bit more animation at Newtonmore, where the Macphersons have a clan museum and an annual rally. This is the place for walkers and pony trekkers exploring the wild country around. Kingussie, next down the line, is more of a resort, with hotels and shops, and even bravely supports a little industrial estate.

On finally to Aviemore, by now 47 minutes late, the first time any of the trains on my travels had been significantly behind time. It was not the day for Aviemore. The sun had disappeared and a cold drizzle was falling. I was perhaps lucky to be spared 47 minutes of it. I left the comfortable train with some reluctance.

Aviemore, between the Monadhliath mountains and the Cairngorms, is a major tourist, sports and leisure centre. It is Britain's most important skiing resort, with lifts to mountaintops and facilities for winter sports enthusiasts at the modern Aviemore centre, a complex of hotel, leisure and catering facilities within a few minutes' walk of the station. The centre is in use all the year round, catering in summer for walkers, climbers and tourists of all kinds.

For railway enthusiasts there is the preserved steam railway to Boat of Garten, operating from its own station a few minutes away (signposted) from the BR station. For a short summer visit Aviemore offers a nature trail, a Highland craft village, excursions into the Cairngorms and the Glen More Forest Park and immense views from the top of the chair-lift.

My own sampling of the centre's lunch facilities was not encouraging: quite the worst casserole of alleged Scotch beef I have ever failed to get my teeth into.

When it was time to catch a train south again the station provided soothing entertainment, the arrival of a goods train of six coal wagons, two flat cars and a van. The locomotive left the wagons at a platform, ran round the train and detached the guard's van, shunted this on to the end of some waiting wagons, attached these and the van to the original train and ran back round to the front of the train ready to move on. This little scene used to be common at most country railway stations but is now quite rare in England.

My train had come in and I was glad to see a buffet ready to help travellers keep out the cold. We ran back over the same route to the edge of Falkirk, then through Croy and Lenzie, the train threading its way among the tower blocks and tenements of north Glasgow and finally into the tunnel to Queen Street station, the last few miles a sad anticlimax after the glories further north.

Having previously stayed most comfortably at the North

British, Queen Street's station hotel, I now sampled the Central, attached to Central Station a few minutes' walk away. A bus runs between the two station but unless the weather is very bad or you have heavy luggage the walk down pedestrianized Buchanan Street is a pleasant one.

The Central Hotel, wrapped around a corner of the station, was built in the heroic days when railway companies competed for custom by the sheer size and magnificence of their establishments. The Central is huge, its corridors long and its bedrooms marvellously spacious, but it mercifully avoids overbearing grandness; its bar and dining room are on a quite human scale and its prices fortunately bear little relation to the scale of its architecture. Underneath all that bulk it turns out to be a friendly, relaxed place.

Excursions from Glasgow

The Trans-Clyde service of interconnecting suburban electric trains centred on Glasgow gives the people of the city and its spreading suburbs and dormitories a swift and convenient means of getting to and from work. It also enables people of the area and visitors to the city to get out quickly to the traditional playgrounds of Loch Lomond, the Clyde estuary and the seaside.

From Central station trains run in something under an hour along the south bank of the Clyde to Gourock for ferries across

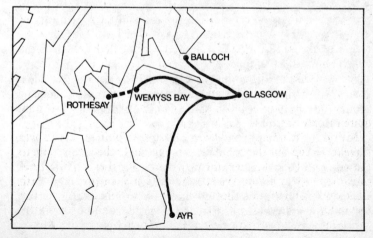

the Clyde to Dunoon and Kilcreggan; and to Wemyss Bay for ferries to Rothesay on the island of Bute. A line a little further south takes an hour to Ardrossan beach on the Firth of Clyde or Ardrossan harbour for ferries to Brodick on the island of Arran and ships to the Isle of Man. It then turns up the coast to Largs for ferries to the island of Cumbrae. A line branching south from this one serves the seaside resorts of Troon, Ayr (for paddle steamer excursions in the Firth of Clyde) and Girvan (for trips to Ailsa Craig) before running south over the moors to Stranraer for ships to Larne in Northern Ireland. All these offer day-out possibilities, the trip to Ayr taking about an hour and to Stranraer two and a half hours.

From Queen Street (or from Central, changing at Partick) there's a half-hourly service along the north bank of the Clyde to Craigendoran and Helensburgh, on the river at the entrance to Gare Loch. A similar service goes to Balloch at the foot of Loch Lomond and this is extended to Balloch pier to connect with the morning trip by paddle steamer.

In addition to the main line from Glasgow to Carlisle and the south, a secondary line reaches Carlisle by way of Kilmarnock, Kirkconnel, Dumfries and Annan. For Glasgow-based tourists day trips to Dumfries are possible, though the trains are not frequent. Burns spent the last years of his life here as an exciseman, wrote many poems and is buried in the churchyard. His favourite pub, the Globe, still has his chair and the house he lived in is a museum.

Ayr

Frequent service, about an hour

I began with a seaside outing to Ayr from Glasgow Central. This is a run through a mainly industrial landscape, some of it bleak, until the coast is reached at Barassie. Paisley, the town that gave its name to the pattern, presents a grim and grimy look, though its Gilmour Street station shows traces of some style. Irvine is a New Town of 60,000 people with plans for this number to be doubled, but shows nothing very striking to the train traveller. Troon and Prestwick (where there is an international airport close to the station) look quiet places catering chiefly for golfers and fishermen besides being Glasgow dormitories.

Ayr is the most considerable town and resort along this coast and gets off to a good start with a poet to greet travellers leaving the station. The statue is of Robert Burns, who was born here, and the old Tam o' Shanter Inn, recalling one of his best-loved poems, is now a Burns museum. Ayr is a pleasant town, with some interesting old buildings. The beach is about fifteen minutes' walk from the station.

Rothesay

Journey one and three quarter hours, approximately every hour and a half

A day trip to Rothesay was the classic day out for Glasgow city dwellers and it's still a marvel how quickly you can get out of the city centre and away across the Firth of Clyde for a day or an afternoon at a seaside resort which hasn't changed in essentials since the last century. The day I went there were plenty of family parties.

The route out of Central station by electric train took us out through Paisley again but this time along the south bank of the Clyde, with views across the mighty river and a touch of salt in the air. There was even a sight of romantic Newark Castle with its fifteenth-century tower before we reached the shipyard cranes and docks of Port Glasgow. We climbed up a single track behind Greenock's waterside industry and had a taste of countryside, with grazing cattle and a wooded valley, before passing the power station at Inverkip, with its massive chimney, and running down to Wemyss Bay, looking out over the upper waters of the Firth of Clyde.

Wemyss Bay station, built for the ferry trade, was determined to give us a festive day out. Its delightful little circular concourse, with elegant glass roof, was hung with baskets of flowers and a wide curving covered walk led down to the landing stage. On the walls were preserved the carved wooden and painted coats of arms which embellished the paddle housings of the steamers which used to ply from here, together with photographs, taken in their pre-1914 heyday, of the graceful old vessels to which they had belonged.

Waiting for us today, though, was not an old paddle steamer but the modern car ferry *Saturn*. All the time-honoured pleasures of a day out at Rothesay were still here. The Firth of Clyde, ringed by hills and with islands at its mouth, made a sparkling inland sea with a flotilla of yachts racing down from the north and industrial Glasgow nowhere to be seen. To complete the picture, there passing us as we crossed the seven miles of water to Rothesay went the double-funnelled *Waverley*, Britain's last sea-going paddle-steamer, which makes excursions from Glasgow to Ayr.

The *Saturn* had a bar but there would be more conviviality on the last passage back at night. This afternoon most were happy to spend the half-hour of the miniature voyage taking in the beauty of the sea, the yachts and the distant hills.

Rothesay was a delight as we passed the headland and sailed into the bay in which it stands — a line of proper Victorian hotels ranging from the grand to the small and fanciful and making up a cheerful whole in which there were few jarring notes of unwanted modernity. This is still a lively and stylish family resort. It has a romantic ruined castle with round walls unusual in Scotland.

Unlike Dunoon, which stands on a peninsula, Rothesay is on an island, Bute. This has helped to preserve its style and prevented it being overrun by motor traffic. It still makes a first-class day out. For a family party a not-too-long train ride, a short sea voyage and an afternoon at a lively seaside resort make a formula that's hard to beat. Both the freckled Glasgow kids and the black-eyed Malaysian boy and girl who were fellow-passengers on the way back were having a great time.

Loch Lomond

Glasgow to Balloch Pier three quarters of an hour
My third outing from Glasgow started from Queen Street low level, not to be confused with the city underground railway. This time I travelled out along the north bank of the Clyde but soon turned inland through forbidding stone tenement blocks and treeless acres of small terraces and semis. We were soon back to the Clyde with brief hints of its beauty seen between tenements and factories. A quick look, too, at the Erskine road suspension bridge, a marvel of economical elegance and the last bridge across the Clyde going downstream.

A train runs to connect with the steamer from Balloch pier but I had caught an earlier train and stopped off at Dumbarton, at the end of Glasgow's sprawl and pleasantly placed on the Clyde with the Kilpatrick Hills behind. The River Leven from Loch Lomond falls into the Clyde here. The town has a pleasant anchorage for yachts in the river and a peaceful quay.

It was a short ride from here to Balloch pier down a single-track branch from Dalreoch. Balloch is the normal terminus but when the boat is in, the train runs a little further on to the pier at the southern end of Loch Lomond.

The *Maid of the Loch*, waiting for us at the pier, was built at Greenock in 1953, the last paddle-steamer to be built in Britain. She absorbed us easily, having a capacity for 1000 passengers, and set off punctually for her morning cruise up the biggest and most beautiful of inland lochs to Inversnaid, near the northern end. From Balloch the loch opens out into a wide stretch of water, laced with numerous wooded islands, set about with green hills and presided over by the 3192-foot bulk of Ben Lomond to the north.

The *Maid* was to call at Luss on the west bank and Rowarden-nan on the east, reach Inversnaid at noon and return almost immediately. She would make a similar trip in the afternoon so that a variety of trips was possible. You could stay aboard until the ship returned, get off at Inversnaid and return on the second trip or get off at Rowardennan and walk through the Queen Elizabeth forest park to Inversnaid, about three and a half hours, to catch the second boat.

The top of the loch is seen from the railway to Fort William, which runs beside it from Tarbet to its head at Ardlui. So I went ashore at Rowardennan in company with many young walkers in ragged shorts and heavy boots who planned to walk in the forest or up to the summit of Ben Lomond. I walked far enough through the forest to attain a modest hilltop from which there was a magnificent view up and down the loch. I had time then to return to Rowardennan for a drink at the Rowardennan hotel, and return to the pier in time to board the *Maid* on her return trip. For lunch the *Maid* offered a cafeteria and a restaurant. I chose the restaurant and enjoyed one of the best-value meals I had in Scotland.

Back at Balloch pier we found a much larger crowd waiting for the afternoon cruise. Our morning trip had never been crowded and must have been more comfortable.

Carlisle to Stranraer

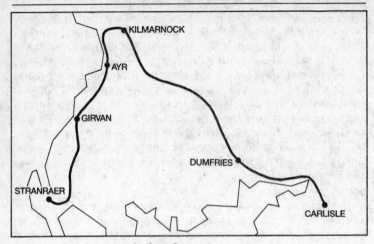

One train a day, nearly four hours

South-west Scotland is a rewarding area often missed by train explorers, there being only one train a day that does the interesting run of 166 miles from Carlisle to Stranraer at the head of Loch Ryan. Most places on this route can be reached from Glasgow but trains, are infrequent between Ayr and Stranraer and between Kilmarnock and Carlisle.

I joined the Northern Ireland boat train from Euston at Carlisle, where it shed four of its coaches and its main-line locomotive and settled down behind a leisurely diesel workhorse, crossing the River Esk at the head of the Solway Firth, leaving the main line at Gretna junction immediately after crossing the border into Scotland and taking the single track to Annan through flat country beside the firth. The going got more interesting when the line, now double again, turned north-west to Dumfries with blue hills appearing to the north and the great mass of Criffel, 1868 feet high, to the south.

The train began to move up through a forest landscape here. Beyond Dumfries, as we climbed Nithsdale following the course of the river through the hills, the country began to look more distinctly Scottish with white farmhouses set among intense green woods, the hilltops crowned with pines. From our side of the valley we could see across to the left the hills and woods of the

Galloway Forest Park, with peaks in the distance rising above 2000 feet.

A tunnel and a wooded hillside in a narrow valley took us to Kirkconnel, a seemingly isolated town in sparsely settled country. At this point I was reached by a charming girl with a tea trolley; she and her brother were operating a freelance refreshment business on this portion of the journey, the BR buffet having been taken off at Carlisle. The journey is a long one, taking all the afternoon, so she was welcome.

We parted from the River Nith at Cumnock and ran down from the high country to Kilmarnock, forbidding in a shower of rain with looming stone institutions but a place of some individuality with a large distillery, a curious turret in a park and a pub near the station called Fiftywaistcoats.

We were now approaching the edge of the greater Glasgow conurbation but our train turned off down a single track to join the Glasgow—Ayr line on the coast of Barassie, near Troon, and soon ran down through Prestwick to Ayr.

Beyond Ayr our line left the coast to wind through low hills with wide sweeps of farming country and neat huddles of villages among the folds of land. After the small town of Maybole we ran through moorland beside Girvan Water past three romantic castles to Girvan, the resort guarded by a hill that looks across ten miles of sea to Ailsa Craig – Fairy Rock in Gaelic but looking more like a monster plum pudding. There were further glimpses of angry waves on the seashore before our train turned inland and climbed back into the hills for perhaps the most beautiful part of the whole journey, an area of wild moorland fells criss-crossed with streams and rent with narrow wooded fissures. Here, as the train struggled through a rock cutting and over high, windswept country, there was a sense of travelling in a strange, unknown land, penetrating deeper into the ancient kingdom of Galloway. Far away to the left the hills of Galloway Forest Park were topped by the summit of Merrick, rising to 2766 feet, and in this still untamed country red deer, wild goats and even the golden eagle might be seen: magnificent walking country. From the train we could see whole valley vistas with scarcely a human habitation, only an isolated farmhouse here and there.

The train glided unhurriedly through gorse-covered cuttings, over grass and scrub, to join the ambling Water of Luce. Past an oak forest and down through grassy hills we ran out at last for a view of Luce Bay before turning west for the last few miles past Castle Kennedy and on to the Stranraer harbour mole sticking out into Loch Ryan.

Most of the passengers, bound for Belfast, transferred to the Larne ferry waiting on the other side of the jetty but I returned up the line to Ayr on a Sealink boat train for Glasgow decked out in red, white and three shades of blue. The new taste for trains in distinctive liveries is nowhere more advanced than in Scotland: it is said that you can see six or seven different train liveries at Glasgow Central station.

There was just enough light to enjoy the run back to Ayr after a trip through some of Scotland's secret beauty.

My tour of Scotland was a quick one. The train makes it possible for the visitor to cover a great deal of ground in a matter of days, enjoying every minute of it and getting an impression of the country as a whole. This can be rewarding and exciting – Edinburgh's stunning townscape, the peace of Loch Lomond, the glories of the glens and their mountains, the confident sweep of the Forth and Tay bridges, the desolation of the remote moorlands and the blue mystery of the Cuillins of Skye all reverberate in the mind long after you have seen them. The effect is so powerful that after a quick train tour of Scotland you are never quite the same person again.

Beyond these abiding visual impressions I took away with me a warm appreciation of the relaxed courtesy of Scottish people and a sense of the country's living history. It's not just that everywhere you go there's a castle or a battlefield or the site of a massacre, but the people still know and care about the events of which these are reminders. It gives an extra resonance to everything you see.

So much for a quick visit, well worth taking if that is all you have time for. But to get the best of a visit to Scotland you need all the time you can find – time to stop moving and drink it in, time to walk in the hills, time to get to know people and places. My tour left me wanting to do it all again, slowly.

5

Eastern England

BR Eastern Region broadly consists of England east of the Pennines and north of the Thames, its backbone being the East Coast main line from King's Cross. It offers a bit of everything – high-speed trains, the beauties of the Dales, the industrial North-east and Yorkshire, agricultural Lincolnshire, the Fens and East Anglia, a knees-up at Southend. Good centres for day trips are Newcastle, York, Leeds, Norwich and Cambridge, and included in this chapter are journeys between Eastern Region centres and

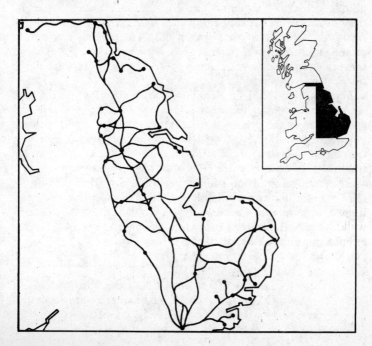

the north-west. Touring tickets are available for several areas in the region.

Leeds to Carlisle

Three trains a day, about two and a half hours

One of the most continuously beautiful train rides you can take in Britain is across the Pennines from Settle in North Yorkshire to Carlisle in Cumbria. In climbing over the Pennine hills the line rises to a height of 1167 feet above sea level and stays at over 1000 feet for 16 miles. While the country never quite achieves the bleak grandeur of the Highlands it provides scenes of great beauty for mile after mile as the train mounts up through the dales to the high moorlands and then drops down through the Eden valley towards Carlisle. The engineering on the line is as spectacular as the scenery, involving 22 viaducts and 14 tunnels in 70 miles of double track.

Although most of the route falls into the London Midland Region it is most easily considered as an extension of eastern journeys from Leeds. To catch the 16.05 train from Leeds the most convenient approach from London is by the 12.30 from King's Cross, a 125 express which leaves the East Coast main line at Doncaster. From here we ran through coal-mining country, stopping at Wakefield, where the train came in on a high embankment giving views of the town centre and over the surrounding country.

Shortly afterwards another curved embankment brought us into Leeds, home of Headingley cricket ground, with a fine panoramic view of modern towers and the dome of a majestic hall set out on a ridge. Leeds is rather a dull name for a major city that makes an immediately favourable impression on the southerner, the people brisk and cheerful, the public and commercial buildings on a scale to match big ambitions. There's a large gusto about the place.

There was an hour to wait before my train to Carlisle pulled out. When it did, the interest was almost immediate. In addition to their other virtues most Northern towns are easy to get out of and we were into the Yorkshire Moors within minutes of leaving Leeds station.

For first-time travellers in these parts it's a revelation how clean and pleasant these woollen towns are. The industrial North no longer consists of dark Satanic mills under a pall of black smoke. Bingley looked smilingly clean among its hills, with an intriguing glimpse of a five-rise lock on the Leeds and Liverpool canal.

Keighley is the terminus of the Worth Valley steam railway which goes to Oxenhope through Haworth, where the Brontës lived and wrote. As we came into the station a train of coaches in the old LMS maroon livery behind a black engine with steam up waited on the Worth Valley platform.

On the right was the legendary quintessence of Yorkshire, Ilkley Moor itself, the perils of walking on which bareheaded, or baht 'at, have been much celebrated in song.

Soon we were at the watershed on the spine of England. At Hellifield we had left the River Aire flowing away to the North Sea and here was Ribblesdale, where the river flows down to the Irish Sea.

We were now well into the Yorkshire Dales National Park. At first there was rolling grassland, rising on either side to fells which on this cool, damp day receded into mists – Pendle Hill, notorious for the witches said to live there (I was told of a vicar driven out of his parish by them in recent times), followed by the great green and blue masses of Ingleborough and Pen y Ghent, both well over 2000 feet above sea level.

From the train as we ran up Ribblesdale the view was of green fields criss-crossed by stone walls, lined and set about with trees, an occasional white or stone farm building, black and white cattle on a hillside sharing grazing with sheep – the picture of timeless beauty, rightness and content. This was the incomparable English farming country at its most beautiful. If Britain is in decay, beset with social and economic problems beyond solution, nobody has told them up there, thank goodness.

A sign on the station at Settle records the opening of the Midland Railway extension, the Settle and Carlisle line, in 1876, and this little town is where the spectacular engineering feats of the Carlisle line really begin. A line had reached Settle from Leeds some years earlier; it branches off just before Settle to climb over the Pennines to Carnforth and Morecambe.

The town's present-day importance is that it is on the edge of the National Park. From the train, when it stops at the platform, you can see the fields and hills starting right at the station gate. You could step off the train, walk out of the station and straight into marvellous country. To the north, as far as the eye can see, there is nothing but grass and trees and rock, rising seductively into the fells – a great escape route for all oppressed by the strains of city life.

This is one of the wonderful things the train can do: take you swiftly and cleanly away from the city and set you free to walk without encumbrance.

Now the line began a steady rise to the summit. It passed through a long tunnel from North Yorkshire into Cumbria and climbed high on the fellside to 1169 feet at Aisgill before dropping steadily down among majestic heights, cloud-topped today. A series of tunnels and viaducts took the line over dales peacefully remote from the workaday striving of the town left far behind. For a time the train ran along a shelf high over Dentdale with all that green loveliness spread below, swelling and falling like sea waves.

At intervals the wall of hills gave way to views up valleys to even more remote and romantic fells and peaks.

At Appleby, where a small, discreet caravan park was the first real sign of tourism to be seen on this line, the train crossed the River Eden and thereafter followed it down the beautiful wooded Edendale to Carlisle. Isolated Appleby was so delighted when the Act authorizing the railway was passed that the church bells rang in celebration. Now there are roads but in winter the railway must still be the most reliable link with the outside world. Snow fences guard the line on the high moorland.

After Lazonby the great sweeps of the dales narrow down and the river runs through a deep, thickly-wooded gorge, the railway high above it. Throughout the length of the line from Settle every viaduct presented a superb view on either side until finally the train joined the main line and crept into Carlisle station.

The run provided a sense of exhilaration such as I had never expected to experience on a train in England. For two hours I had been taken through a country of a perfection of beauty I had never realized could be reached by train, complemented rather than marred by the graceful stone viaducts of the railway. It was a day to be treasured.

A first experience of the line must be an end-to-end unbroken journey to get the full effect. But there are several places inviting a stop on a subsequent trip. Settle offers an irresistible invitation to get out and walk; Appleby is a pleasant old town topped by a Norman keep, and has nature trails. Several stations on the line are closed to regular services but open in the summer for special trains of the Dalesrail service operated on behalf of the National Park. These stations give access to the dales for walkers.

Carlisle was a good place to end the journey. It has a strong, distinctive character and never forgets that it is a border city with the Scots just up the road. Bonnie Prince Charlie's men captured the city in 1745 and a garrison of troops was kept here until quite recent times. The squat, businesslike castle is still in part an army establishment.

The main buildings of the city – except for the Gothic station – are built in the local red stone: the castle, the fat round towers of the citadel and the small but intriguing cathedral built on to a Norman priory whose stout round pillars and odd-shaped arches can be seen. Instead of the usual soaring Gothic pillars and vaulting there is a wonderful painted ceiling.

The city was a Roman station near the western end of Hadrian's great wall, built across the top of England from the Solway Firth to the Tyne. Many Roman pillars and memorial stones with carved inscriptions can be seen in the museum and the red local stone of some of them, matching the stone of the city's existing buildings, gives them a curious feeling of closeness in time to ourselves.

I stayed at the Cumbrian Hotel, next to the station. It makes a comfortable stopover and its adjoining café serves reasonably priced local dishes.

Skipton to Lancaster

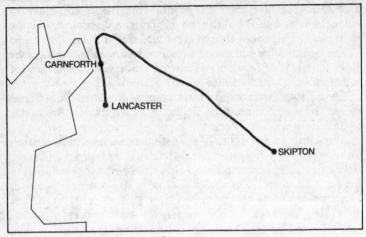

Five trains a day, about an hour

Trains from Leeds over the Settle and Carlisle line being infrequent (though extra chartered trains also run – inquire at Leeds or Carlisle), an alternative taste of the route's beauties can be obtained by travelling from Leeds to Lancaster by a line which branches off before Settle is reached and runs over the south-west corner of the North Yorkshire Pennines. It is not a substitute for the grandeur of the Settle and Carlisle line but offers some hint of its pleasures.

The two-coach local from Leeds, well filled on the morning I travelled, follows the Carlisle route to Skipton and passes up Ribblesdale through Long Preston to Settle junction, just before the town's station, then continues to Giggleswick while the Settle line climbs away to the north for some of its most spectacular engineering feats. The Lancaster line chooses an easier way, shortly finding the River Wenning and following its valley down to cross the Lune to the Keer and so across the West Coast main line to reach Carnforth before doubling back on to the main line and running south to Lancaster. Some trains reverse here and go on to nearby Morecambe on the coast.

From Giggleswick, of which nothing is revealed to train travellers, the train runs between the great bulks of Burn Moor to the south and Ingleborough Hill to the north, cutting through rocks to offer vistas of splendid lines of shrouded hills. Soon the toiling climb is over and the train runs cheerfully down the valley past young conifer plantations. Clapham offers no sign of a village except an inviting stone pub by the station, the Flying Horseshoe. This could be the place to get out and take to the hills – such fine country makes one's feet itch. Away to the south is the glorious forest of Bowland with hardly as much as a village for many miles.

The hills fall back as the train canters down the broadening valley through Bentham, Leck Fell and Crag Hill to the north, Mallowdale Fell and White Hill to the south. From Wennington the old Midland line followed the Lune valley down to Lancaster. This has now gone; the line we take, through a tunnel and over the Lune, was built jointly with the old Furness Railway to join that line at Carnforth. This we now do before turning south to Lancaster.

Carlisle to Newcastle

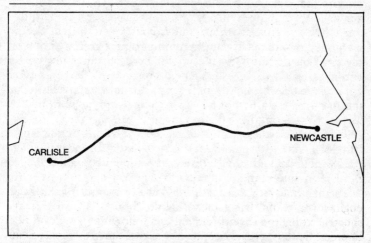

Eleven trains a day, about an hour and three quarters
The line from Carlisle to Newcastle runs for 61 miles across the neck of England. For most of its length it runs south of Hadrian's Wall, looping briefly to the north just before Haltwhistle. There's little to be seen of the wall from the train, but several stops along the route offer convenient transport to points of interest.

Vindolanda, a Roman fort with a well-preserved headquarters building, is close to Bardon Mill, and near Corbridge, a town on the Roman road from York to Edinburgh, a Roman military supply depot can be seen. One of the best preserved stretches of the wall is at Housesteads, where there is also a museum. It can be reached from either Haltwhistle or Haydon Bridge. You can stand on the 10-ft wide wall at Housesteads and look out over the wild, beautiful country to the north, just as the men of the second-century Roman legions did. Begun in AD 122, the wall marked the northern limits of settled Roman civilization. Away to the north was the wild country of the barbarians. Even today it looks like a remote frontier, though in fact there are a good many miles of unspoilt Northumberland hills before the Scottish border in the Cheviots is reached. The Pennine Way, the great footpath up the spine of England, leaves the wall at Housesteads and goes up through Redesdale to the Border.

The little train left Carlisle well filled, with numerous children and a few girl walkers with rucksacks and neckerchiefs. We crossed the River Eden by a viaduct and bridge giving a lovely view and then plunged through forest and fell, secretive cuttings and woodland glades in which our railway line seemed as closely integrated into the landscape as a footpath, the green relieved by the psychedelic purple of the willow herb on the banks of the cuttings.

The Romans were not the only people to build forts or castles in this part of the world, nor to fear invasion from the north. After leaving Brampton, the first stop, the train ran past the solid keep of Naworth Castle before running up the valley of the River Irthing. Haltwhistle and Prudhoe also have castles, of which Prudhoe, which withstood a three-day siege by the Scots in 1174, is the more interesting.

The line follows the South Tyne down to join the North Tyne near Hexham and then runs beside the Tyne itself. Up here it's difficult to believe that this is the same river that will run out between the coal wharves and shipyards of the lower Tyne. Its course is like a man's life – a carefree youth in the hills, gathering maturity as it broadens in the lower reaches, taking increasing responsibility with small boats at first before doing a man's job carrying barges and ships, making its contribution to the life of the country, getting dirty and losing youthful beauty, then falling exhausted into the eternal sea.

Hexham is a gem of a town, built of stone on a hill with narrow streets, a fine abbey and a fourteenth-century Moot Hall. It's at its delightful best on market day, Tuesday, and makes a good centre for walking or outings.

Corbridge came next and then, past Prudhoe, the great industrial conurbation of Tyneside began to make itself felt. The train passed through Wylam, where, it could be argued, the rapid industrialization of Britain really started. It is the birthplace of George Stephenson, father of the railway even if he did not actually invent either railways or steam locomotives. The unpretentious cottage in which he was born, now owned by the National Trust, is 300 yards east of the village on the banks of the Tyne. There is a Stephenson Trail around Wylam linking places associated with his early days. He was the engineer for the Stockton and Darlington and many other lines and built his successful locomotives in this area.

Soon after passing Wylam we plunged into industrial Tyneside, with coal between the sleepers in the sidings, serried ranks of slate-roofed terraces giving way later to tall blocks of flats, warehouses, coal quays on the river, tiny back gardens with home-made wooden sheds for pigeons.

We stopped at Blaydon but there was no sign of a course for the races made famous in the song that has become the Geordie anthem: 'Lots of lads and lasses there, all with smiling faces, ganning along the Scotswood Road to see the Blaydon Races'. They clank out the tune, in funeral time, from a carillon at Newcastle City Hall.

Blaydon Races was written in 1862 in the heyday of Newcastle's rich music-hall culture. It was first sung at Balmbra's music-hall in the city and was an instant smash-hit. Balmbra's still survives in Newcastle, a few minutes from the station, and is still a delightful little hall where you can drink while you watch the performance.

The line crosses to the north bank of the Tyne a little way beyond Blaydon and runs along the sloping hillside on which Newcastle is built. On the south side of the river is Gateshead, joined to Newcastle by six bridges but at one time in another county, Durham. Both the great Tyneside towns are now in the county of Tyne and Wear, which takes in South Shields and Sunderland as well, but Gateshead is still separate from Newcastle, with its own atmosphere.

By the time my train had run past the old terraces and the new blocks and into the heart of Newcastle at the station I had done more than cross England from the Solway to the Tyne along a route constantly traversed since Roman times and earlier. I had come through some of the most sparsely-populated country in England to densely populated and industrialized Tyneside, which could hardly present a more violent contrast. This movement from wild country to teeming city is an important part of getting to know Britain. The country of fells and dales, moors and valleys, is incomparable in its quiet beauty. But the industrial centres, where people live, work, formulate their ideas and start new enterprises, make Britain essentially what it is. To be put off by factories and colliery tips, chemical works, power stations, mean streets and industrial grime is to miss a vital part of the essence of Britain. The urban prospector who perseveres is often rewarded with unexpected treasures.

The North-east

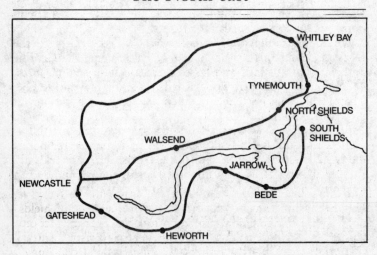

Tyne and Wear and Cleveland

Newcastle can always be enjoyed: its position, its solid public buildings, its scale and the outgoing enthusiasm of its people all mark it with an individuality that ensures the visitor a stimulating experience.

The station has one of the finest portico fronts in the country, matching the neo-classical dignity to be found elsewhere in the city centre. It was opened by Queen Victoria in 1850 and a statue of George Stephenson stands nearby. In this city, as is proper, the railway station is very close to the centre of things. The Royal Station Hotel, adjoining, is not only a sensible stop for travellers but is itself one of the centres of city life, managing to be dignified without being gloomy. Probably every Prime Minister for the past century has stayed here and it is easy to imagine Gladstone descending the remarkable grand staircase.

To get a quick fix on Newcastle, go out of the station, turn right and walk halfway across Stephenson's double-decker High Level Bridge. The railway runs over the top with the road underneath. From here you get a panoramic view that gives a sense of the city at a glance. There are the other bridges linking Newcastle with Gateshead, one of them a low-level swing bridge on a site where the Romans first bridged the river. Directly below are the quays where ships tie up. Tower blocks and streets of small houses cover the hillside on the north bank of the Tyne and a train of clanking coal wagons completes the scene.

A walk back up the road passes the forbidding castle, new in the twelfth century, and the cathedral, its distinctive tower topped by a pinnacle mounted on flying buttresses, to reach Balmbra's music-hall and several old pubs and eating-places.

Newcastle is a good place to stay for a few days and get the feel of city life in the North-east and is a fine centre for touring. Travel in the immediate locality is made easy by the modern, separately run Tyne and Wear Metro city and suburban service, which is cheap and efficient. Running mostly on old BR lines, its distinctive light four-coach electric trains link the city with the coast at Whitley Bay and Tynemouth north of the river and South Shields to the south, bringing new animation to large, near-derelict old stations. It joins the main railway system at Newcastle Central, where it is reached by a rather eerie underground concourse. Tickets, change and information are obtained by inserting coins or pressing buttons but if you turn up, as I did, needing change for a note, a voice from a grille informs you that you will have to go back to the main station.

Frequent trains serve Tynemouth and Whitley Bay, the latter a windy cliff-top resort of forbidding red-brick houses. I preferred Tynemouth, where the Metro trains run into the echoing shell of a large once-busy station, with birds twittering in the girders of the glass roof. The town has a castle and priory ruins on a promontory and a pleasant main street of solid old houses. Looking across the mouth of the Tyne towards South Shields is a huge statue of Lord Collingwood with four guns from the *Royal Sovereign*, the ship in which he was the first to engage the French at Trafalgar. Under his gaze ships batter their way in and out of the river between protecting piers. Food in the High Street pub is indifferent but the political discussion to be heard there is judicious and well-informed. The line to Tynemouth gives views of Newcastle's Byker Wall, a brave attempt to make municipal housing exciting and colourful, and passes through Wallsend, the eastern end of Hadrian's great work.

The line south of the Tyne to South Shields passes through Jarrow, where the Venerable Bede wrote his history and where the most memorable of pre-war hunger marches started; one of the Metro stations is named Bede. This traditional shipbuilding part of Tyneside once rang to riveters' hammers from many busy yards but the pre-war and post-war depressions have hit hard round here. South Shields has some pleasant houses near its cliff top and offers a good vantage point for watching shipping. It was the site of a Roman fort and has an excellent museum of Roman relics.

Local trains on the main line to Scotland serve the pretty little resort of Alnmouth and the historic border town of Berwick.

No one could pretend that train rides in the industrial North-east are a constant delight. On the other hand, real life is not all pretty views and rural seclusion. The traveller with an open mind and a desire to understand how Britain works can find a great deal of interest here. It is also a fairly dependable rule of thumb that the more inhospitable the industrial surroundings, the more hospitable the natives will turn out to be.

Newcastle to Saltburn

Hourly to Middlesbrough via Sunderland, then half-hourly, two and a quarter hours

Away from the main line through Darlington and Newcastle, the North-east has a small but complicated network of passenger lines linking these two places with Sunderland, Hartlepool,

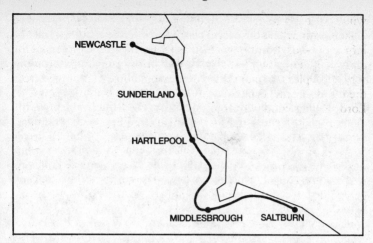

Middlesbrough and the seaside resorts of Redcar, Saltburn and Whitby. The centre of this system is Middlesbrough, whose link with Darlington extends to Bishop Auckland. I took an early afternoon local train from Newcastle Central which rumbled slowly between the small houses and rubble-strewn waste ground of Gateshead's suburbs, interchanging with the Metro to South Shields at Heworth and toiling across a forlorn landscape of mining gear and very small allotments fenced with waste wood and supporting a shanty-town of greenhouses, sheds and pigeon lofts. This was the North-east at its least attractive – down if not entirely out.

Crossing the River Wear at Sunderland was a scaled down version of the Tyne crossing at Newcastle – a bridge, a ship in the river, a busy urban scene – but closer and more intimate, another shipbuilding and coal centre but more densely packed and nearer the sea. Beyond Sunderland the train followed the bleak seashore – grey sea breaking on a dark grey beach with coal mines and their attendant small towns the main features.

Hartlepool, once the third busiest port in England after London and Liverpool, suffered decline but is now somewhat revived by North Sea oil. We could see shipping in the harbour as the train approached the station. We now ran into the Teesside complex of Billingham, Stockton and Middlesbrough. This area of chemical industries and steelmaking showed an impressive urban land-scape of engineering works, chemical plants, great warehouse sheds, cylinders, pipes, chimneys, cooling towers, gasworks, power stations. I had met most of these shapes before – industrial scenes, unlike nature, are not infinite in their variety – but what came over with extra force here was their assembly into one of the vast internal organs that keep the body politic alive.

Unlike some other great centres of heavy industry this area has large-scale modern industries as well as older ones. The predominant impression is not of decay but of a great complex of enterprises keeping Britain going. For a picture of what industrial activity means in Britain today this seemed a good place to come.

One surprise was how quiet it all was. Not inactive – chimneys and cooling towers were steaming away – but modern industry does not have the clanking, bumping and thumping of the old works.

A change of train at Middlesbrough. It's worth a bus-ride, if you have time, to see the Captain Cook museum in Stewart Park which traces imaginatively the local hero's extraordinary career. Middlesbrough has a transporter bridge, built in 1911 and still a landmark and in use although there is also a modern bridge further up the river. The town's steelmaking was established originally by the availability of ironstone, coal and the railway, an early extension of the Stockton and Darlington.

The Saltburn train ran near the river out through South Bank and Grangetown, through docks and chemical works, to the coast at Redcar. This is a little resort with good sands, used by local people and best known among outsiders for its racecourses.

After nearly an hour in the train, we could see the Cleveland Hills ahead. A bit further through a thinning-out series of small places and we were at Saltburn, perched on a cliff over a turbulent, romantic sea.

Saltburn was created as a seaside resort by the railways and the original railway hotel had its own platform, a few yards on from the station, so that Victorian holiday-makers could be carried right to the hotel door with their bulky luggage. This does not happen now; the hotel is no longer in railway ownership, holiday-makers no longer have such bulky luggage, and the station is not what it was.

The resort still has solid gothic stone charm, the sea views and air are as invigorating as ever, and you would never guess that a great industrial complex lay a few miles at your back. Under the cliff in a small cove you can have a drink at a pub on the beach beside the fishing boats and enjoy a seaside scene of vigorous beauty.

Hartlepool, my overnight stop, is to my mind one of the most interesting places in the area and knows how to make visitors feel welcome. I stayed at the Grand, near the station – living up to its name with spacious public rooms but also offering friendly service.

The older part of the town on the headland is worth exploring. A memorial marks the spot where German shells fell in the First World War. The extensive harbour is full of interest and not shut off from view, as so often. At the Maritime Museum you can pick up a radio telephone and listen to real – not simulated or recorded – messages being passed between ships and harbour authorities.

Darlington to Whitby

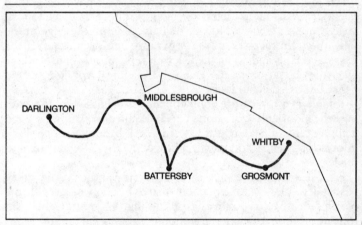

Six trains a day, two hours

A good example of how it can pay the train traveller to persevere despite a forbidding start was provided by a journey from the main line at Darlington to the coast at Whitby.

We ran first over country of no great interest – country only in the sense of keeping Darlington and Teesside apart with nothing much having been built on it. I had achieved one ambition of every tourist, which is to get away from all others: there were plainly none but local people besides myself on this train.

Urlay Nook, the name of a signal box, suggested rural peace but was in fact an outpost of an industrial landscape that would stretch down the Tees to the coast. Eaglescliffe, where the line from Northallerton joined, was equally deceptive: no eagles, no cliff, only long, windswept platforms with terraced houses beyond. I saw a power cable looped low over a playingfield, a wrecked car abandoned in a lane, a battered caravan in a shed. A thin, misty drizzle, blown by the wind, helped to set the scene of a dour world of harsh struggle. This was how southerners often imagine the North-east and I was sorry to see it living up to its image for the moment.

But better times were to follow when we had struggled through the Teesside industrial area. From Middlesbrough the train quickly leaves the chimneys and cooling towers and takes to the hills. Soon after leaving Nunthorpe a big conical hill can be seen on the left. This is Roseberry Topping and if you want to walk up it Great Ayton is the station. Soon after, you pass the granite obelisk the Australians left in exchange for being allowed to take away Captain Cook's cottage. At Battersby, on the edge of the hills, the train reverses on to the Whitby line for a run over the Cleveland Hills and down the Esk valley, beautiful country all the way and as far from the steel and chemical conglomeration behind us as you could wish.

Kildale is a taking-off point for the Cleveland Way footpath over the moorland. Commondale, Castleton and Danby are good walking centres. Danby is the North York Moors National Park information centre and there's a beacon nearly 1000 feet high to the left.

From Castleton the railway follows the Esk down the valley past quiet villages. At Grosmont there's a connection with the North York Moors Railway to Pickering. Soon after, the train runs into Whitby, where the station is close to the harbour.

Whitby lies in a break in the cliffs where the Esk runs out to the sea. The ruins of the abbey which dominate the town from the clifftop, the harbour with its fishing fleet and some fine old houses make it one of the most attractive and characterful places on this coast. Captain Cook, who started his working life as a shop assistant at Staithes, a little village up the coast towards Saltburn, learned seamanship on a boat trading out of Whitby before joining the navy.

Humberside and Yorkshire

By way of a change from the East Coast main line which links London with Yorkshire, the North-east and Scotland, I decided to approach a tour in Humberside and Yorkshire on a cross-country route from Nottingham. This would take me across north Lincolnshire, once known as Part of Lindsey, before crossing the Humber and taking in some of the great variety of travel pleasures Yorkshire offers.

Nottingham to Cleethorpes

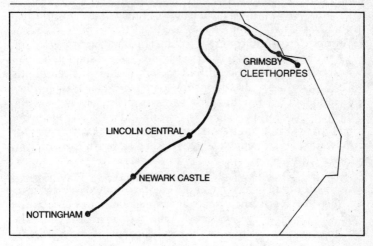

Five trains changing at Lincoln, one through, two and a quarter hours

I had come to Nottingham from Derby in a three-coach local boasting elegant oval mirrors and full of middle-aged ladies on a jolly outing. There was much talk of the Skeggie, the through train to Skegness, which is a seaside lifeline for the people of Derby and Nottingham.

Between Derby and Nottingham is a jumble of canals, complicated railway junctions and old quarries filled with water, but we were soon into the imposing red-brick Midland Railway station of the Queen of the Midlands, Nottingham's own name for itself. It is, in fact, a stately city, with a big chunky castle, statues of

Robin Hood and his band and a spacious market square.

One of the many caves and passages under the castle rock is said to have been used by Edward III to enter the castle and arrest his mother, Queen Isabella, and her lover, Mortimer. Other caves in the rock are used by the old *Trip to Jerusalem* pub to keep its beer cool.

Nottingham is famous for the traditional independence of its girls, its test cricket ground and its lace. The old lace-makers' quarter still has some interesting old buildings. There is still a Sheriff of Nottingham, no longer resident in the castle, but Sherwood Forest, to the north, is no longer the impenetrable haunt of outlaws it once was.

East of Nottingham is the flat side of England and my journey to the coast at Cleethorpes was by diesel train down the Trent valley and across the county into Lincolnshire. After leaving the city, the line crosses a plain and passes a big power station to reach Newark station. King John built the castle and you can see its bulky ruins straight ahead for some time before the train reaches the station just a few hundred yards from it. Just beyond the station the line to Lincoln crosses the main East Coast line from King's Cross on a level crossing, a fairly rare occurrence. Our train waited at a signal while 125s flashed across in front of us in both directions.

Now we crossed a stretch of flat country, keeping company with the Roman Fosse Way on our right. I counted a dozen level crossings, each governed by its automatic gates and bell, as the roads between villages swung to and fro. In many cases the crossing had a neat little villa originally provided for the crossing keeper.

Lincoln, standing on a hill from the plain in front, is a fine sight, topped by one of the most beautiful and interesting cathedrals in the country and a castle planned by William the Conqueror. Slightly off the main north–south lines of communication, Lincoln has a good deal of modern industry but still has the feel of a city of an earlier age, a feeling specially strong in the area of old houses surrounding the cathedral. This was a Roman city, a junction of the Fosse Way and Ermine Street, and it has kept its dignity and its head ever since. On the cathedral a gargoyle devil looks out at Lincoln and grimaces.

Lincoln is on the River Witham, which runs down to Boston and out to the Wash through the Haven. It has a little inland port,

Brayford Pool, for river craft and connects by canal with the Trent.

At Lincoln Central, now the only station in the city, it is usually necessary to change and wait for the best part of an hour for a train from Newark North Gate. One train a day runs through from Crewe, Derby and Nottingham.

We now had to make a sweep round the northern edge of the Lincolnshire Wolds.

As we moved across the fertile land I could feel again that we had left modern industrial England and moved into an agricultural England of a century ago, modernized in equipment but not in atmosphere.

The Lincolnshire Wolds are small, dumpy hills, attractively wooded. They formed a line to the right as the train ran briskly up the straight from Cherry Willingham to Market Rasen, where it stopped half in and half out of the small platform. We were right on the edge of the Wolds here and Market Rasen was clearly a good starting place for walking in them. Several young people got out and made for the hills.

We were back in today's industrial world when we joined the lines from Doncaster and Retford at Barnetby and turned round the top of the Wolds into Humberside, with the towers, cranes, docks, chemical works and oil tanks in the distance. We still ran through golden wheatfields and villages half drowned in trees and we did not actually go into dockside Immingham but we were out of secret Lincolnshire.

Grimsby announced itself with a white lighthouse and followed up with tall chimneys and big industrial buildings. It was once the most important fishing port in Britain but more recently has fallen on difficult times. However, there are still cargo ships, fish docks, ice factories and trawlers to be seen. The train ran past all this to Cleethorpes, where it pulled into a long open platform at the terminus on the promenade.

Cleethorpes station incorporates an amusement arcade, fancy ironwork and an ornamental clock tower, fully entering into the spirit of seaside jollity of which it is part. You step out of the station straight on to the promenade close to the pier and the donkey rides. The vast sands are the main attraction but the resort's Victorian origins make it worth exploring beyond the honky-tonk.

Among the crowds thronging promenade and beach I noticed

an Indian family sitting on the beach, the women sitting tranquil and motionless, swathed from head to foot in beautiful rose and gold-trimmed saris while the near-naked English scampered around them. The effect was surreal and charming.

Cleethorpes to Hull

Hourly, taking about an hour and 20 minutes

From Cleethorpes I went on to Hull, now a swift and easy journey no longer involving a ferry boat trip across the Humber estuary. The little train ran back along the line to Habrough, the station for Immingham, and then turned off north for New Holland on the south bank of the Humber. Lines around here are busy with many freight trains on the move.

The line narrows to single track to run up to New Holland. It used to go on a few hundred yards to a second station at New Holland pier, already crumbling long before the ferry services ended, and paddle-steamers used to ferry passengers across to Hull's corporation pier. Now the line turns west at New Holland to run along the bank of the Humber to Barton. Hull can be seen across the wide estuary while the train is running up to New Holland, and the ghostly shape of the new suspension bridge.

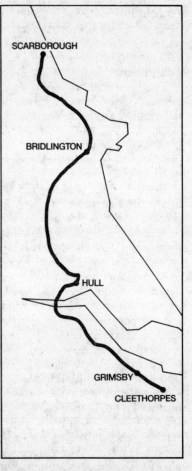

From New Holland, passing the tiny boat anchorage of Barrow Haven, passengers get magnificent views of the new bridge, a miracle of grace and slim, delicate strength, the longest suspension span in the world and perhaps the most beautiful piece of engineering created in Britain this century.

The Humberlink bus which connects with the train at Barton whisks the railway traveller into Hull. As the bus leaves the bridge the old ferry paddle-steamer *Lincoln Castle* can be seen below, now retired and used as a restaurant and bar. The bridge passes over the railway from Selby and Leeds which runs along the north bank of the Humber into the terminus in the middle of Hull.

The bus stops next door to the rail terminus. The Royal Station Hotel, where I stayed, stands beside the station and is right in the middle of the action. It faces the main shopping streets and is just a short walk from the principal buildings, the old town and the pier.

Hull is really Kingston-upon-Hull, the king being Edward I, who laid out the original port in the thirteenth century, and the Hull being the river which comes down to join the Humber on the east side of the town. I rate it highly as an exciting and agreeable place to visit. The business and administrative area has wide streets and some late Victorian and Edwardian public buildings in the grand manner – the guildhall has two embattled female figures with horses, brandishing spears in fearsome style. The Jubilee statue of Queen Victoria, instead of looking bored as in Manchester, here looks arrogant and triumphant. The old town, heart of the port and once surrounded by docks, has narrow streets full of old buildings, many lovingly restored. One street is intriguingly called 'Land of Green Ginger', though it fails to live up to the romance of its name.

The corporation pier where the ferries once landed passengers has been replaced by a new pier where you can watch shipping on the Humber. The River Hull, with an impressive lifting flood barrier at its mouth, is a haven for inland waterway barges and behind the river warehouses runs the interesting old High Street.

Andrew Marvell, the poet, used to be the town's Member of Parliament. Another local character was William Wilberforce, the anti-slavery campaigner, to whom a museum is devoted. Just across the High Street from his museum, ironically enough, is the pleasant Black Boy, which describes itself as a heritage pub; its heritage being, I was told, that it used to be a brothel. Broadminded, friendly, with a cheerful sense of humour, Hull is an absorbing place to wander about in.

Around Yorkshire

The best of Hull's three through trains to King's Cross takes two hours 44 minutes but the port's main links with the rest of the country are its services to Sheffield and Manchester, via Doncaster, and to Leeds with onward connections to Manchester and Liverpool. The journey between Hull and Liverpool takes you across the Pennines and through the two great northern centres of population, Leeds and Manchester, and gives you a chance to compare the very different life-styles of Humberside and Merseyside. A coast-to-coast through train runs between Scarborough and Liverpool via Leeds and Manchester. However, I wanted to see more of Yorkshire before going west, so I planned a journey by secondary lines that would take in Scarborough, York, Leeds and Bradford.

Hull to Scarborough

Eleven trains a day, about an hour and a half
The line from Hull to Scarborough takes you up through Humberside into North Yorkshire – not that it matters, they're all Yorkshire folk here. Since the line serves the three popular resorts of Bridlington, Filey and Scarborough the train was naturally full, mostly of young people, on the sunny summer day I travelled in the four-coach train from Hull's spacious station.

What riches they have here! We had no sooner got clear of Hull's suburbs and crossed a few miles of country to the north than we were at Beverley, the pale cream stone of its minster well displayed to us. I once stumbled over a kerb while staring in wonder at the minster and laid myself up for a week. So I was relieved to be able to remind myself of its powerful charm from a safe seated position. Beverley is a lovely old market town and not all that dangerous if you look where you're going.

The train continued to fill up as we stopped at villages and small towns in flat country on the edge of the Yorkshire Wolds to the north. At Great Driffield the line turned east and we ran into Bridlington, first of the three resorts, where half the passengers got off. There is an old town with a harbour, sands to the south and Flamborough Head to the north. The train goes along an embankment behind the cliff before turning away and running over country stretching away in gentle swellings and dips, with views for miles to the west, each trim farmhouse protected by its own little copse of trees.

Filey has long been associated with a big holiday camp but there's a quite gracious little Victorian resort here. But the queen of this coast is undoubtedly Scarborough, where we arrived after joining the line from York at Seamer.

Scarborough is a seaside resort in the grand manner, with two bays, a headland with a castle between them, clifftop hotels of imposing splendour, a small harbour and the Yorkshire Moors outside its back door. It's been in business since the eighteenth century and is everything that a solid, respectable family resort should be.

Scarborough to Bradford

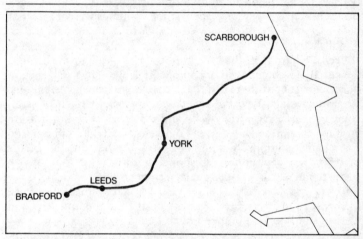

Hourly service to York, change at Leeds for Bradford, whole journey two hours

From Scarborough it was down the line to York and on to Leeds in a cross-country train bound for Manchester Victoria and Liverpool. Soon after Seamer we picked up the Derwent valley. We ran down it with the Wolds on our left and then, beyond Milton, the Howardian hills to the right, with Castle Howard itself somewhere up there, the magnificent Vanbrugh house of the Howard family. Here in North Yorkshire everything is on a big, solid scale.

Malton is an old market and cattle-dealing town not keen to reveal much of itself to railway travellers. We had to be content with some good agricultural industrial buildings and the old brick premises of the Malton Manure and Trading Co.

The river now ran through a narrow valley and the train followed on the valley hillside, with the occasional big house and the ruins of Kirkham Priory on the other side of the river. Once through the hills the line parted company with the Derwent, which flowed off south to join the Ouse while we ran across Strensall common and into York, properly dominated by its minster whichever way you approach it.

We left the main line and ran through mining and industrial country into Leeds. We burst into the city suburbs quite dramatically, riding in on an embankment to see them spread out in a bowl in the hills. We entered the station past a forbidding black stone church. A few years ago all stone buildings were this colour but now most of them have been cleaned up and clean air established by law.

Leeds, where I left the Liverpool train and caught the local, is the centre of a big industrial complex in which one needs the eye of a keen local patriot to distinguish one town from its neighbour. We ran through New Pudsey, through a brief stretch of semi-country — industry with cows — and then there was Bradford in another bowl in the hills spread out below us. The train ran into Interchange station down a slope so steep that the end of the platform was bent up to correspond with it.

Interchange is the city's main terminus, with some through trains to King's Cross. There is also a Forster Square terminus, from which trains run to Keighley, on the line to Lancaster and Carlisle, and down a branch line to Ilkley.

Bradford Interchange station shares a concourse and amenities with the bus and coach station with which it is integrated, to the great benefit of users of both. You step from the station right into the centre of the city, with the towered city hall, the crown court, the fine concert hall and shopping streets all at hand. This was J. B. Priestley's town — they made him a Freeman — and the city very sensibly invites you to walk round the German quarter where the rich wool merchants did business from palatial warehouses. With that, brass bands, an industrial museum, the Dales on its doorstep, the Brontës, Ilkley Moor and much else round about, Bradford's emergence as the first industrial city to cater for package tours begins to look like rational enterprise instead of a joke. I like Bradford and prefer its genuine Victorian grandeur to the phony antiquities sometimes found elsewhere.

York and the Railway Museum

For the railway tourist York is the city not to be missed on any account. It has everything for the ordinary tourist – and then special railway virtues on top of all that. York was the capital of Roman Britain; the Emperor Hadrian was here. And so, in due course, were the Saxons, the Danes and practically everybody else. Dominated by the huge, stately minster, biggest medieval church in Britain, the city has something to show for almost every people, building style or cultural force that has played a significant part in the national history. City walls, castle, medieval streets, museum – York has them all in one harmonious and compact whole which still manages not to be swamped or made into a museum by the armies of visitors from all over the world.

York's special railway importance derives from the activities of George Hudson, the former linen-draper, three times mayor of the city, whose speculations made him the Railway King of the 1840s. By promoting the amalgamation of many small lines he helped to speed up the formation of a national railway network and ensured that his home city had an important place in it.

Hudson overreached himself and when the railway mania of the time collapsed he was ruined with thousands of people who had trusted him. The deposed railway king fled to the Continent when his fraudulent practices were uncovered. Hudson Street was hastily renamed Railway Street by red-faced city fathers.

Nevertheless the railway remained, the network grew and York maintained its importance as a railway town astride the main line from London to Scotland. It became the headquarters of the powerful North-Eastern Railway, which ran the east coast line from London to the North, and the new station built in 1877 was claimed to be the biggest in the world. The North-Eastern's handsome rosy brick head office, built in 1906, is now the headquarters of British Rail Eastern Region. London is just over two hours away, Edinburgh under three and the station is an important junction for trains to Manchester, Birmingham and the South-west.

In 1971, the centenary of his death, the city decided that

Hudson could come back, all was forgiven. Railway Street had its name changed again – to George Hudson Street. A pub in the street, embellished with prints of early railway carriages, is called the Railway King.

Today York is also the home of the National Railway Museum, opened in 1975 as part of the Science Museum. There are now railway or transport museums in many towns, nearly all of them of some interest, but this is the queen of them all, the best presented, the most comprehensive – and free. All the history of the railways of Britain is illustrated in a big building which used to be a locomotive running shed, just around the corner from the station.

There is an impressive collection of steam locomotives, beautifully painted in their original liveries and ranging from the very earliest to the ultimate in British steam engine design, the 126 mph *Mallard* which hauled the Coronation expresses between King's Cross and Edinburgh in 1938. The engine's streamlined shape was reckoned to be worth 500 extra horse-power when travelling at 90 mph.

You don't have to be a railway buff to appreciate these locomotives, though after an hour in here you may easily become one. Their first appeal is that of sheer elegance and grace, marvellously vindicating the old engineers' dictum that if it looks right it probably is right. The High Speed Train (its wedgeshaped front harking back to *Mallard*) and the Advanced Passenger Train have a beauty of their own but these old steamers have something more – an individual character that makes them a delight.

Almost as fascinating is the collection of old passenger coaches, especially those of the royal trains. Victoria was not the first railway queen. There's a coach here built by the London and Birmingham Railway in 1842 for William IV's widow, Queen Adelaide. It looks like three stage-coaches put together. The handles are gold-plated but the sleeping accommodation involved the not very royal procedure of arranging cushions on poles and webbing and sticking your feet into the boot of the vehicle.

They got it right for Queen Victoria in 1869, with a saloon that was a lushly upholstered royal drawing room on wheels. The Queen loved it and used it to the end of her life. It is one of the two most popular exhibits in the museum – *Mallard* is the other.

I stayed at the excellent Royal Station Hotel, which fully lives up to its responsibilities as the railway hotel in a great railway city.

It stands next to the station in its own well-tended park — much too big to be called a garden — and from your spacious bedroom you look out over the lawns to the minster, towering in solitary state over the trees, floodlit at night. The hotel has one of those grand staircases railway hotel architects loved and a fine big airy dining room and lounge. In the basement Railway Mania bar there are pictures of famous old locomotives, station signs, railway companies' coats of arms and other items of railway interest.

York to Leeds

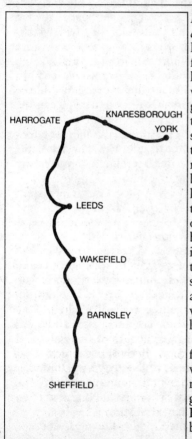

Hourly service, an hour and a quarter

In addition to the main line from York to Leeds there is a longer but prettier route by way of a branch line to Harrogate and I took this route for a trip to Leeds and Sheffield instead of the more direct route to Leeds or indeed the still more direct route to Sheffield by way of Doncaster. This local line is served by two-coach trains which consist essentially of bus bodies on railway coach bases. These have bus-style seating, shake rather more than the old diesel units and are not so comfortable. But they are acceptable on short trips and will be seen increasingly on local routes.

The line first goes through flat fields and passes a village with old maltings but after 25 minutes, having been climbing gently, the train crosses the River Nidd on a high stone bridge into the picturesque old market town of Knaresborough. The town sits on a rocky bluff by the river.

Mother Shipton, the fifteenth-century prophetess, is said to have been born in a cave here and the town has made a good thing out of witches and caves ever since. Eugene Aram, the eighteenth-century murderer celebrated in a poem by Tom Hood, buried his victim's body in a cave here. In other caves any object hung up will be turned to stone by the action of lime dripping on it.

A little further on is Harrogate, once the biggest spa in the north of England, now a conference centre and inland holiday resort. The pump room and big hydros associated with the spa look pompous and stuffy but in fact the town today is quite lively with good pubs and attractive old houses. A big open space called the Stray brings the moors right into the centre of the town, which is perched on a plateau. This is a good touring centre and starting point for walks. The station is in the centre of the town.

From Harrogate the run down to Leeds is through beautiful country. At Pannal the line crosses a tributary of the Nidd on a fine stone viaduct and then takes a sharp turn so that you can see it by looking back to the right. Shortly after this there are fine views to the right up Wharfedale and the line passes through the edge of the moors on its way down from the heights around Harrogate to Leeds. Tunnel entrances on this line are built like castle gatehouses, complete with turrets and arrow slits.

Leeds to Sheffield

Approximately hourly, taking an hour and a quarter

At Leeds I changed to a hard-worked three-coach diesel for Sheffield, where I planned to take the train to St Pancras. I could, of course, have got to London in less than half the time taking the 125 to King's Cross but I wanted to go down the old Midland line.

Struggling from Leeds through the coal of Wakefield and Barnsley to the steel of Sheffield cannot be anyone's idea of a scenic route. It's a sombre landscape of coal tips and water-filled holes intersected by muddy lorry tracks, dispirited, half-abandoned sidings and the occasional ghostly power station. At Normanton the platform was a sea of rubble and the whole area is perhaps best appreciated on a day of low visibility. The train was fairly full of people not much inclined to speak.

We crept through Wakefield and shortly afterwards our diesel lay down and quietly died on us, like an old horse worked beyond endurance. Crigglestone Junction on a wet Saturday afternoon seemed as appropriate a place as any for it.

What was surprising was not the breakdown, given the advanced age of these diesel units, but the speed with which it was dealt with. A cheerful Indian guard came through the train to tell us what had happened and I settled down with a book for a long wait. But within twenty minutes a diesel locomotive had arrived behind us and we were pushed cautiously on our way. At the next station a loop enabled the locomotive to run in front of us and from then on we moved faster than we could have done on the diesel unit's engines.

None of my fellow passengers seemed at all moved by our little crisis or its resolution. The silent ones kept silent and the few talking kept on with their private conversations with no general exchange of experiences. We ran into Barnsley and most passengers got off.

On the platform opposite was a complete wedding party waiting to see the bride and groom off on the train to Leeds and beyond. Newly-weds in their travelling outfits, carrying a suitcase with 'Just Married' chalked on it, parents and best man with buttonholes, bridesmaids in pretty pink dresses – they kept up the wedding banter gallantly while they waited and brightened up the whole journey for all of us. It seemed the right image for Barnsley – a dour environment transformed by human cheerfulness.

We left the wedding party and went on, our locomotive now really hustling. At Wombwell, amid a scene of dereliction, someone had written on a wall 'Let God in'. At Elsecar, things looked a bit cheerier; a man was walking his whippets on a heath. At Chapeltown there were new houses and a supermarket. We ran into Sheffield past its great cliff of flats, the city council's pride, reputed when they were built to be the biggest development of the kind in Europe.

East Anglia and Lincolnshire

Cambridge and King's Lynn

Good service from London to Cambridge, about an hour; every two hours to King's Lynn, about two hours
There are two main lines from London out of Liverpool Street station, one to Colchester, Ipswich and Norwich and the other to

Cambridge (present limit of the electric line), Ely and King's Lynn. The Cambridge line runs up beside the River Lea through Enfield into Hertfordshire, along the Hertfordshire—Essex border to Bishop's Stortford and then across the north-west corner of Essex.

My train to Cambridge, fairly old coaches hauled by a locomotive, left the Colchester main line at Bethnal Green, ran through Hackney Downs and Clapton and followed the line of the Lea navigation past reservoirs, gravel pits, sewage farms and industrial estates. We ran out into the country beyond Waltham Cross and up beside the River Stort, a tributary of the Lea. Our first stop was Bishop's Stortford, in Hertfordshire, the station for Stansted Airport.

We ran now through Essex with a chance to see some pretty village houses at Newport. For a county so near London Essex has a surprising number of attractive old cottages and villages which have retained their character.

A stop at Audley End, where little is to be seen, seemed puzzling but the station is a mile or so away from the great Jacobean mansion of that name. Also near is the pleasant old town of Saffron Walden.

Crossing Cambridgeshire now, we ran down beside the Cam through flat grain-growing country to enter Cambridge after being joined by the branch line from Royston and Hitchin. Our journey had taken an hour and 25 minutes on a Sunday, but a good train on a weekday does it in a little over an hour.

Cambridge's station is further from the centre than Oxford's and nothing of the colleges is to be seen. These are a bus-ride or a twenty-minute walk away. The station itself is a long, handsome building, its façade embellished with college coats of arms. The platform layout is strange, with one long platform at which main-line trains from both directions arrive and depart. It would not work everywhere but it does have the advantage that there are no footbridges to cross.

The ancient university city of course, demands a full day, if not several, to see even part of its treasures and it is well placed as a railway touring base. A branch line to Ipswich worked by diesels runs through the racing town of Newmarket, the historic and beautiful town of Bury St Edmunds, full of handsome old buildings and well worth a stop, and across some quiet, rich west Suffolk countryside, joining the London–Norwich main line at Stowmarket.

The line to Ely from Cambridge runs across flat fenland to the raised ground on which the city stands. This approach gives the train traveller the best view of the cathedral and it can also be seen from the south end of the station. Ely is a boating centre and as the train for King's Lynn draws out of the city it passes over the Ouse where boats tie up at a pub. A network of waterways can be reached from here in hired or private pleasure boats.

From Ely the line crosses the flat fens with their drainage channels past the pleasant old Norfolk town of Downham Market and on to King's Lynn. The flat countryside gives extensive views and the whole of East Anglia is largely free from the peculiar ugliness and depressing effect of decaying basic industries. There is no dramatic scenery here but with its handsome old towns and cities the area is one of the most rewarding for sightseeing by train.

North of Ely the line crosses the Bedford Level, the fenland area first drained by the Earl of Bedford in 1634 and later by the Dutch engineer, Cornelius Vermuyden. Before the drainage schemes created an area of fertile land the fens were the home of fiercely independent people who lived in marshland that outsiders often found impossible to penetrate. Boadicea fought the Romans from here, Hereward the Wake led a legendary resistance movement against the Norman conquest from a base near Ely and Oliver Cromwell was born on the edge of the Fens at Huntingdon.

The line ends at King's Lynn. Though much built up around the outskirts the town's heart remains wonderfully preserved, with some of the finest streets of old houses, especially of the sixteenth century and earlier, to be found anywhere, as well as many agreeable later buildings. The town has two market places, the Tuesday and the Saturday markets, and the walk between them along King Street and Queen Street takes you past old merchants' houses, a fine seventeenth-century Custom House and a medieval Guildhall. Compact, gracious and dignified, having a lively association with the arts, this old port on the River Ouse is a delight to wander in. The royal estate of Sandringham is a few miles away by bus.

Ely to Sleaford

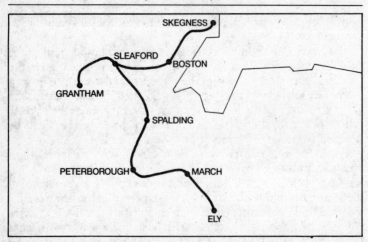

Three trains a day from Peterborough

For an extensive ride around the fens the line to take is that from Ely through March to Peterborough and from there to Spalding and Sleaford. Two of the trains to Sleaford run through from Cambridge and go on to Lincoln; for the third a change is necessary at Peterborough. The fens are still a land apart, with a feeling of being different from the rest of England. And although for much of the way you can see from the train to distant horizons all round, the effect is more of secretiveness than of openness. In flat country, where there seems nowhere to hide, not everything need be revealed to the stranger or the man from the ministry. Farmhouses stand isolated from their neighbours, often wrapped in a covering of trees. Just as you can see far into the distance, so they can see a stranger coming.

From Ely the route follows the Norwich to Peterborough line through March. This was once an important railway junction, as its substantial station indicates, and still has a big marshalling yard. The town used to stand on the Nene but as part of a drainage scheme the river was diverted from Peterborough direct to Wisbech. Deprived of much of its rail and river significance, March manages to thrive nevertheless.

My train ran across the middle of the Bedford Level to meet the River Nene at Peterborough. Another train took me north, soon branching off the main line for a straight run across the fens to Spalding. We were now well into Lincolnshire. When this big county was divided into three parts, this part was called Holland, which it greatly resembles.

Spalding is the centre of the Lincolnshire bulb industry and the time to see the area at its most spectacular is in April and May when it is ablaze with fields of bright tulips. It is a quiet, decent town of suntanned people in no frantic hurry. There are some fine Georgian houses on the banks of the River Welland.

After a stop at Spalding's spacious station our train set off again across the great flatness, although there were now hills to be seen in the distance. No fields of bright flowers at this time of the year, alas, only cabbages, potatoes, and cereal crops. This is one of the great agricultural counties of England, with hardly anything to be seen on this line unconnected with farming.

The train went past Pinchbeck and Donington and even as we crossed a drainage canal we could see the end of the great flatness. The hills to the west were now not so distant. Tree plantations broke up the empty landscape and the train even went into a shallow cutting. We passed a huge maltings, nine interlinked red-bricked buildings now turned to other uses, and then we were in Sleaford, where the line to Lincoln crosses one from Grantham to Skegness.

I left the train here to take a turn in the town before going on to explore the Skegness line. The station is close to the main street and the market place. I walked up the High Street past the elaborate memorial to one Henry Handley, the town's favourite son, and into a small but excellent market in front of the church. I noticed real bargains here in glass and china and the best cheese stall I have seen anywhere.

This is one of those small market towns, minding its own business, where everything looks harmoniously right, the buildings solid and handsome brick, the agricultural storehouses spacious, the pubs welcoming.

Sleaford–Skegness–Grantham

Two-hourly service, one hour 35 minutes from Grantham
The train to Skegness was not the famous Skeggie of which I had heard on the train from Derby to Nottingham but a diesel originally from Nottingham. There were a fair number of holiday-makers but we were nowhere near uncomfortably full.

We ran east across the now familiar flat fenland, though with more trees and more pastures up here. We could see villages scattered in the distance but no communities of any size. Near the village of Swineshead – surely not the most enticing of addresses – we were joined by the South Forty Foot Drain. Again, not a specially attractive name, but in fact it looked quite pleasant with grassy banks and is evidently popular with anglers, several of whom left the train here.

Now we could see ahead that extraordinary 272-foot church tower, the Boston Stump, standing high out of the flat landscape, topped by its octagonal lantern. It can be seen from up to twenty miles away and makes a landmark for ships approaching the Haven, the channel leading to the port.

Boston is a most attractive place and for anyone not passionately eager to reach the seaside it makes a better stop for a day out than Skegness. It has a big market place with handsome old buildings all round. Boston used to trade with the Hanseatic League and in the thirteenth century was England's busiest port. It has pleasant walks beside the River Witham and small boats pass through on their way up to Lincoln and the Trent. There are links with Boston, Massachusetts, and a memorial to early would-be American settlers who were jailed here.

The charm of this old town, as of others in Lincolnshire, is that it has retained its character and very much of its own way of life. Its people go their own way at their own pace. In its quiet way it represents some of the best qualities of England.

In the train we passed close to the Stump, and caught a glimpse of boats on the river and the pleasant riverside walk. Then the train set off again over flat, drained land crossing the Hobhole Drain. We could see now the beginning of the Lincolnshire Wolds to the north.

At intervals along the line we passed little cottages built for railwaymen, each a miniature Italianate villa, recognizably in the same style as some of the grander stations on the old Great Northern Railway, of which this line was once part. Who would put so much style into workers' housing today? The cottages make pleasant punctuation marks along the flat, straight route.

After running straight and more or less parallel with the coast for some miles the line crosses the Steeping River and turns fairly sharply towards the east coast to Thorpe Culvert and Wainfleet. The sharp turn arises because the line used to go further north to Grimsby with a branch off to Skegness. Now only the branch has survived.

And so to Skegness, its presence heralded by a large gasholder. This is a seaside resort built on sand, which for a seaside resort is a fairly firm foundation. I found it packed with holiday-makers but nothing like as noisy and brash as I'd been led to believe. As well as its day-trippers from the Midlands it has big holiday camps nearby and caters for very large numbers. Not a place of any special character but the town has spacious streets and the sands are superb. Its main distinction is the famous old railway poster of the dancing fisherman with the legend 'Skegness is so bracing', one of the classic poster ideas copied by others since. The station is about ten minutes' walk from the front.

I returned by way of Grantham in a train packed with holiday-makers. Back to Boston and Sleaford and then on to country looking more like the rest of England, with small hills, woods, trees and grass, hedges and hollows, small villages among trees in the distance with neat spires on low towers.

At Ancaster, where we crossed the Roman Ermine Street, roses adorned a platform set on an embankment looking over the town. Shortly after, the line crossed the east coast main line and continued to Nottingham. Our train turned on to the main line and ran down into Grantham. It's an agreeable station for a short wait between trains, with a good buffet. But the main-line trains follow in quick succession and I was soon away, bound for Peterborough and Norwich.

Trips from Norwich

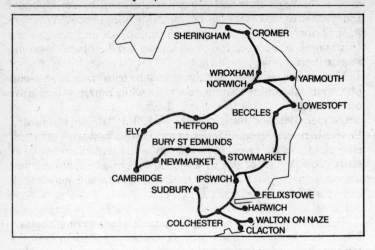

Norwich, principal city of East Anglia, is exceptionally well placed as a rail touring centre. It is two hours from London on the main line from Liverpool Street, an hour and three quarters on a cross-country line from Peterborough and is the centre of a network of local lines. The station is within walking distance of the Norman castle and cathedral.

To my mind, Norwich is one of the three or four best-kept and most attractive cities in the country. Its medieval heritage has been preserved without turning the place into a museum. Its cathedral is one of the finest. Its great square castle on its mound houses a collection of landscapes of the Norwich school of painters – Crome, Cotman and others. The city has great individuality – the Norfolk motto is *Du Different* – and is notable for its rebels as well as its bankers and insurance men.

The River Wensum winds through the city and from the quay opposite the railway station you can board a pleasure steamer for a trip down the Wensum and the Yare; or you can hire a small day-boat at the yacht station.

From Norwich station seaside resorts are within easy reach. One train takes an hour to run through the peaceful north Norfolk countryside to Cromer and Sheringham. It runs beside the Yare, to the boating village of Thorpe before turning north. At

Wroxham, where the double track dwindles to a single, the train crosses the River Bure and you get extensive views up and down the river at this capital of Broadlands yachting. From Wroxham several operators run day trips on the Broads and it's also the starting place for week-long holidays in hired cruisers or sailing boats.

The line now rises gently through trim farmland, with pheasants disdaining to notice the train while rabbits lollop lazily out of range.

Cromer, perched on a clifftop, is full of late Victorian and Edwardian character, which is to say that its buildings are often endearingly ugly. It used to be considered a better-class resort, its Hotel de Paris reflecting its upmarket aspirations. Now it has unbent a little and is all the better for it. There's a pier, good beach and colourful crab boats.

From Cromer the train reverses for a ten minute ride along the cliff to Sheringham, smaller and quieter. The train stops at a new platform a few yards short of the old station, which is now the terminus of the steam-operated North Norfolk Railway. This runs three miles on to Weybourne and has an interesting collection of locomotives and restored coaches.

Another line from Norwich runs east to Great Yarmouth through Acle, a village near the River Bure where sailing boats can be hired.

Norwich–Lowestoft–Ipswich–Cambridge–Norwich

A good round trip by rail from Norwich which can be done comfortably in a day is to go to Lowestoft, then by local trains to Ipswich, Cambridge and back to Norwich, taking in the unspoilt countryside of Norfolk, Suffolk and Cambridgeshire. The first leg of the trip crosses the Yare at Reedham by a swing bridge, giving good views of the village and river busy with holiday craft. The train runs beside the cut which joins the River Waveney to the Yare. This was once an alternative route for wherries from Lowestoft to Norwich, avoiding Yarmouth where port charges were high. Seagoing coasters still ply up to Norwich but now use the original Yare navigation.

The placid Waveney is crossed by another swing-bridge after a run across the reed-fringed marshland of the Broads. I saw a swan's nest here and you are quite likely to spot a heron on the bank.

At Lowestoft the train runs alongside the harbour into a terminus only a few yards from the beach, the yacht and trawler basins and the main shopping street. It is a fishing port and resort with good bathing.

The 49 miles from Lowestoft to Ipswich take you through deepest rural Suffolk, a lovely ride. A local train runs down the east Suffolk line through rolling farmland and a series of small towns. At Oulton Broad there's a glimpse of one of the biggest of the Broads, a favourite venue for sailing races. Beccles, Halesworth, Saxmundham and Wickham Market are small towns with comely old houses set in spacious countryside of which the train frequently offers sweeping views.

Woodbridge is a beautiful little town of Georgian brick buildings standing at the head of navigation on the River Deben. The train stops at a station beside the quay, with an old riverside pub, the Anchor, nearby.

At Ipswich, county town of Suffolk, we're back on the main line. The well-organized station with ornate ironwork, Victorian decorative brick and unusual platform canopy, is on the deceptively unattractive edge of town. A ten-minute walk takes you to the centre, with old merchants' and sea captains' houses, pleasing Victorian public buildings and inviting old pubs. I lunched agreeably at the Swan opposite a corn exchange advertising wrestling and a Bach choir. There's a station hotel with a sign depicting an InterCity 125 and the *Rocket*.

From Ipswich the circular tour from Norwich would take you by local train to Bury St Edmunds and Cambridge, then back by way of Ely. Or you could return direct to Norwich from Ipswich.

Ipswich and surrounding area

Ipswich is little more than an hour from London, with a good electric train service extending to Norwich. It is a considerable port at the head of the Orwell estuary. The coast of Essex and Suffolk is divided into sections by a series of estuaries – the Crouch, the Blackwater, the Colne, the Stour, the Orwell, the Deben, the Alde – so the main line runs some miles inland and the coast is reached in this area by branch lines. From Ipswich there's a short branch to Felixstowe, a small resort and large container and ferry port opposite Harwich.

More rewarding is the Harwich branch leaving the main line at Manningtree, a few miles south of Ipswich. This runs on the south side of the Stour and serves the busy ferry port of Parkeston Quay before going on to Harwich town, still a place of some character. Captain Jones of the *Mayflower* was married, and Charles II took a pleasure cruise here. The busy harbour at the confluence of the Stour and the Orwell is alive with shipping which can be seen from the ferry pier. Next station to Manningtree is the charming little port of Mistley.

From Colchester, further up the main line towards London, a branch goes off to the resorts of Clacton, catering for day-trippers, holiday camps and caravanners, genteel Frinton, and Walton-on-the-Naze (the Naze being a headland with the small harbours and saltings of the Backwaters behind it). One of the most agreeable stops on this branch is at Wivenhoe, a small riverside town on the Colne. Another short branch line goes from Colchester and Marks Tey to pleasant, quiet Sudbury on the edge of Suffolk.

Southend day out

Frequent services

Southend, 36 miles from London, has for more than a century been the East End's favourite day-out spot for a breath of sea air. Few people went there for more than a day at a time. You went there on a Sunday or a Bank Holiday, walked on the pier, ate whelks, had a few drinks and a bit of a knees-up and came home wearing a funny hat, much refreshed and feeling that the sea breezes had done you good.

The town still welcomes crowds of day trippers but nowadays the whole area is a dormitory for City workers and the town itself is a centre of office employment in its own right. It is served by two railway lines, both electric, and there's a connection at Barking with the Metropolitan and District lines of the London Underground. I went out from Fenchurch Street Station and returned by way of Liverpool Street.

Fenchurch Street station, in the heart of the City close to the Tower of London (nearest Underground station, Tower Hill), serves only the Tilbury and Southend lines. It has an attractive

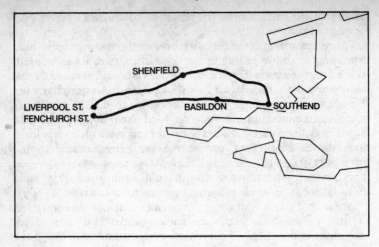

station front with a curved pediment. Inside, on a Sunday morning, before there's been time to clear all the tins and fish-and-chip papers thrown on to the tracks by the Saturday trippers, it is not at its best.

The ride out to Southend Central takes something under an hour. Leaving Fenchurch Street the line goes out on a viaduct to the north of Wapping and Shadwell dockland, now awaiting redevelopment, and parallel with the once-notorious Cable Street and the Highway (formerly the Ratcliff Highway) which was Jack the Ripper's hunting ground. Through Stepney and Limehouse with a distant glimpse of a Hawksmoor church, over the Grand Union Canal and then across the River Lea and past a thousand small back gardens the train runs to Barking, the junction for Tilbury.

As the train moves out through Dagenham and Hornchurch terraces give way to semis and there's a little more space as London gradually loosens its grip. Upminster is the last station in Greater London and the end of the Underground. Branch lines from here connect with Romford on the line out of Liverpool Street and Grays on the Tilbury line.

So far it has been houses all the way but now we are out into Essex with the first hesitant appearance of bushes and trees and the east London child gets a first glimpse of cows and farmland. Basildon was one of the early post-war New Towns and its centre, seen from the train, shows the influence of the 1951 Festival of Britain in its architecture.

The next town, Benfleet, sits pleasantly on top of a hill, confusing to those led to believe that this part of Essex doesn't have any hills. This is the station for Canvey Island, reached by the causeway across the marshes and over a creek. In spite of its oil storage tanks Canvey is an interesting place. East Enders and others determined to have a place of their own bought land that was going cheap here between the wars and built their own little houses without benefit of architects or control by planning regulations. The result is a striking collection of do-it-yourself dream houses ranging from the shack-like to the almost-stately; much more fun than planned and architect-designed Basildon.

At Leigh-on-Sea the train reaches the Thames estuary after passing Hadleigh Castle, on the left, where Anne of Cleves lived after her divorce from Henry VIII. There are yachts here and views across the estuary to the Kent coast. The channel is busy with ships going in and out of the Port of London. Leigh and Westcliff are mainly residential; the Southend of the Cockney day out is reached at Central station. From here, in the main shopping area, it's a ten-minute walk down the High Street to the Marine Parade, the mile-and-a-half long pier, the big pubs, the whelk stalls and the fun area. The pier's great length – claimed to be the longest pleasure pier in the world – is no mere fancy: it is needed to reach over the mud to the water when the tide is out.

Southend is still a favourite fun-by-the-sea place for Londoners, though perhaps not as frenetically so as it was in the days when Sundays and Bank Holidays were all the breaks most people had. It's still a place to let your hair down, buy rock and go for boat trips (the *Queen of Kent* crosses the estuary to Chatham and Rochester).

What's surprising about Southend is not the brashness but the survival of the very pleasant Cliff Town on the height above, now a conservation area. The clifftop terraces of houses, with the Royal Hotel and an assembly room, were built in the 1790s and have been well preserved. Princess Caroline stayed here in 1803 while her errant and bigamous husband the Prince of Wales, not yet Prince Regent, was discovering the delights of Brighton. Two years later in the year of Trafalgar, Lady Hamilton stayed here and held a ball for Lord Nelson in the assembly room. Evidently not quite the spot for married bliss but there's a touch of Georgian grace up here with fine views across the historic shipping highway of the Thames estuary.

I returned to Liverpool Street from Victoria station, a short walk up the High Street from Central, past the tower blocks and big shopping centre. This line runs north to Rochford, for Southend airport, then west on an embankment looking north over flat country with occasional glimpses of the River Crouch in the distance. Rayleigh has a windmill on a hill but any suggestion of rural charm this might produce is soon more than cancelled out by no less than five lines of electricity pylons which trample over the landscape beyond.

At Wickford a much more rural branch line goes off to Southminster with a chance to see the yachts in the river at Burnham-on-Crouch, a notable yachting centre. Billericay is a dormitory town, and then the train reaches Shenfield to join the main line into Liverpool Street. This route takes nearly twenty minutes longer than the other, and is more for commuters than day trippers.

6
London and the South

The Southern Region of British Rail covers the area between London and the coast south of the Thames, from Margate in Kent to Weymouth in Dorset. For the leisure traveller the whole area is pre-eminently day-trip country. All of it is within easy reach of London and there are dozens of seaside places large and small to choose from, almost all served by fast electric trains. As well as the big popular resorts – Brighton, Bournemouth, Eastbourne, Hastings, Folkestone and Ramsgate – the railway serves many smaller ones. Behind the coast resorts, too, there's some fine country – the

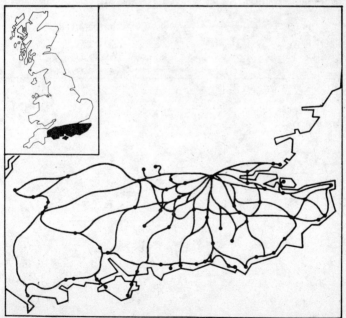

South Downs, the Weald, the New Forest — and some historic
sights — Hampton Court and Windsor close to London, Canterbury, Rochester and Salisbury among the cathedrals and Winchester, the old Saxon capital of Wessex.

The London area north of the Thames is not in the region but
may conveniently be considered with it.

Good touring centres outside central London are Richmond,
Brighton, Southsea, Canterbury and Tunbridge Wells.

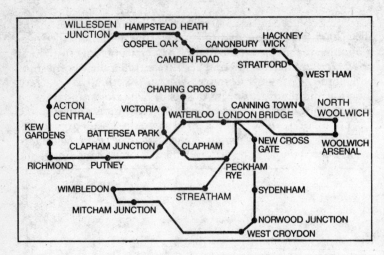

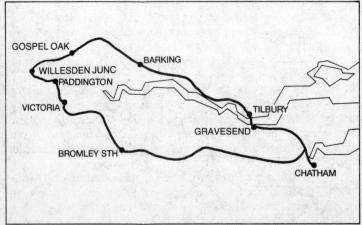

Around London

The lines round London can give the traveller an intimate picture of the capital outside the central tourist area that is not easily obtainable in any other way. It is quite possible to go all round London by British Rail train keeping mostly above ground and more often than not raised well above street level, giving a better view. The key to this is the useful line running from Richmond in south-west London through Acton, Willesden, Hampstead and north London to Stratford and Canning Town in the east, finally joining the Thames again at North Woolwich, close to the free ferry. It serves the two great London outdoor amenities of Hampstead Heath and Kew Gardens, not to mention Richmond itself, a popular day-out resort for Londoners.

For a morning's look round London by train an interesting route might be as follows:

Charing Cross to Waterloo East, walk through to Waterloo main station and take the train to Richmond. Change to the North London line for a train to North Woolwich, where you cross the Thames on the free ferry. Then walk to Woolwich Arsenal for the train back to Charing Cross.

For an extra sweep through the inner south London suburbs, there's a train (Mondays to Fridays only, best taken in mid-afternoon), which runs round from London Bridge, on the Charing Cross line, through Peckham, Brixton, Clapham to Battersea Park and Victoria. For a more extensive tour through the south London suburbs, accomplished in about two and a half hours, take a train from London Bridge to West Croydon and return by way of Wimbledon and Streatham.

Good ideas for quick days or afternoons out in the London area are Windsor, Hampton Court, Richmond for its riverside and park, Epsom Downs, Greenwich for the National Maritime Museum and the old tea clipper *Cutty Sark*, Chingford (from Liverpool Street) for Epping Forest, Egham for Runnymede, Bourne End, Marlow or Henley for the Thames.

I set out for a tour around London from Paddington. Four stations on the London Transport Bakerloo line took me to Queen's Park, where I caught a British Rail train to Willesden Junction. On the way I passed Kensal Green, whose famous cemetery was on Chesterton's route to Paradise in his ballad of the Rolling English Road:

> 'For there is good news yet to hear and fine things to be seen
> Before we go to Paradise by way of Kensal Green.'

Chesterton's rolling English drunkard would surely have approved of going from Paddington to Victoria, as I was, by way of Kensal Green, Gospel Oak, Barking, Tilbury, Gravesend and Chatham, even though nothing much resembling Paradise turned up on the way.

The North London line train took me from Willesden Junction through Brondesbury, where Mr Pooter (of the *Diary of a Nobody*) had his home, under the heights of Hampstead to Gospel Oak at the bottom of Parliament Hill, a good spot from which to look over London. Here a train of refurbished coaches was waiting to run across north and east London to link with the Southend line at Barking.

We set off through Upper Holloway and Crouch End to Tottenham, Walthamstow and Leyton. This line runs further out from the centre of London than the one to North Woolwich. For most of its length it is more suburban and less industrial. It goes through parts of north and north-east London which are little known except to people who live there. For long stretches the train travels through a green avenue, the railway cuttings lush with bushes, trees, willow herb and convolvulus. The railways, in fact, provide some of the wildest country in the London area. Plants, birds and small animals flourish and in railway cuttings in the south London suburbs foxes have been seen.

I knew we had passed from north to east London when the passengers – middle-aged women, mothers with small children – became suddenly more talkative. Notable, too, was the east Londoners' passionate devotion to their small gardens. As we passed through Wanstead on an embankment nearly every back garden was a riot of well-tended roses.

Barking, the terminus for this service, is an interchange with the line from Fenchurch Street to Southend and Tilbury and the London Transport Metropolitan and District lines. The train I caught was one from Fenchurch Street to Southend by way of Tilbury Town, where it is necessary to change to a local from Upminster to complete the last mile to Tilbury Riverside.

The train ran through London's industrial Thameside, with Ford cars at Dagenham Dock, oil depots at Purfleet, containers, it seemed, almost everywhere, a huge gas works and a power station away across the marshes by the river. The Port of London has moved down the Thames to Tilbury and this is now London's chief outlet to sea trade, the old docks further up the river now being redeveloped.

Even among all this industry there are distinctive little towns and villages – Rainham, with a pretty church and fine Georgian house, Grays, with a High Street running down to the river that must be worth exploring, and Tilbury, the port town itself.

At Tilbury Riverside station I stepped out into a large concourse, this being the passenger terminus for cruise ships. A Russian ship was tied up at the landing stage. This is a good viewpoint for the Thames and its shipping.

On the landing stage here I found a Norwegian cyclist sunbathing and anointing himself with lotion. A perfectly rational place to sunbathe on a Sunday when you thought about it – quiet, plenty of space, ships to watch, a fine view of Gravesend on its hill across the river. The ferry to Gravesend is run by British Rail and takes five minutes, just long enough to get a breath of sea air and take in the river scene.

Gravesend is an historic old town and port. East Indiamen used to sail from here and Queen Elizabeth used to come here to welcome important foreign visitors. Forts on both sides of the river guarded the entrance to London. There is a riverside park with fine views of the shipping. On my way up past the old church to the railway station I looked into the churchyard to pay respects to Princess Pocahontas, the Indian chief's daughter from Virginia who married a settler and died here in 1617. There's a lovely little statue of her.

Gravesend station is about a quarter of an hour's walk from the ferry. Here I caught a train to Chatham which took me over the River Medway, full of small ships and barges, closely past the fine and often overlooked Rochester cathedral and the very solid remains of a splendid Norman castle and priory. This is Charles Dickens country. The writer spent some of his childhood at Chatham and the last years of his life at Gadshill Place on the Rochester-Gravesend road.

Chatham is on the main line from Victoria to the Thanet resorts. Before reaching the north Kent coast with its string of resorts, starting with Whitstable, a fine old town worth a visit is Faversham, which has a very well preserved old town centre with some excellent old pubs. Small coasters still creep up the creek on the tide and tie up at the town wharf.

From Sittingbourne, a few stations down the line from Chatham, a branch line runs to Sheerness on the Isle of Sheppey, crossing the Swale, the channel between the island and the Kent coast, by a bridge with a span that can be raised to allow ships to pass underneath. Sheerness is a ferry port and a small resort. More interesting is Queensborough, an almost forgotten little port which has some handsome old houses and an anchorage where you may sometimes see some of the last remaining Thames sailing barges.

I rode back to London from Chatham in style. A sleek, fast train from Ramsgate whisked me to Victoria in 46 minutes with only one stop, at Bromley South. We ran through Sydenham Hill and Brixton and over the Thames with Chelsea Bridge to our left and a view up the river to Albert Bridge and the Chelsea reach Whistler painted so often.

Wales to the Isle of Wight

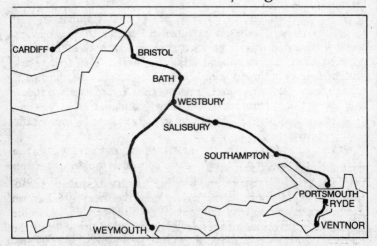

Hourly service, three and a half hours

London is not the only gateway to Southern Region. There's a very good approach from Wales and the west of England (as well as from the Midlands and the North by way of Reading). From Cardiff to Portsmouth on the south coast takes us the last few miles in Gwent, then through the Severn Tunnel into England and through the counties of Avon, Wiltshire and Hampshire. It's an easy run between breakfast and lunch and can be done in a through train, although I had to change at Bristol. There are connections at Westbury for the line to Weymouth.

I caught a train from Cardiff Central at 9.05 and was in Bristol about an hour later. From Cardiff to the Severn Tunnel is on the Paddington Main line and presents little of interest as it runs along flat industrial land bordering the Severn estuary.

It takes only minutes to go from Wales to England by the Severn Tunnel, saving the long detour by way of Gloucester that would otherwise be necessary. When the train emerges at Pilning the countryside looks quite different, the fields and hedges and buildings all subtly changed from those on the other side of the Severn.

The train ran quickly down into Bristol through Patchway and Filton, close to the home of the Concorde aircraft. From Patchway the London trains go off to the east.

The change at Bristol Temple Meads was an easy walk across the platform with time to get a cup of tea at the platform buffet before joining the Portsmouth train. There is no buffet on this two-and-a-half hour cross-country run. As far as Bath the train followed the Bristol-Paddington main line, then branched off to follow the Avon valley into Wiltshire. Bradford-on-Avon, inevitably overshadowed by its grander neighbour and much less well known, is a delightful little town of stone houses spread over a hillside looking over the Avon and its water meadows. The fourteenth-century stone bridge has a curious structure on it, originally a chapel but later used as a lock-up.

Soon after Trowbridge, a sleepy little country town, train travellers get their first view of the Wiltshire downs, the great rolling grassy hills that help to give the country its special character. On one of them, as the train nears Westbury junction on the Exeter main line, you can see a fine white horse carved in the chalk. There are four of these on the downs in this part of the country. On the hill above the Westbury Horse are the prehistoric earthworks of Bratton Castle.

From what's visible from the train there could hardly be a more peaceful town in a more peaceful setting than Warminster, the station for the popular stately home, Longleat, four miles away. There is, however, an army training ground a few miles to the east, on Salisbury Plain.

Now the train ran down the valley of the River Wylye past the old carpet town of Wilton into Salisbury. This took us through tranquil country with broad sweeps of downs, deep grass and trees. The train passed a string of small villages in which peace and contentment seemed to hang in the air. Wiltshire is one of the least industrialized and commercialized counties.

The run through Wiltshire came to a climax at Salisbury, where our line crossed one from Waterloo to Exeter. The cathedral spire, highest in England at 404 feet, is a reminder to train travellers that the city not only has perhaps the finest early English cathedral in the country but a wealth of other picturesque and historic old houses of different periods that make it a city to stop and stoll in. Iron Age folk and the Romans were here, Stonehenge is not far away.

It was just a short run now through the last stretch of real country on this route, as the train moved east into Hampshire and then dropped down through Romsey to Southampton. Romsey has a twelfth-century abbey overlooking the market place. Broadlands, the late Lord Mountbatten's Palladian house, is just outside the town.

When the line joined the River Test the complex of docks that make Southampton one of Britain's great ports was already in view. On a main line from Waterloo, Southampton is the port from which the Atlantic liners used to start. Nearly all those have departed, but cruise ships, ferries to France and Spain and freighters still make their way up and down Southampton Water. There was more to see after the train left Southampton station – barges and small ships up the River Itchen when the train crossed it and ran down beside the river.

Crossing the River Hamble was a reminder that we were into yachting country, then we were through Fareham and running across the top of Portsmouth harbour with a view of the city across the water. Portsmouth itself occupies an island between Portsmouth and Langstone harbours and the line drops down through the middle of it, mostly with little to see, until it emerges from Portsmouth and Southsea station for a short elevated stretch to Portsmouth Harbour station.

Most of what's best worth seeing in Portsmouth is around here:

the old town, Nelson's *Victory* in her dry dock, and some of the navy's more modern ships in the harbour itself – the guided missile destroyer *Bristol* was moored next to the ferry the day I was there. With the constant coming and going of naval pinnaces and ferries the harbourside is always full of interest. Southsea is really part of Portsmouth and adds watching ships and yachts to the normal seaside resort amusements.

From the Harbour station, where I now left the train, a walkway leads down to the landing stage where the Isle of Wight ferries tie up.

The ferry *Southsea* was not due to leave for half an hour but I could go aboard and have some lunch in the buffet on the lower deck. I was ready then to enjoy the 25-minute voyage across Spithead to Ryde, Isle of Wight, four miles away. This was an exciting sea experience. Our little ship had to steer a zigzag course through a sea alive with other craft – freighters outward bound from Southampton, other ferries on routes crossing ours and a fleet of about 70 big yachts racing. There's always something to see in the Solent. On an earlier trip I had seen former prime minister Edward Heath at the wheel of his yacht *Morning Cloud*, the *Queen Elizabeth II* off on a cruise and a fleet of racing yachts all with their colourful spinnakers up – not bad for one crossing.

Ryde is an almost perfectly preserved Victorian resort. Not that there aren't new buildings – and indeed a hovercraft on the beach ramp – but the feeling is of solid comfort, simple pleasures and the fun of being beside the seaside. There's no mistaking you're on an island and somewhere else when you come over the water. It feels different, the pace is different. The people, though friendly enough, take folk from the mainland for foreigners, *overners* they call them. Crossing to the island is a miniature trip abroad without the bother of different languages. But no customs concessions, alas.

On Ryde pier two trains stood waiting, one to take people for Ryde down the long pier to the esplanade, the other going on to the resorts of Sandown and Shanklin. Though done up in BR colours these were unmistakably old London Underground trains, built in the Twenties and put out to end their days in peaceful semi-retirement after years of pounding up and down the Piccadilly Line, like aged pit-ponies being put out to grass. They worked well enough and rattled us along in fine style. The island can easily be explored by bus from any of these resorts and a cheap bus-and-train rover ticket is available. Places worth visiting include the famous yachting centre of Cowes and nearby Osborne House, one of Queen Victoria's favourite residences; the traditional seaside resort of Sandown; Shanklin, another popular seaside town; and sheltered Ventnor, with palm trees growing in the Botanic Gardens.

Westbury to Weymouth

Eight trains a day (two through from Bristol), an hour and 40 minutes

From the junction for the Exeter main line at Westbury in Wiltshire, another cross-country route to the south coast takes you to Weymouth, harbour for the Channel Islands boats and terminus for the main line from Waterloo through Southampton and Bournemouth. The local train runs down the main line to Castle Cary, a small place not visible from the station but having the remains of a Norman castle. The train now turns off through the Somerset countryside of intensely green fields and trim stone houses with lichened roofs. Yeovil Pen Mill station is in a beautiful setting in the Yeo valley with the old town perched on a hill. The town is noted for milk and cheese, and the poet T. S. Eliot is buried at East Coker nearby.

Our branch line then crosses the Salisbury-Exeter line and burrows among the sleepy villages and small towns of Dorset – Thornford, Yetminster, Chetnole. There is a friendly lack of assertiveness here, the church towers are squat and fat, the hills small and rounded. Shortly before Maiden Newton the line joins the River Frome and follows it to Dorchester, the county town. It figures as Casterbridge in the Wessex novels of Thomas Hardy; there is a statue of him in the town and a reconstruction of his study in the museum. Judge Jeffreys held his infamous Bloody Assizes here in 1685, when 74 of those who had taken part in Monmouth's rebellion were sentenced to death.

Shortly after leaving the station the train joins the line from Bournemouth for the final run down to the pleasant seaside resort of Weymouth.

Portsmouth to Brighton

Half-hourly service, one-and-a-half-hour journey

At Portsmouth I was in the long-established Southern electric network covering most of the area between London and the coasts of Kent, Sussex and Hampshire. Portsmouth, Bognor Regis, Littlehampton and Brighton are termini for a rather complicated service of fast trains to and from Victoria and Waterloo by four different but interlocking routes. But I wanted to go along the coast so I took the local train to Brighton, 45 miles away in East Sussex.

Portsmouth Harbour station, from which I started, is built out on piles over the water and from the platform buffet you get a good view of the harbour. My train of suburban coaches had a lot of stops to make but these electric trains accelerate fast; the journey was leisurely but not intolerably tedious.

Although this is a coast line it's surprising how little of the sea can actually be seen from it. There were glimpses of water as we skirted the top of Langstone and Chichester harbours and then nothing maritime, except the names of the stations, until we crossed the River Adur and ran past Shoreham, the small port just before Brighton. It's not, in fact, a line of great visual interest, though the South Downs are to be seen away inland for most of the way. There's a good view of Chichester's green-roofed cathedral.

The names of the stations promise more than they deliver. Surely there should be a nest of song-birds at Warblington. What it offers instead are a couple of grave-watcher's huts in the churchyard, installed in a bid to prevent body-snatching in the eighteenth century.

Emsworth has some good Georgian houses in a beautiful old port area around its harbour. Fishbourne has its Roman mosaics. Chichester is a good centre for the area, Goodwood racecourse, the Downs and Selsey Bill all being handy and it is an attractive and unspoilt city, with a noted summer Festival Theatre season.

From Chichester onwards it's a string of seaside resorts, each with its own personality. Brighton is the liveliest, the most elegant and the most raffish. The Prince Regent gave it style and its marvellously exotic Pavilion. Criminals on the run from the Metropolitan Police, finding this a convenient bolt-hole, added their own special flavour. It's popular with actors – you can get home after a West End performance. French youngsters come here in force. It's a considerable town in its own right, not just a resort.

Bognor, down a branch line, was where King George V spent a long convalescence, hence the Regis. Today its holiday ambience is more fish-and-chips than royal. Littlehampton, on another branch, has a small port and offers quiet relaxation. Worthing is a favourite retirement spot. Lancing has a public school and its imposing chapel can be seen to the left from the train.

Brighton virtually begins with the crossing of the River Adur. From Shoreham onwards is a continuous built-up area, with docks at Shoreham and Southwick and a power station.

I left the train at Hove, joined to Brighton but with its own distinctive Victorian aura, and made my way to the Sackville Hotel on the front within walking distance of the station, quiet and attentively run in a late-Victorian building.

Brighton to Ramsgate

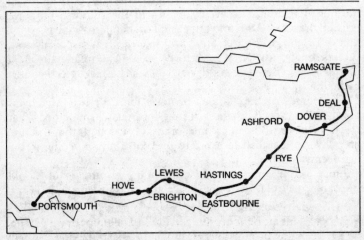

Hourly between Hastings and Ashford, otherwise half-hourly, about two and three-quarter hours

Brighton is an important station and has a fine curved steel and glass roof over its platform and concourse. In addition to its main-line service through Gatwick Airport to Victoria, reached in under an hour, it serves routes along the coast east and west and even has through services to Manchester and elsewhere in the north. This Saturday morning a large party of French schoolchildren were being marshalled on to a special train for Cardiff.

My own immediate destination was Hastings, by the line to the east which runs through the Downs to Lewes, down into a terminus at Eastbourne and then out again along the coast to Bexhill and Hastings. This is an altogether more rewarding journey than that along the coast to the west. For a start the train climbs out of Brighton and over a tall viaduct giving extensive views over the town. Away from the coast the country behind the Downs looks fresher. Falmer is the stop for Sussex University.

Lewes, eight miles from Brighton, is a town of great antiquity and historical importance. William the Conqueror gave it to one of his barons, who built a castle on the hill to guard the pass through the Downs. He also endowed a priory, dedicated to St Pancras, which was blown up at the Dissolution. The railway passes over its site. The castle was the scene of the great battle in which Simon de Montfort defeated Henry III in 1264.

At Lewes the line from Brighton joins the main line from Haywards Heath to Eastbourne before branching off again to Newhaven and Seaford. That line follows the River Ouse through the Downs with some lovely views. Newhaven is a pleasant little port and town, with ferries to Dieppe, a yacht marina and fishing boats.

Our train ran over the main line through some pretty Sussex country, going through Glynde, close to the Glyndebourne opera. At Berwick the train was still up on the Downs, then ran down through Polegate and into Eastbourne.

Eastbourne has been somewhat overshadowed by its flashier neighbour, Brighton, but in fact has a great deal to recommend it besides Beachy Head, which guards its western end. It's a late Victorian resort of solid, well-kept hotels with the station not too far from the sea and beautiful country within easy reach behind. It has a pleasant air of not trying too hard to be smart or up to date.

Between Eastbourne and Hastings the coast line does actually get near the coast, though not near enough for much of a view of the sea. Along here it is possible to get away from it all by train and find your own bit of beach. Pevensey Bay is a very small resort with a pebble beach. William the Conqueror landed here but nothing much has happened since.

Normans' Bay, the next stop, is part of Pevensey Bay and

presumably received some of William's men. There's even less here than at Pevensey and the swimming is good once you get over the pebble beach and into the sea. The country behind is flat grazing land stretching back to a line of hills.

Bexhill is a small resort of no great character which before the war hired a modern architect and built itself the then much-admired De La Warr Pavilion – nowadays it would be called a leisure centre. It still looks quite good and still gives Bexhill its main claim to attention.

St Leonard's is the quieter end of Hastings but it's all one town really, a deservedly popular resort on a direct line a little under two hours from Charing Cross. The Battle of Hastings didn't take place here but a few stations up the line at Battle. Hastings is built on and under high ground, with an old town of pretty houses at the east end. It has a castle, a good beach and is a shopping centre and resort of character.

At Hastings station train announcements in the summer are made in French as well as English. The station swarms with groups of foreign youngsters who take time off from learning English to travel up and down the lines from here. A couple of dozen of them joined the train to Ashford with me, though many of them, being German, still had to ask for guidance.

I wanted to go along the Kent coast and it was necessary to go inland to Ashford, the major railway junction for east Kent, in order to do so. (The coast from Dungeness round to Hythe, next door to Folkestone, is served by steam trains of the miniature but quite businesslike Romney, Hythe and Dymchurch Railway.)

The little train from Hastings takes just under an hour to run the 26 miles through Rye to Ashford. It moves inland at once and follows the broad valley of the River Brede.

Hastings was one of the original Cinque Ports, whose members had to furnish ships for the King's Navy. Winchelsea was one of those added later. But the sea receded and it now has no port. Rye, the next stop, was also a Cinque Port. The sea has gone from here too, but there is a harbour a mile away at the mouth of the River Rother. Rye is a delightful town on a hill, with many beautiful old houses and cobbled streets.

The train now took off across country through sheep-grazing lands on the edge of Romney Marsh. Away to our right were Dungeness with its nuclear power stations, the little town of New Romney and the marshes which for centuries were the haunts of smugglers bringing contraband in from France. This is mysterious, treacherous country where mist can come down suddenly and leave you helplessly lost. But today the sun was shining and I watched a man shearing the last one of a flock of sheep, the others skipping away looking naked but not otherwise incommoded.

The train terminated at Ashford, where two main lines from London, from Victoria and Charing Cross, meet before going their separate ways to Ramsgate; the Victoria line inland via Canterbury, the Charing Cross line by way of Folkestone, Dover and Deal.

I now saw the Southern electric main-line expresses in action, a startling contrast to the coastal ramblers. Southern Region doesn't get much chance to show its paces over the longer distances but on these lines to the Channel ports and the popular Thanet resorts the twelve-coach trains of comfortable rolling stock make an impressive show.

It was a quick run through east Kent to Folkestone. The Central station is perched high above the town giving extensive views both sides. This is one of the ferry ports for Boulogne and Calais and the boat trains go off the main line into a siding and then reverse down a steep line to the harbour. In the days of steam, boat trains coming up the slope would have two or three banking engines pushing from behind, belching smoke. Folkestone has a cliff-top garden and promenade, the Leas, for a walk with a view, and is much favoured by people who only want to look at the sea rather than swim in it.

From Folkestone to Dover the line runs along the chalk cliffs. Dover is Britain's busiest port, a lively and cosmopolitan town rich in places to eat, full of bustle and animation. The train to Ramsgate goes round the back of the town hugging the hillside, giving good views of the town and of the imposing Norman castle high on its rock. France is only 21 miles away and from the castle on a clear day a long stretch of the French coast can be seen.

The town lies in a gap in the celebrated white cliffs and the railway line, having climbed round the hillside and crossed the gap, goes out through a tunnel and emerges behind the cliffs. Dover was the chief of the Cinque Ports but the official residence of the Warden of the Cinque Ports is Walmer Castle. The post is honorific now: Sir Winston Churchill held it and occasionally used the residence.

Walmer, now reached, is a small Victorian seaside resort.

Immediately adjoining it is Deal, an ancient seaside resort town of very great character. Many of its seventeenth-century houses are preserved. The Goodwin Sands, on which many ships have been wrecked, lie opposite the town and between the town and the sandbank is a safe anchorage, the Downs. In the days of sail the fleet used to anchor here waiting for a favourable wind and captains were rowed out to join their ships from the town, which has a steep pebble beach. Nelson is supposed to have dallied with Lady Hamilton here. There are two interesting Tudor forts.

Across flat land now to Sandwich, another of the Cinque Ports which has almost lost its port status, though the occasional coaster comes up the River Stour. Sandwich is a beautifully preserved town of seventeenth- and eighteenth-century houses in narrow streets, with a town wall and a championship golf course.

Across the Stour, past some light industry and the Roman port of Rutupiae (revived in the First World War as the ammunition port of Richborough) and we were on the Isle of Thanet. The trains run across flat land to join the line from Canterbury into Ramsgate. I stopped here but the train carries on round the Thanet coast through Broadstairs to Margate and a main line from there runs along the north Kent coast and back to Victoria.

Of the resorts in Thanet and on the north Kent coast Ramsgate, built on a cliff with some fine old houses, is my favourite. It manages to combine popular resort amenities with a character and personality of its own. There is a harbour and, during the summer, a hovercraft service to Calais. Adjoining Ramsgate is the smaller but perhaps prettier Broadstairs, with a small harbour, a house where Dickens lived on the cliff and a fine sweep of old houses on the front.

Margate is for those who want a convivial holiday, Westgate is the quieter, more select end of Margate; Birchington, sounding more like a place of correction, to my mind has little to offer. Herne Bay, past the Reculver Towers landmark seen from the train, is a little down at heel but has a nice atmosphere, one or two pleasant old houses on the front, and is good for watching shipping making for the Thames. Whitstable is an old Kent fishing port with character and oysters.

With its network of good train services and wide variety of seaside resorts, East Kent is a very good area for taking a holiday runabout ticket.

Rural Kent and Surrey

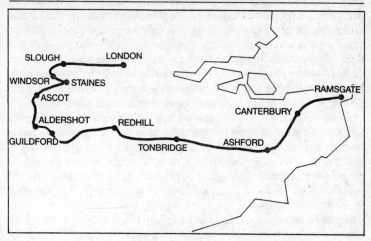

Southern Region are in the business of getting you to and from work in London or to and from the seaside resorts and ports that line the coast from north Kent round to Dorset. This they do with great dispatch and if you find yourself in Ramsgate a choice of fast electric trains will whisk you to Victoria or Charing Cross in two hours or less. If you're making for Paddington, that's seven stops on the London Transport Bakerloo line from Charing Cross, say another half an hour.

But if you've time and inclination for a country ramble, that too can be arranged by train. So I decided to go from Ramsgate to Paddington the roundabout way – through Canterbury to Ashford and across the Weald to Guildford, with the North Downs in view most of the way, and a final spectacular run between Box Hill and Leith Hill before Surrey's commuter land closed in.

From Guildford, if all the trains kept strictly to the timetable, I could catch a train to Aldershot which would then reverse to Ascot. A two-minute change would bring a train to Staines and if I hurried over the bridge there I'd be in time to catch a train down the branch line to Windsor. From Windsor and Eton Riverside, the Southern station, I could stroll up the road, past the castle's great round tower and into Western Region's Windsor and Eton Central. From there the shuttle train would take me to Slough, where I could change for Paddington. Six hours instead of two and a half but you see so much more and who's hurrying? British Rail has plenty of well-publicized scenic routes but it's often more fun to work out your own.

Ramsgate to Tonbridge

Good service, best train just over an hour
My first train was to Ashford by way of Canterbury West. (It's near enough due north of Canterbury East, the other station.) As the train comes in there's a splendid view of the cathedral and a quick look at the gate in the city wall. Besides being the headquarters of the Anglican church and the place where Thomas à Becket was murdered, Canterbury is a very small city of manageable size, focal point and logical touring centre for east Kent.

From Canterbury to Ashford the line goes up the Stour valley through Chartham and Chilham and Wye, through the sort of neat, pretty country which has earned Kent the name of the Garden of England. The main roads and railways from London to Folkestone and Dover pass through Ashford and Canterbury and here in between life goes on without rush, with tile-hung cottages in the villages and cricket played on village greens, great trees giving shade, pubs with benches outside them.

Half an hour of that, travelling south-west to Ashford, and then I began to travel the line that runs almost straight across the Weald from Ashford through Tonbridge to Redhill. This was the time to take in the classical Kent countryside – the line of the Downs to the north, sleek horses in paddocks, a patchwork of greens and yellows in the fields, round oasthouses with conical roofs and white wooden tops seen all over the Kent hopfields. In many cases the hops have gone and the oasthouses have been converted into homes.

Before the First World War special trains used to leave London Bridge carrying East Enders into Kent for their annual holidays picking hops for a week. They actually worked long hours and were accommodated in primitive huts, but the country air was the thing.

By the main lines from Ashford or Tonbridge I was only about an hour from central London, yet this is as beautiful and as peacefully rural as anywhere in England. Pluckley, Headcorn,

Staplehurst, Marden, Paddock Wood – these are the names of unhurried, tranquil Kent.

This is a good time to remember that bicycles can be taken on trains. From any of these stations it would be possible to cycle away and explore real country, eventually finding a station on another line from which to go home: Headcorn to Lenham, Marden to Wadhurst or just take off and see where you get.

At Tonbridge the line from Hastings joins the line from Folkestone and Dover turning north-west to London.

Tonbridge to Guildford

Hourly service, about an hour and a half

From Tonbridge I took the local train that runs straight across country to Redhill, reversing out of there to carry on across Surrey to Guildford and out to Reading to join the Western Region main line. This line is really a continuation of the one from Ashford and was once the main line to London.

The line of the North Downs was closer now. Beyond the hills, invisible from the train, was the southern edge of London's commuter area. None of that was to be seen from the train as it set off for Penshurst, Edenbridge, Godstone and Nutfield. There were no very spectacular views but the country through which we passed was continually pretty, wild flowers on the embankments, trees dappling the sunshine, villages coming and going at decorous intervals. At two or three places we passed I could see a fête in progress, as was only proper on a Saturday afternoon in July. Cricket was being played, school sports were being held.

Outside the small towns and villages, few but farm buildings were to be seen. The wooded heights of the North Downs marched on our right. Gentler tree-clad hills closed the views to the south. And all this beautiful country was only 25 miles from Victoria.

The idyll was only briefly interrupted while we made our way across the main Brighton line into Redhill station and then reversed out through Reigate. We ran along under Box Hill, through Dorking, and then there was a final fling of rolling Surrey hills, Ranmore Common and Hockhurst Down to the north, with the Polesden Lacey National Trust estate up there somewhere, Leith Hill and Abinger Hammer to the south. Marvellous walking country this – coming this way again I would get off at Gomshall and head south.

Then we had run through the trees and into Guildford, with its modern Gothic cathedral, its new university, the Surrey of bridge parties and leaded windows and of London just up the fast line.

Guildford to Windsor

Half-hourly service, good connections, about an hour and a half
A change of train here to a humble one which just links different lines together rather than going anywhere in its own right. It went first to Aldershot, the army's home town, where it deposited a couple of young soldiers and made a link with the line to Alton. Then it reversed and made its way north through Camberley to Ascot. We were still in army country here. The Staff College is at Camberley and across the River Blackwater on the line to Reading Sandhurst is the home of officer cadets. Betjeman country too, this, but those lovesick subalterns and beefy tennis girls rarely travelled by local train and were not to be seen on this one. The pines, however, were on parade.

At Ascot, its station anything but royal, our train joined the Reading-Waterloo line and gave up the struggle, its duty done. It had arrived in time for me to make my connection, though, and so I went up the line to Staines. Sunningdale, Virginia Water – the name suggests a drippy deb and we were into the moneyed classes here, with well-scrubbed, confident girls waiting at the station who looked as if they'd just come from a gymkhana. But between the two stations, a discovery: at Longcross you can walk out of the station, which seems to have no village attached, and away directly into extensive woods.

At Egham there's a view to the left of the incredible towers, spires, gables and fanciful whatnots of Royal Holloway College, founded by the pill and ointment man. Egham is the stop for Runnymede, where Magna Carta was signed. The memorial to the late President Kennedy is nearby.

Over the Thames to Staines and a quick change for a train up the short line, mostly flanking reservoirs, to Datchet and back over the Thames again into Windsor and Eton Riverside, only a minute's walk from the Thames. River steamers can be boarded here.

Windsor to Paddington

Half-hourly service, changing at Slough; about 40 minutes

Riverside is a plain, modest station. For pretensions to grandeur you have to take a five-minute walk up Thames Street round the great mass of Windsor Castle to Windsor and Eton Central. Queen Victoria, who was fond of railway travel as long as trains didn't go too fast, relished having this amenity practically opposite her front door and often boarded her special train here. The Great Western Railway responded with an elaborate canopied entrance, decorated with coats of arms, which today leads to rather a letdown when you find behind it a tired two-coach local on a single track, going only to Slough.

Even this experience has its moment, however, for the train rises to a bridge over the river and continues on a viaduct giving a superb view of the castle and of Eton College before plunging under motorways into Slough.

Windsor is one of those unmissable, almost compulsory sights that the visitor sometimes expects to be a bit of a disappointment. Not a bit of it: it's a delightful little town which handles its crowds of visitors well. The castle is everything a royal castle should be, impressive to look at from outside, historically fascinating within.

And so on from Slough the last few miles into Paddington, into the comfort of the Great Western Royal Hotel with its Brunel bar.

Waterloo to Poole

Hourly service, two hours

For a seaside day out from London I chose the Weymouth line from Waterloo and settled for Poole, two hours and 114 miles away and the furthest you can get on a Southern Region bargain seaside day-out ticket.

Waterloo is the biggest London terminus, serving the south-western area of Southern Region. It was rebuilt in the twenties and has been smartened up internally. Expresses used to run from here to the Atlantic coast of North Cornwall. The line to Exeter is still open, running through Yeovil, Axminster and Honiton, but from Salisbury it is now only a local service. The longest main line out of Waterloo is now the Weymouth line, electric as far as Bournemouth. It's a good fast service, reaching Southampton in a little more than an hour, Bournemouth half an hour later and

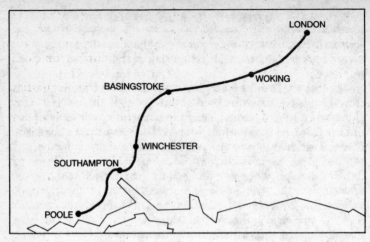

Poole in just under two hours. It goes out through the south-west London suburbs, through attractive farming country in the middle of Hampshire and on to the New Forest and the Dorset coast, a varied and interesting ride.

Waterloo is just across the river from Westminster and you get a glimpse of Parliament on the right as the train pulls out. Another palace comes immediately afterwards, the Archbishop of Canterbury's Lambeth Palace in its park. By contrast with this grand residence, down the line at Battersea are streets of houses submerged in a tangle of railway viaducts. After Vauxhall comes Nine Elms fruit and vegetable market, migrated here from Covent Garden, with behind it the upturned table of Battersea power station, listed for its architectural merit.

Clapham Junction, where the lines from Victoria cross those from Waterloo, is reckoned one of the busiest stations in the world with more than 2000 trains a day passing through. You could sit here for hours and see trains on the move all the time, often several at once on the many tracks from Waterloo.

From Farnborough, where the train breaks out of suburbia, to Basingstoke the line runs straight and level for 15 miles. This is a fast section of the route, and the trains can keep up the maximum permitted speed of 90 mph. Basingstoke is where the lines to Salisbury and Southampton divide and the link line from Reading comes in. Trains from Birmingham and the North use this to reach Southampton and Portsmouth.

Beyond Basingstoke, with its surprising high-rise office blocks set in the Hampshire downs, we were off through traditional southern English farming country of great beauty between the rivers Test and Itchen, with hills away in the distance on either side.

Winchester is a disappointment for the railway traveller passing through. A cutting robs us of much idea of this ancient city, capital of England under Alfred the Great. It's well worth a day out on its own; besides the Norman cathedral there's the Great Hall of the otherwise ruined castle, where there hangs what's reputed to be King Arthur's round table.

Our train continued down beside the Itchen into Southampton and through the port. Just beyond Southampton is the line up to Salisbury. Between Southampton and Bournemouth the train ran through the New Forest; new, that is, when William the Conqueror created it, with great cruelty towards the local people. Both his sons were killed in it and contemporary opinion was that it was God's judgment on him. Today it's beautiful country of majestic beech and oak – it supplied timber for the old navy's hearts of oak – and as the train passed I was able to see that the traditional New Forest ponies still thrived.

Bournemouth, approached through residential suburbs, is a major seaside resort and retiring place for the wealthy. It has a good beach, sub-tropical gardens, parks full of pines, all the amenities of a major resort and a resolute air of gentility.

This is the end of the electric line and the occasion for a neat way of transferring to diesel traction for the rest of the line to Weymouth. The twelve-car train from Waterloo is powered by electric motors in the four-car unit at the rear, but is driven by a man in the cab of the leading car, using remote control equipment. At Bournemouth the four rear cars, with their electric motors, are detached and a diesel locomotive is put on the front. This, too, has remote control gear so that on the return journey from Weymouth to Bournemouth the train can be driven from a cab at the other end of the train from the locomotive. The coaches are simply pushed back to join on the end of the four-car electric unit.

Out of Bournemouth station the line goes across the back of the town by an embankment giving a panoramic view of the residential areas. A stylish brick viaduct, no longer in use but still adding elegance to the scene, curves away to where Bournemouth West station used to be.

Before the train reached Poole I could see the huge harbour, full of yachts, with Brownsea Island, a bird sanctuary, in the middle. At Poole station itself, a view out over what looks like the harbour is actually only a small part of it, but still impressive against the spur of wooded hill beyond. The great harbour is Poole's glory, marvellous in extent and fortunately too shallow to be developed as a major deep-sea port.

I left the train here. It would run on to the pleasant old town of Wareham (the river by the station is the Piddle) and up the Frome valley with Purbeck Hills away to the left, to Wool and Dorchester. Then on past the earthworks of prehistoric Maiden Castle, to be seen on the right, down to Weymouth, where George III popularized sea bathing and seaside resorts before his son, the Prince Regent, had thought of settling in Brighthelmstone. Grateful Weymouth townspeople put up a striking statue of their royal patron which is kept brightly painted and is one of the resort's distinctions. It's an attractive little port (for the Channel Islands) with some fine old buildings and a seaside resort with a bit of a West Country flavour. Chesil beach and Portland Bill are nearby.

Poole has the advantage of being the fairly quiet neighbour of a big resort. On an August Sunday I saw no great crowds as I strolled down from the station through the High Street to the quay, passing handsome Georgian houses near the church. The High Street is pleasantly human in scale. Off to one side, in Market Street, many old houses have been well restored. There's a fine old custom house. The old part of Poole makes an attractive little place away from the main hustle, with amenities available if required in neighbouring Bournemouth.

Richmond

Back at Waterloo I switched to the Staines line for the fifteen-minute ride to Richmond, by way of Clapham Junction, Putney and Mortlake. From the station I walked up the hill to stay the night at the Richmond Hill Hotel (the 71 bus would have taken me). As an alternative to staying in central London, Richmond has much to recommend it. It is an historic old riverside town with many fine eighteenth-century houses. George IV, then Prince of Wales, secretly married Mrs Fitzherbert here in 1785. Richmond Park, once Charles I's deer forest, is London's biggest and finest open space. Kew Gardens and Hampton Court are near and Windsor not far away.

The hotel, put together from several old houses, stands near the park on the brow of the hill, which offers one of the finest views in London – up the Thames and over miles of trees to the west, with the Surrey Hills to the south. Below, in Petersham meadows, cows graze peacefully.

After an excellent meal I walked down the hill for a drink at the riverside White Cross Hotel and admired another fine view, of the classically elegant Richmond Bridge.

The Thames is the heart of London. Many of its riverside villages can be reached by train and are worth exploring – Putney, Chiswick, Barnes, Kew, Twickenham, Hampton Wick (for lovely Hampton Court Park) and Hampton Court. But none offer a better mix of elegance, history and natural beauty than Richmond.

Ways to the Kent and Channel coasts

By my count there are eleven different routes from the London termini of Victoria, Waterloo, Charing Cross and London Bridge by which the coasts of north and east Kent and the English Channel can be reached and more than 30 different seaside places in the area which are accessible by train. Of these, Weymouth, two hours 40 minutes from Waterloo, is the only one that cannot be reached in under two hours; Brighton needs only 52 minutes from Victoria.

From Waterloo smooth electric expresses to Portsmouth for Southsea and the Isle of Wight share the main line with those for Southampton and Bournemouth as far as Woking, then turn south through Guildford, find a gap in the hills and run up the Wey valley through Farncombe, the last of suburbia, through picturesque Godalming and out through the sort of country that gets painted for Christmas cards as the heart of old England – gracious forest heights, ample tile-hung houses nestling among trees. The line joins the River Rother for a short while before Petersfield, which has some lovely old houses, then climbs up into the South Downs and runs down through wooded hollows into Portsmouth.

Victoria is the London terminus for the greatest number of trains to the coast. It is a jumbo-size, satisfying station – formerly two – which still does things in style. Outside, the Edwardian classical façade has female figures brooding over scrolls. Inside, the atmosphere is cosmopolitan with destination boards notifying departures for Paris, Warsaw and Moscow, frequent expresses to Gatwick Airport in distinctive livery and young people in ethnic dress, festooned with rucksacks, seething everywhere. From here the main seaside day-out destination is Brighton. The route goes through the tangle of Clapham Junction, through the south London suburbs and out past Gatwick, briefly through forest and more dormitory towns before finding a way through the South Downs into Brighton. Take the fast train and you're there almost before you've caught your breath.

The Littlehampton trains turn off to Hove and take the coastal line through Worthing. Bognor Regis trains turn off the Brighton line at Three Bridges, just beyond Gatwick, and take off quite rewardingly through West Sussex, passing through Crawley, skirting St Leonard's forest and after Horsham crossing picture-book farming country not yet covered with London dormitories. To the left after Horsham is Christ's Hospital, the Bluecoat school noted for the boys' medieval uniform of cloak, knee breeches and yellow stockings.

From Pulborough the clean lines of the Downs can be seen and Arundel offers the splendid spectacle across the meadows of the hillside town and its great castle guarding a gap. The castle was besieged twice in the twelfth century and knocked about by Cromwell's men in 1643. Since then it has been extensively rebuilt and is the seat of the Duke of Norfolk. The castle can be visited and the town, with many attractive walks, makes a very enjoyable day out from London by train. If you don't get off here the train follows the River Arun through the Downs, then follows the coast line a short way before turning off to Bognor.

The busy Brighton line also carries trains which turn off at Wivelsfield for Lewes, Eastbourne and Hastings, with a branch at Lewes down the Ouse valley to Newhaven and Seaford. Newhaven is a yachting centre and the ferry harbour for Dieppe. King Louis-Philippe of France, fleeing from the 1848 revolution, landed here and stayed at the Bridge Hotel.

Hastings can be reached more swiftly from London by the service from Charing Cross, which runs down the main line to Tonbridge, on the Medway, then branches off to the south through Tunbridge Wells and over the lovely wooded country of the Weald through Battle and on to Hastings. Tunbridge Wells was a fashionable Regency spa and still has its fine seventeenth-century Pantiles promenade and its high rocks: a good centre for walking. Trains on this line have red labels proclaiming the 1066 Route, Battle, not Hastings, being the station nearest the spot where William conquered: fine walking country all round here.

From Tonbridge, main-line trains from Charing Cross serve Folkestone, Dover and Deal and run on to Ramsgate. But the resorts of Thanet – Ramsgate, Broadstairs and Margate – are reached more quickly by fast trains from Victoria, which take in the north Kent coast resorts on their way, with a branch line from Sittingbourne for Sheerness.

7

South Wales and the West

The Western Region comprises the south-west of England and the southern half of Wales. It takes in the Thames Valley, the Cotswolds, Hereford and Worcester, Devon and Cornwall. With Dartmoor, Exmoor, the Welsh mountains and some of the most beautiful coastline in Britain, it is a favourite holiday area.

The main lines to Wales and the south-west are served by InterCity 125s, including the *Cornish Riviera* from Paddington to Penzance. Trains to Devon and Cornwall on summer Saturdays

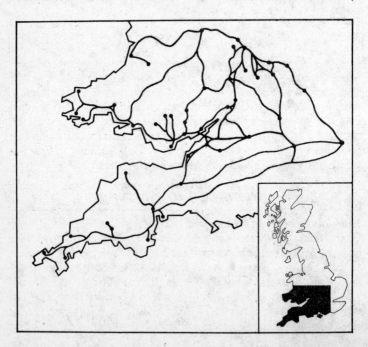

are usually crowded and reservations are required. Local run-about tickets are available in the holiday areas.

Good day-trip centres in the region are Cardiff, Birmingham, Bristol, Oxford, Exeter and Plymouth.

Around the West Country

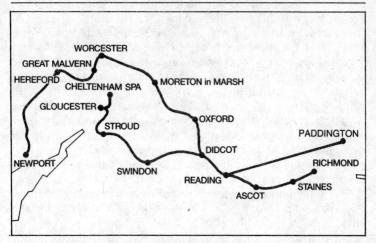

Some train journeys are meant to get you there quickly but it is also possible to ramble enjoyably. I had such a ramble in mind in setting off from Richmond to go to Birmingham by way of Oxford, Worcester, Hereford, Newport and Gloucester. Of course I could have gone to Birmingham direct from Reading up the main line through Oxford, Banbury and Leamington Spa; but why be in a tearing hurry to get to Birmingham?

Richmond to Reading

Half-hourly service, 54 minutes
From Richmond there is a direct line to Reading and I boarded a train of fast suburban electric stock for the run through Twick-enham, Staines, Ascot and Wokingham. Richmond station was busy – it's also the terminus for the North London and District lines – but most people were going into London; the trains out were nearly empty. Through Twickenham and Whitton the line is classic suburban back-garden; not to everyone's taste but I find

suburbia's back-gardens much more interesting than its shopping centres – more character, more variety. Back gardens gave way to the scrubby edge of Hounslow Heath, a poor vestige of a once romantically wild area infested with footpads. Then we ran by way of gravel pits to Staines on the Thames. We were officially out of London and soon across the tip of Surrey into Berkshire, running through tall forest trees and pines beyond Ascot. Trees are the glory of this part of the country.

Bracknell was one of the post-war New Towns, founded in 1949, and today is the home of the Meteorological Office. Wokingham next, with rosy red brick and a neat church by the station, is the very heartland of the prosperous south, where the depths of depression in the north are only traveller's tales. In Royal Berkshire the towns are like parks, set about with trees, with neat, clean houses in immaculate gardens, roses climbing the walls. Whatever economic problems the town has it is keeping to itself, not advertising to the passing traveller.

This Southern electric line ends at Reading. It used to sneak into a little station of its own, suitably cowed by the mighty Great Western main line. Now the Southern train is permitted to climb on to the main line, to be hustled quickly off it again and into a bay.

The real life of the station happens on the main-line platform 4, where 125s from Paddington pause briefly before taking off to Cornwall, South Wales or Bristol. On this summer day the platform was thronged with young people, elderly couples, Americans, a few Japanese tourists.

Reading to Hereford

Infrequent, about two and three-quarter hours
The Cotswold and Malvern Express from Paddington is the only through train of the morning picking up at Reading for the beautiful line through the Cotswolds between Oxford and Worcester. The Bristol main line carried us through the Goring gap in the Chilterns and as far as Didcot; then we took off to the north on the Oxford and Birmingham line. Passing Didcot on the east side showed us briefly the Great Western Society's collection of rolling stock in the old GWR livery – chocolate and cream coaches with romantic old destination boards like 'Torbay Express', and green tank engines.

The line crossed the Thames twice as it went north through Oxfordshire between fields of golden straw. Then we were at Oxford, less than an hour from Paddington, with the dreaming spires clustered excitingly only a short way down the road.

There was a big exodus here, the most important destination on this line. We left the Americans to tour the colleges while we pulled away past an impressive pile of scrapped cars. Shortly afterwards we left the Banbury line and struck out for the Cotswolds.

Quite soon we were into very pretty wooded country tracing the River Evenlode up towards its source. Villages of stone houses nestle among trees on small hills around here, each village with its needle-spired church. Charlbury station, on the edge of the Cotswolds, has a cared-for, well-tended look with flowerbeds on the platform and an attractive little chalet station house. This is beautiful walking country and some of those getting off here were making for Blenheim Palace, seat of the Dukes of Marlborough, seven miles away.

After Charlbury the train continued up the Evenlode valley past what is left of Wychwood, once a forest in which Henry VIII liked to hunt. The names of villages, Shipton under Wychwood and Milton under Wychwood, are reminders of it. This is a quiet, comfortable land that doesn't flaunt itself. There are hills on both sides of the train and soon after passing the station at Kingham I could see Stow on the Wold away to the left.

At Moreton-in-Marsh we had left the Evenlode close to its source and were in flat pasture between the hills, Bourton-on-the-Hill on one side, Barton-on-the-Heath on the other. Here the train crossed the Fosse Way, the Roman road from Exeter to Lincoln which runs through the High Street at Moreton. A building near that station proclaimed itself the home of Spook Erection, whatever that was – could there be a CIA build-up here?

Now in wooded cuttings we seemed to be penetrating deeper and deeper into a private England; an effect enhanced by the railway's single track between trees that sometimes brushed the sides of the coaches, and by the misty vagueness of the hills on either side.

Then we were through a tunnel out of the hills and out of Gloucestershire into the flat, fertile Vale of Evesham, with Bredon Hill in front of us, where Housman's couple used to lie on Sunday mornings, and Shakespeare's Stratford a few miles up the Avon to the north. This is market gardening country with greenhouses and orchards, a picture of peaceful industry.

Evesham revealed little significant of itself to us and Pershore even less. But now we could see the great cathedral tower of Worcester ahead and the Malvern Hills in the distance.

It was at Worcester that Cromwell routed the forces of Charles II in 1651. Charles watched the battle from the cathedral tower and many of his soldiers were afterwards imprisoned in the building. The city has an apple and a sauce named after it and apart from this has managed to keep itself pretty much out of the news, living a quiet life and minding its own business in spite of being only a short drive down the M5 from Birmingham. Between the two Worcester stations the train ran over a red-brick viaduct giving wide views over the town and its bulky cathedral. We left the city, crossing the River Severn, and made for the Malvern Hills. The spas which once flourished in the hills no longer attract visitors in the numbers that once flocked here but the water is as pure as ever and the hills strange and beautiful in contrast to the flat country the train has crossed to reach them.

In Great Malvern station, where our train terminated, one remnant of past smartness remained: round the capital of each canopy column was a circle of painted yellow leaves, a different arrangement for each column. After half an hour a train from Birmingham came to carry us out of the town under the great swell of Worcester Beacon. We plunged through the line of hills, climbing through tunnels to Colwell, then out to Ledbury and beyond.

Rolling through this agreeable rural landscape from one sleepy cathedral city to the next I was just about to fall asleep myself when we ran into Hereford, with a good view of the cathedral and the spires of other churches. It looked a nice open town with no tall building. Its chief glories are the cathedral's chained library and its fourteenth-century map of the world. It is the centre of a lush agricultural area and has given its name to a breed of cattle. You can almost hear how quiet it is. Its station, with flowers in red and white tubs, goes into a timeless hush when no train is in, reminding you of how country stations used to be.

On another occasion I took an alternative and equally beautiful route through the Cotswolds, travelling down the main Bristol line to Swindon before turning off. The most comfortable train to take is the morning Cheltenham Spa Express from Paddington, calling at Reading. From Swindon the train takes off on a single track between dense hedges and high banks, across farm land to the stone-built village of Kemble, close to the source of the River Thames.

The Cotswolds start here and the train climbs among wooded hills, through the mile-long Sapperton tunnel and then down the side of a narrow valley through Chalford and into Stroud. This was the centre of a thriving woollen industry; there are some fine old warehouses and splendid views from the hillside. The train runs on down the valley, shortly joins the Bristol to Birmingham main line, goes in and out of Gloucester and terminates at Cheltenham Spa, from where it is possible to go on to Worcester and Hereford by other trains. Both Gloucester, cathedral city and terminus of a ship canal from the Severn, and Cheltenham, which has many fine eighteenth-century terraces, are well worth a walk-round.

Hereford to Newport

Infrequent, under an hour

A train came in from Crewe and Shrewsbury to take me down into Wales through Abergavenny and Pontypool to Newport, a hauled train of none-too-new coaches fairly full. My fellow-travellers were holiday-makers and Welsh people going home, unbuttoned in the heat and plainly not posh like some of the folk who had been going to Worcester.

The train slid away into the sun-dazed afternoon with no fuss and we seemed almost to have dropped out of the inhabited world. We crossed the River Wye on leaving the city and passed through country between hills where there seemed to be hardly a village, only a few scattered farm houses, a land even more remote than those I had passed through earlier.

The map showed that there were villages – Madley, Ploughfield, Eaton Bishop and Wormbridge were all somewhere around – but contented-looking cattle provided most of the visible animation. The fields began to rise and fall, covering small hills with a patchwork of cultivation, and then the hills closed in and we sank into Wales as into a warm sea, pushing through the foothills of the Black Mountains under the Sugar Loaf mountain to Abergavenny, a popular walking centre.

Down the edge of the mountains then to Pontypool and into the classic Welsh industrial landscape of mining valleys, industry in the valley bottoms and houses climbing the hillsides, down past Caerleon to Newport on the muddy Usk, where the station seems to have a constant stream of coal trains rumbling through.

Newport to Birmingham

Eight trains a day to Gloucester, three through to Birmingham
Finally, north to Birmingham by a train leaving the Paddington main line at Severn Tunnel junction to run up beside the river instead of plunging under it. From the train I had a fine view of the estuary, mysterious, dreamlike, and of the graceful road suspension bridge. Expanses of mud on the banks showed what a great rise and fall the tide has.

At Chepstow we passed close to the castle glowering on a rock, separated from the town by the Wye in a deep ravine. Further up the Severn on the far bank was a different fortress, the nuclear power station at Berkeley.

The train followed the bank of the Severn before cutting across to go over the now much reduced river at Gloucester. Gloucester is a seaport as well as a cathedral city. Ships can reach its quay and docks by way of the Berkeley and Gloucester canal, which we had seen running close to the Severn's far bank.

As the train came in we were offered a wonderful sight of the cream cathedral riding high above the town, the intricate lace-work of decorative stone on the tower seen to best advantage with daylight visible through the openings. There is an odd station here with one of BR's longest platforms, 1977 feet, used by trains in both directions.

Out of Gloucester station the line joined that from Bristol. With a stop at Cheltenham Spa we ran back past the other side of Bredon Hill and across the Oxford-Worcester line to Birmingham. I had marked down some places to visit later at leisure: Charlbury, Great Malvern, Chepstow. But mostly this was a trip for exploring the country from the train, getting the picture of a lovely land.

South and West Wales

For railway purposes, North and South Wales are two quite distinct areas. Their lines were developed by different railway companies as extensions from England and to get from one to another it is necessary to pass through Shrewsbury, in England. This was my starting point for a trip in the south and west of the Principality.

Shrewsbury to Llanelli

Five trains a day, about three and a half hours
At Shrewsbury the two-coach diesel waiting in a bay was well filled. When we started the guard checked the passengers' destinations; at more than half the 32 stations on the Llanelli line the train stopped only on request.

The line from Shrewsbury to Llanelli – the train reverses there and goes on to Swansea – is a remarkable one that runs 110 miles through the heart of Wales, through Llandrindod, Llanwrtyd, Llandovery and Llandeilo down to industrial west Wales at Ammanford, Pontarddulais and Llanelli. From Shrewsbury the line first runs south between two long hills, the Long Mynd and Wenlock Edge, through Church Stretton to Craven Arms, named after a pub. This is on the main line to Hereford and Newport, but once through the station the train stops and the guard gets out to throw the points for the train to move on to the branch. The train moves over the points and waits for the guard to switch the points back and rejoin his train.

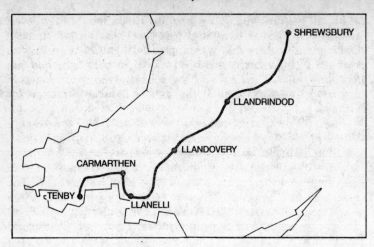

Now we were on our way into the hills and soon found ourselves over the border into Wales at Knighton, in Welsh Tref-y-Clawdd, the town on the dyke. Offa was the eighth-century King of Mercia who built a skilfully engineered dyke from the Dee to the Severn to mark the border with the Welsh. It was mostly a rampart with a ditch on the Welsh side and much of it can still be seen. Knighton has an Offa's Dyke information centre.

The line runs up into the Welsh hills and has to climb to a height of 980 feet above sea level before it can find a way over into the Towy valley. At Knucklas station, just before the line curves round, you can see the impressive Knucklas viaduct with its thirteen high stone arches and a tower at each end. A tunnel follows and then the summit and the little train picks up speed down the other side. There's a marvellous section of line when it clings to a hillside going down a narrow valley with wooded hills and crags. This is deepest Wales, revealing itself more easily to the train traveller than to anyone but the most energetic walker.

The train now runs down through steep hills, green and secret, and out into more open country at Llandrindod. This is the largest of several places in the area which enjoyed some popularity as spas. Drinking the waters here is still thought good for gout and rheumatism but Llandrindod has blossomed out into an all-round holiday centre, the abundant hotel accommodation left over from its spa days making it a popular centre for sightseeing tours, fishing, walking and golf.

Builth, the next spa, is bypassed by the railway, Builth Road station being about two miles from it. Then through tunnels, cuttings and scenery that is a continual delight the train goes on through Llangamarch, another little town that once had spa ambitions, and on to Llanwrtyd, which has given up spa waters in favour of pony trekking in the hills as a main attraction for visitors.

After the stop at Llandrindod at about 12.30 I unpacked a simple picnic bought that morning before setting out – cold meat, bread and cheese, an apple and wine. Having a meal on a train while going through some of the most beautiful countryside to be seen anywhere is to my mind one of the great pleasures of life. The meal does not have to be elaborate – the view makes the occasion – and from Llandrindod to Llandeilo I enjoyed a feast for the eyes and the appetite. Not everyone can afford the full British Rail restaurant car treatment (even if it were available on this line) but this simple pleasure is within reach of most of us.

After Llanwrtyd the train plunged into a tunnel under the Sugar Loaf mountain and then ran down over another viaduct, longer and even more impressive than the first, though lacking towers. This was the Cynghordy viaduct and as the train went in and the line curved a look back gave a view of the mountain and the viaduct. Our train followed a hillside in a steep valley covered with trees; at Cynghordy station two young walkers with rucksacks got off and disappeared into the woods.

At Llandovery we were in the valley of the River Towy, a great river for salmon and trout. This is a pleasant market town and further down the line, as the valley begins to open out into broad farmlands, came another little market town of neat houses, Llandeilo. We were running through a series of small farms which seemed to be sleeping peacefully through the afternoon.

Having come through the central mountains of Wales we were now running down into the industrial south. Ammanford was the beginning of coal mining, with sidings full of coal wagons; Pontarddulais followed with its tinplate works. We had transferred from the River Towy to the River Loughor and we ran beside its estuary and the Burry inlet, with the Gower peninsula across the water, into the tinplate town of Llanelli.

By this time our line through the mountains had joined the main line from Cardiff to Milford Haven and Fishguard. Our train would reverse and go back up the main line the two stations to

Swansea. I left it at Llanelli, feeling I had had a privileged view of some of the beauties of Wales.

Llanelli to Tenby

Infrequent, an hour and a half

There was time to look round Llanelli before I caught my next train. A few years of modest prosperity had made this industrial town into a cheerful-looking place, all the old terrace houses rendered and brightly painted and a fine market area and town centre built. There was not very much wrong with Britain that full employment could not cure, it seemed. And then, as the train taking me on to Whitland passed the town's closed and silent steel works, we were reminded of the other side of the coin – the bitterness that unemployment could bring. The baleful message chalked on a wall was big enough for all train passengers to read: 'It could be your job next.'

Carmarthen, sitting on top of a hill, is the county town for Dyfed and has a ruined castle. There was a Roman fort here, part of the foundations of which can be seen. Trains coming into the station here have to reverse out to continue.

Tenby is usually reached by leaving the Milford Haven train at Whitland and changing to the Pembroke Dock branch line, although there are two through trains from Swansea and on Saturdays even an express from London.

I arrived at Tenby just before six o'clock and walked to the Imperial Hotel, high on a rock looking out over the sands and the sea to Caldy Island, an unbeatable position giving a superb view. Thoughtful service matched the position: a delightful place.

Perched on a cliff and divided by a headland with a castle, Tenby is a lovely little resort, certainly among the half-dozen most charming in Britain. It has a small harbour, clifftop views, ancient town walls, miles of sandy beach, brightly painted houses of style and charm and a miraculous ability to provide family holiday amenities without being swamped by bingo parlours.

Pembroke Dock to Cardiff

Infrequent to Swansea, then main line, three and a half hours

The south-western peninsula of Wales, formerly the county of

Pembrokeshire but now part of Dyfed, has long been known as a land of mystery and magic. The whole coast from the mouth of the River Teifi near Cardigan round to Amroth on Carmarthen Bay has been made a national park to preserve the beauty of its headlands, cliffs and beaches. A path follows the coast for the whole 148 miles. The main railway line to Haverfordwest and Milford Haven runs through the area, with branches off at Whitland for Tenby and Pembroke Dock and at Clarbeston Road for Fishguard, the ferry port for Rosslare in Ireland.

Haverfordwest is the most central point for exploring the area. Milford Haven is an oil tanker base; the haven stretches back seventeen miles from the sea and is the largest natural harbour in Britain. Pembroke Dock and Pembroke are at the eastern end of the haven.

Pembroke is an ancient town built round a castle in which was born the Henry Tudor who became Henry VII, the first Welsh king of England and the founder of a royal dynasty. Naturally, medieval revelry is a local tourist attraction. Pembroke Dock adjoins the old town at the end of Milford Haven and with neatly painted terraces is more attractive than it sounds. The wooden ships of Britain's eighteenth century navy were built here and it was an important naval dockyard until the 1920s.

I started here on a rail journey to Cardiff, 108 miles away. The local train runs through Tenby to rejoin the main line at Whitland, goes in and out of Carmarthen and terminates at Swansea. Here the 125s take over that can whisk you to London in something under three hours.

From Pembroke Dock's neat little stone station the train ran to Pembroke, with a fine view of the castle. At Manorbier it stopped at a level crossing for the guard to get out and close the gates against road traffic.

Then it was back through pleasant country, into Carmarthen over a lifting bridge, and out again, and on through Pembrey and Burry Port. Napoleon's Empress Josephine's niece went down in a shipwreck near here and Amelia Earhart landed in Burry inlet in the first seaplane to cross the Atlantic. Matters to brood on, these, or we could turn attention to fellow passengers and note the frequency among people in these parts of red hair and freckles and of prematurely white hair. This latter makes Welshmen look intellectual and poetic even if they're not (but perhaps they all are).

An Irishman on the train told me, 'The Welsh are so friendly,' as indeed they are. However, my railway peregrinations have taught me that virtually all people are friendly when not harassed or being put upon, Scots, Welsh, Northerners, even the dreaded toffee-noses of the Home Counties.

Back through Llanelli to find another silent steel works on the other side of the town, surely one of the saddest sights in Britain. Then the mid-Wales line to Shrewsbury branches off to the left and we crossed the wide River Loughor and over the top of the Gower peninsula.

Now the train ran down near the River Tawe into the terminus at Swansea. This is the metropolis for south-west Wales, industrial city, shopping centre, university town, port and seaside resort by virtue of its connection with the Mumbles a little way along the beach at Mumbles Head. It is also, of course, the birthplace of Dylan Thomas and a memorial to him stands appropriately in Cwmdonkin Park.

It had taken a little more than two hours to get here from Pembroke Dock: time now for lunch in a pub across the road. Then away on a 125, lolling in luxury while being whisked past an industrial landscape including an oil refinery and giant chemical complex, also steel mills – presumably still working, thank goodness, there was steam coming from the cooling towers – piles of wrecked cars and endless sidings. At Neath I could hear faintly from the buffet car the sound of Welsh male voices raised in serious song. At Port Talbot streets of low houses crouched in the gap between big hills and a monster strip mill.

The West Wales industrial belt ends before Bridgend. The line leaves the coast and turns inland through farms and forest. But up there on the left are the hills that hide the Rhondda and Taff valleys, heartland of the old coal-mining and iron industry. And now, under an hour after leaving Swansea, the 125 glided through the old suburbs and into the high-rise blocks at the centre of Cardiff, with just a glimpse of the crowd in the stands at Cardiff Arms Park as we went by.

Cardiff, the Welsh capital, is a good place for a stopover. Its centre is the large, partially phoney but beautifully-kept castle with adjoining park. On the castle tower coats of arms and figures are picked out in brilliant colour. The castle is an easy walk from the station and in the area between the two is the main shopping centre and most of the amenities a visitor needs. I stayed at the friendly Royal Hotel, just a minute from the station and two or three minutes from the castle. There are an exceptional number of reasonably priced eating places in the area, no doubt due to the proximity of the rugby ground.

Some cities take a lot of getting to know. In Cardiff the traveller soon feels he knows his way around. Worth seeking out and visiting, besides the castle, are the National Museum of Wales, with a collection of French Impressionist paintings, and the Maritime and Industrial Museum in Bute Town near the docks entrance.

Outing from Cardiff

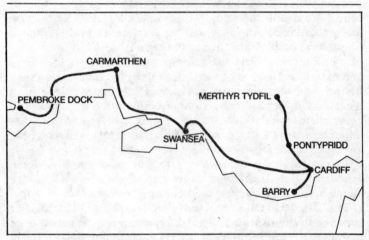

Fair service, about an hour and a half

For a better understanding of the area and some of its history, it's worth leaving the grandiose buildings in the city centre, taking the train from Cardiff Central Station to Barry and then travelling the length of the line through the city and on up the Taff valley to Merthyr Tydfil.

From the footbridge over the tracks at Barry station you can see a great panorama of industrial transport – railway sidings, docks, cranes, flour mills, oil tanks. This was once the busiest coal port in the world. Across the road from the station is the faded grandeur of the Barry Hotel, which must once have accommodated rich coal and shipping magnates. The ornate port office building is also now a little tatty.

Although the port has declined from its great days there is still activity here. There are ships in the docks and coal trains rumble through to supply a power station.

In the train all the passengers are locals – a man with a deeply seamed coal-miner's face, a mother discussing with a friend her son's career: 'He got his first degree at Oxford and then did research at Cambridge but he's had to go abroad for a job that suits him.' The two ladies got off the train to walk to their homes in one of those back street terraces that still produce clever young men.

The train runs back through Cardiff Central, through the city and out to the north. Soon it begins to climb out of the Cardiff suburbs and into the mining valleys. On a station platform a mother stands holding a child in her arms with a shawl wrapped round them both. Along the line our train is passed by long trains of coal wagons. Others are waiting on sidings.

At Trefforest industry covers the floor of the valley, terraces of houses climb the hillside on either side. The valley is wide here but it narrows as we continue to climb. At Pontypridd a line branches off up the Rhondda Valley to Tonypandy (where striking miners once faced troops sent against them), Treorchy and Treherbert, all one-time mining towns.

This pattern is the same in the Taff valley which we now ascend, a colliery or two in the narrow bottom of the valley, with attendant coal-tips and wagon sidings, terraces of two-storey houses clinging to the sides of the valley, following the contours or climbing steeply upwards. Beyond the terraces and in between the mines are the green mountainsides – the train goes occasionally through wooded ravines that give a hint of the glories of the mountains beyond these valleys.

Finally, an hour and a half up from Barry, the train reaches the top of the valley at Merthyr Tydfil. There was once a great iron works here – in the early nineteenth century the town was bigger than Cardiff, Swansea and Newport combined. Trevithick built a steam locomotive here in 1804, the world's first. Keir Hardie, founder of the Independent Labour Party, was its MP. Now it's a pleasant little town and on its doorstep to the north is Brecon Beacons National Park, a wild place, with mountains up to 2,600 ft, good for walking, riding and birdwatching.

Devon and Cornwall

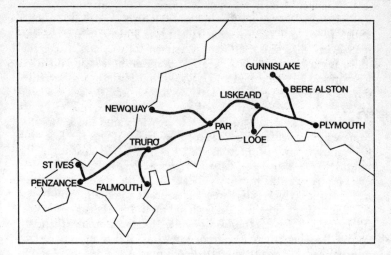

St Ives to Plymouth

Good service, under two hours

After industrial South Wales Cornwall offers a complete contrast. St Ives is a delightful little port, pretty as a picture and prettier than some of the pictures innumerable artists paint there. With its narrow streets, miniature harbour, Atlantic breakers crashing on the sands and hills climbing round the bay, it's just what a Cornish fishing port ought to look like. The only trouble is that thousands think so. During the summer the little town is bursting with holidaymakers to such an extent that you have to jostle your way along the main street and use your elbows to get at the bar of the Sloop Inn on the harbour edge.

There are two ways to deal with this problem. One is to go there out of season: in the winter St Ives has all its charm without the hassle; you might even meet and speak to some genuine locals. Or if you must be there in the summer, find accommodation outside the crowded area and go in for short visits.

I chose the latter course and decided to rise above the problem. The Tregenna Castle Hotel, complete with castellated parapet, stands at the top of a hill overlooking the bay, with perfect views of the harbour. From here you can take in the beauty of the situation in comfort, then walk down into the town for closer acquaintance. Tregenna Castle was originally built in 1774 as a home for one Squire Stephens, descendant of an Irishman who landed here from a shipwreck. The branch line from St Erth was opened in 1887 and the Great Western Railway took over the house for a hotel the next year. Hitler's ambassador von Ribbentrop stayed here often and it's said that Hitler promised it to him as a private residence. Luckily for us, the occasion never arose.

The hotel car takes guests to St Erth to catch the main-line trains which start from Penzance, a few miles down the line and 305 miles from Paddington. In 1904 the GWR instituted its famous crack train, the *Cornish Riviera Express*, which took seven hours over the journey via Bristol, 19 miles longer than the present route which runs direct between Reading and Taunton.

Modern 125s take just under five hours. Nearly two hours of this is taken up with the last 79 miles from Plymouth through Cornwall, when there are frequent stops and many curves to reduce speed. While the modern diesels put on an impressive show of speed today they are not quite such a revolution in travel as might be supposed. Today's *Cornish Riviera* covers the 226-mile section from Paddington to Plymouth in three hours at speeds up to 125 mph, though it is capable of 140 mph. Yet as long ago as 1904 the steam engine *City of Truro* became the first locomotive to travel at over 100 mph, while taking a mail train from Plymouth to Bristol. Hauled from there by the *Duke of Connaught* the train reached Paddington by the longer route in three hours 47 minutes.

Whatever speed you get there Penzance is a good place to be. It's an excellent centre for touring the small fishing villages of the Penwith peninsula. Land's End is ten miles away. St Michael's Mount, seen from the train as it runs the last mile or two along the shores of Mount's Bay, was once a monastery. It got its name from the saint appearing in a vision to a hermit who lived there. Cornishmen believe that Christ visited this part of the world with Joseph of Arimathea, he being in Cornish legend a tin miner. Another belief is that the lost land of Lyonesse lies under the bay, the great rock of St Michael's Mount being the only part left visible.

I went the other way and stopped at Plymouth. For me it was a revelation. From near the station in about ten minutes you can walk straight down a broad way through the modern shopping centre, between the civic centre and the guildhall and up the rising ground to the Hoe. Here, with dramatic suddenness, you get one of the finest views any city can offer in its combination of beauty and historic significance.

For you are standing on the Hoe where Drake played bowls before setting off to deal with the Spanish Armada. Before you is Drake's Island; beyond is Plymouth Sound with a breakwater guarding the harbour, hills enclosing it – and probably a naval vessel anchored in it.

Out to sea on a clear day you can see the Eddystone light. To the right is the entrance to the Hamoaze, the anchorage between Devonport dockyard and Torpoint into which flow the Rivers Tamar and Lynher. To the left is the Citadel and below it the Mayflower steps from which the Pilgrim Fathers sailed to America in 1620.

On the Hoe itself stands the Royal Navy memorial, a rather jolly statue of Drake, and Smeaton's lighthouse, removed from Eddystone when the rock on which it stood became unsafe. In its beauty and its pride the scene speaks for England simply and directly.

Plymouth to Gunnislake

Every two hours or so, 50 minutes
One of the most rewarding trips out of Plymouth is the ride up the branch line to Gunnislake. I joined the two-coach local train leaving from the bay platform, my fellow passengers nearly all tourists with maps and binoculars to make the most of the views.

We ran through Devonport and at Dockyard halt we could see the naval vessels there, with others anchored in the harbour. After leaving the main line we ran through a cutting and emerged on the bank of the Tamar underneath the Royal Albert railway bridge and the road suspension bridge. A plaque near here marks the spot where some of the American forces embarked on D-Day in 1944.

We ran close to the water up the bank of the Tamar and over the mouth of the River Tavy. This gave us a great panorama of the river – wide, stately, stretching up into the hills with another river emerging from the gorge. These deep fjords, with anchorages penetrating far into the hills, are among the glories of this coast.

Bere Ferrers station, on the outskirts of the village, seemed deep in the country, though only a few miles from Plymouth. We climbed steadily up through a green tunnel of trees to reach Bere Alston at what looked like the end of the line, a decayed station high in the hills with little sign of life. Already the country seemed as far from urban life as it was possible to get.

But there was more. We reversed out with Dartmoor brooding to our right and a series of inviting valleys closer to hand. We dropped down a little to cross a high viaduct and bridge over the Tamar into Calstock. The village of white cottages clung to a steep hillside and boats were busy on the river. This was once a busy little port serving mines, quarries, timber yards and brickworks.

The train now climbed on again to Gunnislake, running high on a hillside from which we could see a wide curve of the river below, with an old steam launch among the boats, and a backdrop of steep wooded hills.

We passed the old stone chimneys of abandoned mine workings in an area where lead and copper were once produced. There are no automatic crossing gates or flashing lights on this line, so at each road crossing the train stopped and hooted before moving cautiously across. Gunnislake is a village on a hill. From here we could see a turbulent sea of blue and green hills, Bodmin Moor to the west, Dartmoor to the east, the Tamar valley reaching to the north between its hills.

Close by and well worth a visit is Morwellham Quay, once a busy copper port on the Tamar. Its quays have been restored and a small railway takes visitors underground into an old copper mine.

Falmouth, Newquay and Looe

From Plymouth, Falmouth about two hours, Newquay two hours, Looe one and a quarter hours

The Cornish branch lines make delightful days out from Plymouth, the local connections usually being timed for travellers from that direction. A conveniently timed morning train from Plymouth takes an hour and ten minutes to Truro, the county town of Cornwall, where you join the local for the 12-mile, 24-minute run to Falmouth.

This is the sort of cosy ride where the ticket collector chats with the customers, mostly elderly ladies, calling them 'my dear'. The line starts on high ground with a good view of Truro's Victorian gothic cathedral – the only one in Cornwall – and then extensive views of small hills and occasional villages of trim white houses. Later, there are glimpses of shipping in the harbour before the train terminates at a rather rough-and-ready halt looking over the estuary. It used to run a little further into an impressive ocean terminal, for Falmouth was once a port of call for transatlantic liners which anchored in the bay and discharged passengers by tender.

Falmouth Bay looks out into the great expanse of Carrick Roads. It is a busy harbour scene; you can take a ferry across the bay to Flushing or across Carrick Roads to St Mawes in the delightful Roseland peninsula. Each side of the sea entrance is guarded by a castle. From the station a half-mile walk up a cliff-top road giving splendid views takes you to Pendennis Castle, 200 feet above sea level and built by Henry VIII.

Par, about an hour from Plymouth, is the changing point for the line to Newquay on the north Cornwall coast.

The train toils up a single track beside a stream through a green, mysterious valley with the great bulk of Henbarrow Down rising to 1027 feet on the left. This is strange, foreign-looking country and a rake of old-fashioned, tarpaulin-covered china clay wagons is hauled by a locomotive marked 'Cornish Railways'. High on the downs there are extensive views to the right over fields and woods in remote, sparsely settled country before the train canters down to the north Cornwall coast.

At Newquay the train reaches a modest terminus near the edge of high cliffs. Up here powerful winds can sweep you off your feet. Down below, magnificent Atlantic rollers crash on a fine wide sandy beach; this is a favourite surfing resort. The town is notable mostly for the seaside architecture of the Thirties. There is a small harbour.

A shorter, easier and prettier branch-line trip from Plymouth is to Looe. From the station at Liskeard, less than half an hour down the main line, the local train takes just over half an hour to run down beside the River Looe through a wooded valley of great beauty. After leaving Liskeard the train dives back under the main line in almost a complete circle to Coombe, where it reverses for the valley run. The little port of Looe was once a haunt of smugglers. Today it offers old-world charm and shark fishing.

Exeter to Barnstaple

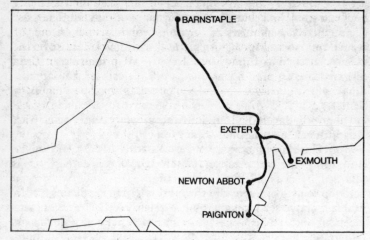

Every two hours, about an hour

Exeter, 52 miles up the line from Plymouth, is a rewarding centre for day trips by train in Devon. It is convenient for outings to Barnstaple on the north Devon coast, Torquay and Paignton to the south and Exmouth on the Exe estuary. Bristol, Bath and Salisbury are within easy day-trip reach.

St David's is the main-line station but Central (on the line from Waterloo) is nearer the centre of the city. Exeter is the county town of Devon, was a Roman station and has many agreeable Georgian houses and the distinctive Devon early Victorian. Its cathedral can be seen from the train after leaving St David's for the west. There is a medieval guildhall but nothing much is left of the castle. Some of the old warehouses on the quay now house the Exeter Maritime Museum, with a collection of more than a hundred boats.

For the trip to Barnstaple I started from Exeter St David's in a train of five elderly coaches hauled by a diesel locomotive. This should have been a quiet and uneventful run across the width of Devon, up the gentle valley of the River Yeo and down the valley of the Taw: mild, pleasant country, nothing dramatic.

This country of woods and pastures has a feeling of deep tranquillity. The heights of Dartmoor are a distant presence, as they are over most of Devon. The small hills covered with fields, the narrow lanes, the shorn sheep with comical black faces and legs, the mare trotting with her foal, all suggested nothing much happening and everybody being quite happy about that. The most exciting things hereabouts, it seemed, were the names of some of the villages: Zeal Monachorum, Black Dog, Woolfardisworthy, Honeychurch and Broadwood Kelly – all promising in their different ways.

Stations on the line couldn't quite rise to this but I had high hopes of King's Nympton, which suggested royal dancing girls. No nymphs appeared but it looked a nice place all the same with lush pastures, a hotel and the promise of fishing.

From Eggesford on there were areas of dense forest and wood-land. Eggesford has a nature trail through the forest and a picnic site.

Umberleigh had flowers of the most intense violet I'd ever seen – ultra-violet indeed. Chapelton had a battered old station sign in the green and white colours of the Southern Railway of long ago. From lace-making Crediton onwards none of the stations appeared to be anywhere near the villages they purported to serve. Or perhaps there was not very much to be near – it was difficult to tell.

Barnstaple is an ancient town, once a considerable port on the River Taw, and still has a good riverside walk. There's a bus connection to Ilfracombe on the coast, north Devon's largest resort, where you have to go through rock tunnels to reach two of the beaches. The railway station is a little out of the centre.

We had been bowling along the single track with nothing to stop us, keeping well up to time, when we were held at a signal just a few hundred yards from the terminus. The driver got out and telephoned the signal box and word was passed down that there was a points failure ahead, preventing us from getting into the station and the train already in from leaving.

The driver fetched from his cab a large crowbar, apparently carried for just such emergencies, and attacked the points with this, helped by the guard and advised by the signalman. The points refused to budge. The signalman went back to his box to phone for assistance. The driver kept up the attack with his crowbar. No luck, but you had to admire his persistence.

After a while those in a hurry stopped admiring the driver's persistence, jumped down on to the permanent way and walked on to the station. I followed suit. I had planned a short look around before returning on the next train and catching a connection at Exeter to Dawlish, where I was to stay. Sure enough, a train was waiting in the station and had been for half an hour.

After some time the expert arrived in a small yellow van with a large and businesslike gripping instrument. Whatever it was, it worked; within minutes the stranded train had come in and the waiting one pulled out for Exeter.

The guard now came down the train asking us where we were going. The driver, he said, would try to make up as much time as possible. I explained which train I had hoped to catch at Exeter. It was just possible that I still could.

And so the creaking old local became the Exeter Flyer, determined to break the track record for the 40 miles ahead of us. We let off an elderly lady at Umberleigh. After that we stopped only when the driver saw a passenger on the platform or when he had to hand over the single-track token to the signalman. We stopped twice for passengers and each time our guard leapt out with vigorous gesticulations to urge the driver on as soon as the passenger was aboard. Forty, fifty, sixty miles an hour – it felt much more hair-raising than the effortless 125 mph of the main-liners.

We got on to the main line and into Exeter St David's without a hold-up in what must have been record time, just at the moment when my train to Dawlish ought to be going. I raced over the bridge to retrieve my bag from a locker, raced back again to the far platform with it. Our guard had evidently passed the word and the train waited until I flung myself aboard.

So I travelled over the peaceful rural branch line to Barnstaple and back, feeling, as I caught my breath, as exhausted and triumphant as if I had just brought the good news from Ghent to Aix.

Other branches from Exeter

The other two branch lines conveniently explored from Exeter are also of interest. One runs the ten miles from Exeter Central to Exmouth (most trains run through from Exeter St David's and some from Barnstaple or Paignton). After clearing the suburbs the line follows the eastern shore of the Exe estuary. From Topsham on there are extensive views across to the wooded hills behind the western shore. Exton is right on the riverside, giving a splendid panorama – the views are better from this side than from the main-line trains on the opposite shore. One station it is *not* advisable to alight at (unless you are one) is Lympstone Commando, the halt for a training establishment which threatens dire consequence to intruders.

Exmouth, where the train stops an easy walk from the front, is a quiet, pleasant, well-kept resort of mostly Victorian hotels, with views from a hilltop walk and sandy beaches. A pub by the station is called the South Western, correctly recalling that this railway owned the Exmouth branch line – but carries a mural depicting a train in Great Western colours.

For the other branch you have to change at Newton Abbot, 20 miles down from Exeter, to a train serving Torquay and Paignton. Unlike the other branches, the ten-mile-long Paignton line takes holiday trains from Paddington and Birmingham as well as locals. Torquay is a stately queen among seaside resorts, magnificently spread over seven hills on the sheltered Torbay. It enjoys an exceptional climate in which sub-tropical plants flourish. It has hotels of suitable grandeur to match its status. Paignton next door is not quite so grand but has the very fine Torbay and Dartmouth Railway, on which you can run under steam in Great Western livery for the seven miles to the Kingswear ferry for Dartmouth.

Main line to Paddington

Good service, two hours from Exeter St David's

And so back to Paddington on one of the great main lines of Britain. When Brunel laid out the route to the west he swept it in a curve north of the Berkshire downs to Bristol and later extended the line from there to Taunton, Exeter, Plymouth and Penzance. When the London and South-Western completed a direct line to Devon through Salisbury there were jeers that GWR stood for Great Way Round. To answer that, the Great Western completed its own direct line from Reading to Taunton, in effect creating a 107-mile Bristol bypass. It shortened the route to Exeter by 19 miles but passed through no important towns on the way. And it was still, irritatingly, a mile or two longer than the Waterloo route to Exeter Central.

No need to worry about that, though, as the 125 purrs smoothly back through Castle Cary, junction for Weymouth – don't look for a castle, only a grassy mound is left. Charles II, escaping from

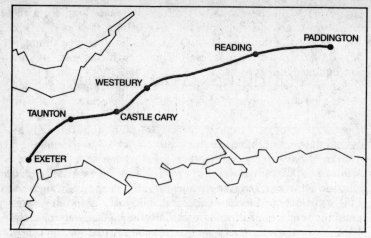

the battle of Worcester, spent the night at the manor here disguised as a lady's servant – but the manor is demolished, too.

Westbury station, junction for Salisbury, is bypassed as we are
not stopping there and we get a good view of the White Horse on
the chalk hill to the right, 166 feet long and 163 feet high. There's
another, smaller one at Pewsey. Both were originally created in
the eighteenth century.

From Newbury, with its racecourse, the line keeps company
with the Kennet and Avon canal. And then we're in among the
red-brick fortress factories of Reading for the final high-speed
dash into Paddington. The station here was planned by Brunel as
the gateway to London for passengers coming from America by
steamer to Bristol. Built in 1854, its triple canopies owed much to
the inspiration of the Crystal Palace. The present concourse, still
called the Lawn, was built over cottage gardens.

When you come back from a tour of Wales and the West you
know you have been somewhere different perhaps because, next
to the Highlands of Scotland, this part of Britain is furthest away
from most of the main population centres. Apart from south
Wales, perhaps, life seems a little more relaxed, moves at an easier
pace and is more closely in touch with country ways. There's
magic out there in the soft air of the West.

8
Midlands, North-west and North Wales

London Midland Region includes lines from the capital to the Midlands, the north-west of England and North Wales. It takes in the major centres of Birmingham, Coventry, Manchester, Liverpool, Nottingham and Leicester, the beauties of Snowdonia, the Lake District, the Peak District and tourist favourites like Stratford-upon-Avon and Oxford.

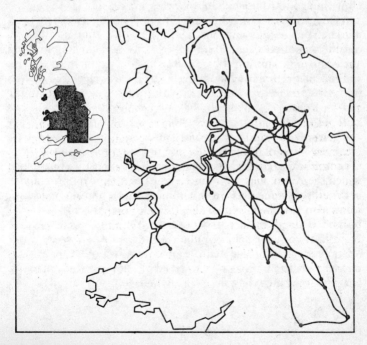

As well as the big cities, good centres for day trips are Shrewsbury, Chester, Preston and Carlisle.

London Midland derives its name, of course, from the old
London, Midland and Scottish railway grouping, whose main line
forms its spine and whose Scottish end was hived off to a new
region. Inevitable, perhaps, but after riding around the region you
will think the name very unfair to North Wales and the north-
west of England, which supply at least half the joys of a region in
which large concentrations of population contrast with areas of
superb natural beauty.

Birmingham area

The natural centre of the region, certainly the one with the best
connections, is Birmingham. It makes an excellent base for train
excursions. Stratford-upon-Avon is an hour away, Warwick 40
minutes (both from Moor Street); Lichfield is 40 minutes from
New Street. Matlock, Oxford, Chester and even Aberystwyth are
all within comfortable day-out reach.

As in all big cities, the choice in Birmingham is between being in
the centre of things and finding an agreeable spot not too far
outside. I chose the centre and stayed at the Midland, a rambling
Victorian pile comfortably modern inside. Here, next to the
station and the Bull Ring shopping centre, I was well placed both to
take trips and to enjoy the big-city amenities. The second largest
city in Britain, Birmingham has two cathedrals, excellent art
galleries and a rich industrial history.

Alternatively, the best choice for a base nearby would be
Lichfield, a quiet, unspoilt little city just escaping engulfment by
the conurbation centred on Birmingham. Dr Johnson's birthplace
is a museum and there are statues of the doctor and his biographer
in the market square. The city has many handsome old buildings,
some associated with Johnson. The choir school, formerly the
Bishop's Palace, in the cathedral close contains the salon where
David Garrick gave his first public performance. There are many
other literary and stage associations. This is a quiet place with
pleasant walks among well-preserved old houses, with three old
coaching inns including the Swan, where Johnson stayed.

Bradford to Blackpool

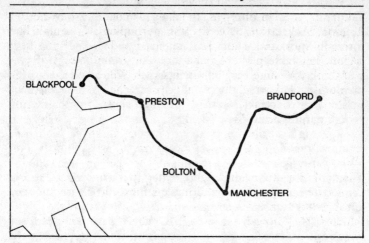

Seven trains a day via Blackburn, hourly via Manchester

There's a train that does the journey from Bradford to Blackpool in under two hours, cutting across the moors from Hebden Bridge to join the line running from Colne through Blackburn to Preston and on to the resort. Other trains take the same route but involve a change at Preston. Otherwise it's a longer journey changing at Manchester Victoria; this was the route I chose.

The first leg, to Manchester, is only 40 miles but it means crossing the spine of England from the old wool capital to what used to be called Cottonopolis, from the land of the White Rose to the Red. All this in an hour in a local train.

The run to Halifax is through a string of small towns and villages, never quite making it into real country. Halifax was the centre to which weavers used to bring their cloth for sale at the Piece Hall. The old beggars' and vagrants' prayer, 'From Hell, Hull, and Halifax, good Lord deliver us,' referred to the town's harsh way with cloth thieves. 'Theeves ... stealing cloth, are instantly beheaded with an engine,' the historian Fuller recorded in 1662. (Hull was feared for its good government.) Today many of the large mills are put to other uses but it still looks a formidable place.

The town stands under a cliff with hills around and from here to Rochdale the line tackles the problem of getting over the moors.

First, it runs up the Calder valley through small hillside towns. Sowerby Bridge looked bleak with high hills all round, its station decayed. At Mytholmroyd, its names suggesting a legendary Priestley character, care seemed to have returned. The station had roses on the platform and a painted fence and a respectable little town could be seen.

At Hebden Bridge high hills flanked wooded valleys as the train worked its way round the moors, climbing all the time. Here we could see the special Northern mixture of natural beauty and industry, mills and close-packed houses in the narrow valley and the splendour of the moors above on both sides. The higher we climbed, the more beauty took over from industry. Shortly after Hebden Bridge the line crossed the walkers' Pennine Way and the train continued to climb up the valley to Todmorden – still in Yorkshire but already into cotton spinning – and then we were into the long tunnel under the summit.

When we emerged we were in Greater Manchester and the landscape was by Lowry – panoramas of square red-brick mills with tall chimneys looming out of an undergrowth of fierce terraces. I half expected to see Lowry-like matchstick figures in the streets of Rochdale, the town which gave us Gracie Fields and the Co-ops. Disappointingly, Rochdale's magnificent Victorian town hall is not to be seen from the railway.

Down from the high ground we dropped into Manchester, its tall buildings visible from miles away, through the forest of warehouses, a tangle of railway viaducts and office buildings of various ages from blackened brick Victorian to modern. Not beautiful but demanding respect, like a lined old face.

A change at Manchester Victoria and I was off again from the next platform on a six-car diesel for Blackpool North. From Manchester to Bolton the train traveller is offered close inspection of a range of industrial buildings from early nineteenth to the twentieth century. Then, after Bolton, we were quite suddenly in the country, with young girls learning to ride in a paddock, cows chewing, the moors away to the right.

We ran out through Chorley and joined the main line from Euston; a stop at Preston to fill the train with holiday-makers and we were off the main line and running out to the west through Fylde, the flat area between the Rivers Wyre and Ribble. At Kirkham a following train from Preston could run passengers down a branch line to Lytham St Anne's and Blackpool South, but our train ran on through flat country, taking a curve to the north so that we could see the famous Tower in the distance some time before we reached Blackpool, an hour and a half from Manchester.

Blackpool really does have it all – sands, three piers, the Tower (like the Eiffel, only smaller), illuminations, trams, scenic railways that turn you upside down, millions of visitors and every known device for parting the cheerful holidaymaker from his spending money. It's the ultimate in popular British seaside resorts, wholly dedicated to the purpose of filling the week with fun during the season, with no la-di-da nonsense about history or high culture.

If Blackpool is where it all happens, Lytham – round the corner facing the Ribble estuary, its back squarely turned on its kiss-me-quick neighbour – is where they're glad to say it doesn't happen. Lytham St Anne's, as it's called on maps, is a bit of a misnomer. St Anne's is one place, nearer Blackpool, offering seaside pleasures of a less hectic nature and genteel relief from the full treatment further up the beach. Lytham, further into the estuary, offers virtually no excitement at all, apart from occasional Morris dancers. There's a stretch of greensward and a promenade along the front, facing the river, some moored yachts and the sea to be seen when the tide's in. You can walk up and down the promenade, watch the boats or go and play golf. Or, as I did, you can admire the town's streets full of charming small Victorian gothic cottages. I found these even more satisfying than the imposing but predictable specimens on the front. Quiet Lytham was a discovery for me. For those who want them, the amenities of Blackpool are within easy reach by public transport.

I stayed at the Clifton Arms Hotel on the front, a few minutes' walk from Lytham station: comfortable, agreeable, very well managed, a good place for a week-end break.

Lytham to Chester

Mostly suburban services, fairly frequent

Between the Ribble and the Mersey west of the Euston main line is a network of lines based on Liverpool. From Preston a line runs to Ormskirk to connect with the suburban service through Aintree and Walton to Liverpool Central, though you get a better view of the Grand National course coming in from Kirkby, reached by a line from Wigan Wallgate. A line from Wigan North Western joins the line from Manchester Victoria to Liverpool at Huyton to run through Edge Hill, one of the earliest passenger stations and now a museum, to Liverpool Lime Street. The last mile is through a deep cutting down a steep incline; trains used to be hauled up it by a stationary engine.

From Lytham, with its long, low, rather grand station façade, now sadly crumbling, I decided to make for Liverpool by way of Southport. It involved going back up the branch line to Preston, up the main line as far as Wigan North Western and taking a short walk up the road to Wigan Wallgate to catch a train from Manchester to Southport. This is not an inspiring line. We ran through nondescript country with occasional industry, in mist and persistent rain.

Southport, across the Ribble estuary from Lytham, is to Liverpool and Manchester what Brighton is to London; a seaside resort which is also a superior commuter town, retirement place and shopping centre. Its mile-long Lord Street with arcades of fine ironwork comes off magnificently as one of the great shopping streets of the country. There's much solid stateliness in evidence: it was all built to last and not offend the susceptibilities of the well-to-do. It's not as lively as Brighton, or as elegant, but it's not as brash and violent as Brighton sometimes is either. The station is in the centre, a few minutes from the promenade, and the resort makes a respectable day out for Liverpudlians and Mancunians. Queen Victoria, presiding in a 1901 statue, seems quite at home here today.

The line from Southport to Liverpool Central is part of the Merseyrail network of modern suburban electric trains. Other lines on the network link with Liverpool Lime Street and run under the Mersey and out to New Brighton, West Kirby and Rock Ferry in the Wirral.

This line is much like suburban lines anywhere, a succession of small dormitory places, some fiercely neat and well-kept, some old and worn. Formby, conjuring up visions of the grinning maestro of the ukulele, offers the passers-by ageing semis and bungalows which don't look as if cleaning windows here would be as exciting as George used to claim.

The interest of the ride lies almost entirely in the chance it gives to see in action the indomitable Liverpool grannies with the young charges who plainly adore them. Children who might reasonably have been expected to howl or grizzle throughout the journey if they had been with their mothers behaved perfectly with their grans. The secret seems to be that the grannies can concentrate love and attention on their grandchildren in a way that harassed and distracted mothers can't.

Waterloo showed exhausted-looking, gloomy old houses, and then we were into the Liverpool complex, flats and offices towering, Mersey docks away to the right. Here it always seems to be dark, sooty, gaslit and raining even when it isn't.

And yet Liverpool hits you as an exciting, alive city, whatever the current economic or law-and-order situation. It comes across to the visitor not as a great city like Manchester or Birmingham, where vast numbers of people in modern offices are pursuing money with a proper seriousness, but as a shabby but not defeated place whose inhabitants are determined to get something out of life. Once it was a very prosperous city, and the magnificent civic buildings are a legacy from those days before pop and football fame.

For anyone passing through, the pubs are Liverpool's glory – the most lavishly decorated, wildly extravagant licensed premises in the country. From the riot of mahogany panelling, engraved glass and fancy plasterwork on offer I chose the Philharmonic, one of the most ornate of them all. Its main room is 20 ft high with richly panelled walls, gilded floral plasterwork, caryatids, assorted goddesses, massive chandeliers and a stained glass sky-light. Even the solid marble gents' lavatory is a showpiece.

It seemed an appropriate place to ponder, without unravelling, the tangled symbolism of the location. The pub is in Hope Street, which has the Roman Catholic cathedral (designed by an Anglican) at one end, the Anglican cathedral (designed by a Roman Catholic) at the other, and a big police station in between.

The underground line took me from Lime Street's cavernous gloom under the Mersey to Hamilton Square in Birkenhead. The square itself was a surprise, a fine classically laid out piece of architectural theatre, still more or less intact, dating from the days when Birkenhead was Liverpool's rival and very much a separate entity.

Just a short walk from here is the ferry stage, once a scene of frenetic bustle across the Mersey to Liverpool Pier Head, focal point of the city, where the Liver birds perch on the Cunard building. The *Royal Iris* pleasure boat was due in shortly, so I chose a cruise on the Mersey in her as a way to get an idea of what Liverpool is about. In a cruise of about two hours to the mouth of the Mersey we passed tankers and container ships coming and going, spotted the big ventilators of the road tunnel and saw the extent of the docks.

The real life of Liverpool was going on inside the *Iris*. In the main saloon a three-piece band was playing while children from four to fourteen were dancing their feet off, many in white party frocks, the older ones instructing the tiniest in the art of flinging arms and legs about. It seemed a popular way to give the children a treat while the mothers relaxed with a drink. Other children ran happily all over the floating playground while grandfathers (who seemed to have taken over from the grans) kept watch on deck.

From Hamilton Square I made my way to Chester by way of the Merseyrail line to Rock Ferry and a local service on from there. On this suburban line the train was full of people going home from work; small, wiry girls with muscular legs, a man reading a Japanese newspaper, young men with mild faces and small moustaches.

As we pulled out of Birkenhead there was a chance to see the Mersey again, with a big tanker at her moorings. Shortly after, we passed Port Sunlight, Lord Leverhulme's model town for his workers, built in a variety of styles from half-timbered Tudor onwards. The houses looked solid and well-cared-for. The Lady Leverhulme Art Gallery here has some fine works by British masters.

The train lost most of its passengers at Bromborough, found a little bit of Cheshire countryside and ran happily across this before getting to Chester, where long trains of tanker wagons trundled over the wide triangle of lines.

Chester's confident station (big red BR emblem, flag flying) stands at the end of a road from the city centre. There are some hotels by the station but I took the bus into the town centre. It dropped me in Eastgate Street, opposite the Grosvenor Hotel where I stayed the night.

Chester stands just outside the Merseyside dock complex. Its railway position at the meeting place of six lines brings a large amount of the freight traffic of the area rumbling through the lines on its outskirts. But the heart of the city, inside its medieval walls, is magnificently aloof from all this. It was once a Roman city – the Twentieth Legion was here and there are remains of a large amphitheatre. It was a medieval port on the Dee before the river silted up and has some fine examples of the black and white half-timbered houses characteristic of Cheshire.

In Victorian times many of the medieval houses were restored and new ones built in the same style. The result is one of the finest medieval cities in the country, none-the-less so for the fact that many of the 'medieval' houses are only a century or so old. A special feature of the city centre, within the inner walls, is the Rows – galleries at first-floor level that run the length of the streets and enable you to shop under cover. It was raining when I was there and it is one of the very few cities you can walk around in the rain without getting wet.

In total effect the city succeeds triumphantly. Whether you view it as a medieval city restored here and there or as the working out of a Victorian fantasy it gives tremendous pleasure. The city walls of red sandstone make an interesting walk. The cathedral, in the same stone, expresses devout strength but to my mind does not soar. There are riverside walks, a racecourse and a zoo.

The Grosvenor Hotel is itself a successful part of the medieval effect, a large building in flamboyant half-timbered style with turrets, gables and tall chimneys put up in the late nineteenth century. Its standards are high and it is in the best possible position from which to explore the houses, shops and pubs of the city.

Chester to Shrewsbury

Two-hourly service, taking one hour

The line from Chester to Shrewsbury is the only one that actually takes you *through* Wales, beginning and ending in England. Chester is a border city only a few miles from Wales and the line runs to the Welsh border before turning south across the Cheshire countryside. After a few miles it crosses into Wales, which here thrusts a beefy arm into England, crosses the county of Clwyd to Chirk and then runs through Shropshire to Shrewsbury. It takes a leisurely hour in a two-coach diesel and could form part of a circular tour of north Wales from Chester or Shrewsbury, the other legs being the mid-Wales line from Shrewsbury to Pwllheli, the Festiniog railway from Minffordd to Blaenau Ffestiniog, the Conwy Valley line to Llandudno Junction and the Holyhead-Chester main line.

The train took me very quickly out of the industrial belt and into the Cheshire countryside. Moving along the side of a valley among trees on a sullen, overcast day, I had the impression of entering a remote country. A chapel or two hinted that we had crossed the border as we headed for distant Welsh hills. We passed into mining country, not as stark and hemmed in as that of the south Wales valleys, and then past overgrown coal tips to Wrexham, the first stop, where a line comes in from Bidston, the connection for Liverpool. You know Wrexham is in Wales because the name is given on the station in Welsh green above the English version. Its fifteenth-century church of St Giles is one of the seven wonders of Wales.

The best part of this journey came as the train moved south from Wrexham, close to the Ruabon mountain and going past the dauntingly named little town of Rhosllanerchrugog to Ruabon and Chirk. The sense of remoteness was stronger here. Nothing much seemed to be happening but this could have been deceptive: the Welsh here are not people to let it all hang out; they live their lives in ways not revealed to passers-by in trains.

From Ruabon the train descended through a series of stone bridges to cross the beautifully wooded Vale of Llangollen on a high viaduct, with lovely views up and down the fast-moving River Dee. Up the valley to the right was another long stone viaduct of 19 arches, 127 feet high and 1007 feet long. This early nineteenth-century engineering masterpiece by Telford and Jessop is the Pontcysyllte aqueduct, carrying the Llangollen canal over the valley in a cast-iron trough made watertight with Welsh flannel. Opened in 1805, it is still in use by pleasure-boats on the canal and the towpath makes an excellent walk – even if you don't meet the lady in a crinoline who is said to haunt it.

The canal swung round to join the railway and they ran close together until they crossed the River Ceiriog at Chirk, each on an impressive stone viaduct but not so dizzyingly high above the valley bottom as at Pontcysyllte. In this area the line of Offa's Dyke comes close to the railway and about a mile from Chirk railway station stands a border castle founded by Edward I, now a private home.

At Chirk the train crossed back into England and ran through the forgotten countryside of this north-west corner of Shropshire between the Dee and the Severn, dozing peacefully since the decline of the canals.

We had been a quiet train until Gobowen, but there a group of chattering schoolchildren scrambled aboard, laden with rucksacks almost as big as themselves, and cheered the whole train of silent folk through the morose weather and the quiet Shropshire plain to land us in Shrewsbury in excellent humour. Every train should have a group of schoolchildren aboard and a surprising number of them do.

The Cardigan Bay line

Up to six trains a day, change at Machynlleth, two and three-quarter hours

Much of Britain's coastline is accessible by train but there's no doubt which is the most beautiful seaside train ride in Britain. It's the Cambrian coast route between Aberystwyth and Pwllheli, a continual delight for all its 70-mile length as it follows the shoreline of Cardigan Bay and Tremadog Bay between the sea and the mountains of the Snowdon range. It finds its way across three great estuaries, runs sometimes almost on the beach and sometimes climbs up the cliffside. For more than two hours it treats the train traveller to magnificent panoramas of sea and mountain, estuary sands and castles. In this one train ride you can see examples of all the grandeur and beauty of Wales.

Presiding over the southern stretches of the line is Cader Idris, the mysterious mountain of basalt and porphyry. The name

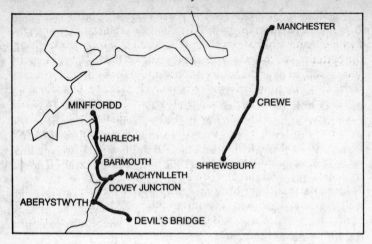

means chair of Idris and this traditional Welsh figure is supposed to have had his rock-hewn throne on its summit. Idris had the power of conferring poetic inspiration or of sending people mad and whether the builders of the railway were inspired or mad, or both, must have been a subject for debate.

I started from Aberystwyth, having stayed overnight at the Belle Vue Royal, a very pleasant hotel on the front a few minutes' walk from the station. Aberystwyth is a quiet, substantial resort and university town, with a castle on a headland from which there are wonderful views down a beautiful rocky coast. You can go shark-fishing, pony-trekking or walking in the hills and forest behind the town. The station for the Cambrian coast line is also the terminus for the magnificent Vale of Rheidol narrow-gauge railway, BR's only steam line (see page 219).

The four-coach diesel began by running inland and in the early morning mist the peace of the countryside was palpable. Sheep grazed on the steep, rounded hills and the train plunged every now and then into a silent green tunnel of trees, whose leaves brushed our windows. We were back on the coast at Borth and then ran across marshy grazing land lined with drainage dykes, with the flat sands of the Dovey estuary on one side, the colourful little resort of Aberdovey on the far shore and the dreamy shapes of misty mountains closing the scene. At this time of the morning nothing seemed to be moving except our train and the air was full of Welsh magic.

The line from Aberystwyth joins the line from Pwllheli at Dovey Junction and the mid-morning train connects here with the Pwllheli train from Shrewsbury. I secured a seat on the left side, the better to see the estuary birds feeding on the sandbanks as the train rumbled over the bridge and ran close to the shore through a series of short tunnels in the overhanging rocks to Aberdovey.

There's a legend at Aberdovey that a rich and fertile land lies sunk beneath the sands of the estuary, a drunken watchman of the gods having failed to close the dyke against the sea. You're said to be able to hear the bells of a lost city in the murmur of the sea. Among these mountains and mysterious expanses of sand it's easy to believe this and much more Welsh legend.

From Barmouth the train moved inland and the scenery became a little less spectacular. The mountain backdrop was there but caravans, golf courses and chalets occupied the foreground. Never mind, entertainment was now provided by a party of schoolchildren who had got on at Barmouth and were going to school in Harlech. Bright-eyed and mischievous, several of them had come without their rail passes. The guard tried hard to sound convincingly stern when he warned them that he would put them off the train if they did not have their passes tomorrow. The children didn't believe a word and neither did I.

At Harlech the station is under an outcrop of rock on which stands the still-impressive castle built as part of Edward I's plan for subduing the Welsh after he had defeated Llewelyn, the last Welsh prince. At one time the sea came right up to the castle walls, making it all but impregnable. From the castle walls there are marvellous views of the Snowdon range of mountains and the Lleyn peninsula across Tremadog Bay.

We were moving inland now, the grassland beside us alive with sheep newly sheared. We found the sea again as we ran up beside the third great estuary of the journey, the Traeth Bach, which reaches up into the Vale of Ffestiniog. Across its sands I could see the graceful and fanciful towers and dome of Portmeirion. This delightful Italian-style fantasy village can be visited, the nearest station being Minffordd. After Penrhyndeudraeth there was another bridge to cross, with tremendous views down over the estuary and up the vale into the mountains. Then we were into Minffordd.

I left the train at this point to join the narrow-gauge railway to Blaenau Ffestiniog (see page 225). I had left only six minutes for the connection but my train, though leisurely, was on time and I made the connection easily.

The train I had left went on round Tremadog Bay, to Criccieth, close to Lloyd George's boyhood home and grave, and on past a big holiday camp to Pwllheli, the terminus, a popular holiday resort with fine sandy beaches and magnificent views across the bay to Snowdon. It makes a train ride of unmatched enchantment.

Blaenau to Manchester

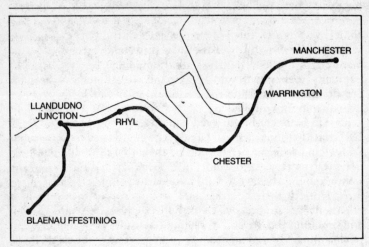

About an hour to Llandudno Junction, then about two and a quarter hours
BR's Conwy Valley line shares a station with the narrow-gauge Festiniog Railway. Before joining the Llandudno train I lunched at the North Western, named after the company which built the line to compete with the Festiniog for what was then, over a century ago, the very substantial slate traffic out of Blaenau. The single track runs up from Llandudno for 28 miles and passes nearer to Snowdon itself than any other BR line (though if you want to go up the Snowdon mountain railway take the bus to Llanberis from Bangor on the Holyhead line).

On the two-coach local, fellow passengers were holidaymakers with rucksacks and a local lady, not a native of the area, who as well as helping me to identify things seen on the way told me how neighbourly Blaenau folk were. It was the practice even today, she told me, when a man was in hospital for neighbours to call there and leave small gifts of money for him and call on the wife with groceries, a custom going back to the days when injury or illness for the breadwinner meant hardship and possibly starvation for the family unless neighbours rallied round.

The train plunged almost immediately into a tunnel more than two miles long through the mountain. We came out into a valley and ran down through a mountain landscape of peace and beauty in which no roads or houses could be seen. Roman Bridge station seemed to serve only one house – no village was visible – and we moved briskly down the valley of the little River Lledr, passing wild Dolwyddelan Castle, where Llewelyn the Great, Prince of Wales, was born. Snowdonia was Llewelyn's stronghold and many of the castles around the area, including Conwy, Criccieth, Harlech, Aberystwyth and Welshpool, were built to withstand attacks from the Welsh in these mountains. Dolwyddelan is about a mile from the station.

The valley narrowed down and we ran through the great Gwydyr forest into Betws-y-Coed which is a centre for touring Snowdonia and has a railway museum in the station goods yard, housed in old coaches – one of them a veteran Pullman. Llanrwst followed, with a bridge by Inigo Jones and an abbey nearby where Llewelyn is buried.

Now we were in the Vale of Conwy and the line followed the wide river until we could see the estuary in front of us with the powerful towers and walls of Conwy Castle on the other side of the river. As we ran down we could see the Euston-Holyhead express run across an embankment and into Robert Stephenson's tubular steel bridge which spans the estuary to a point under the castle walls. Seen across the river the town, its castle and the bridge made a noble sight. Our train ran into Llandudno Junction, where I left it. The train was going on to its terminus at Llandudno itself, biggest of Welsh holiday resorts and the one offering the most hotels and greatest variety of entertainment. A tramway takes you to the top of the Great Orme headland for extensive views.

Llandudno Junction is the station for Conwy, an historic and interesting town. The railway line goes through the town and along the coast to Bangor, university town and shopping centre, and over Robert Stephenson's second tubular bridge, the even finer Britannia bridge across the Menai Strait to Anglesey.

The first station on the island, dismissed in BR timetables as mere Llanfairpwll, is really the impressive LLANFAIRP-WLLGWYNGYLLGOGERYCHWYRNDROBWLLLLANTY-SILIOGOGOGOCH, properly identified as such, I'm glad to say, on the station sign itself, though you'd be hard put to copy it down as the boat train to Holyhead runs through. Local trains stop there, however, and there's a brisk sale in souvenir tickets.

Eastwards from Llandudno Junction the InterCity trains from Holyhead run through Chester and Crewe and down the main line to Euston. Local trains run to Chester and then go by way of Warrington to Manchester Victoria. I opted for the latter as being the natural line of communication for this holiday coast. While getting annual holiday-makers from further afield it owes much of its popularity to being within easy day-trip distance of Greater Manchester and Merseyside. The line runs along the holiday north coast of Wales and down the mostly industrial Dee estuary before running out of Wales to Chester, then turning north-east to Warrington and Manchester.

The local train had some recognizable North Country types aboard, people who knew how to make themselves at home like the man who made a leisurely picnic out of paper bags and then removed his shoes before composing himself for a postprandial nap.

This North Wales holiday coast is for families who want good bathing and extensive sands, together with all the traditional amenities of a holiday resort – bands, piers, discos, bingo, summer shows. All this these resorts provide in abundance and if a break from these delights is wanted there are plenty of coach tours into the mountains which loom behind the coast.

The train took us through Colwyn Bay and past lines of holiday chalets and caravan parks to Rhyl, the next major family resort. Here on the large station our train was met by a man with a trolley selling drinks and chocolates. This seemed a good idea and I wondered why this sort of train-side service is not seen more often in Britain.

Prestatyn, the next stop, has a big holiday camp and then the line cuts across behind a headland to follow the shore of the Dee estuary. After the beauties of the Conwy Valley line this coast offers little of visual interest to the train traveller. On the Dee estuary we had left holiday land behind, except for a brief reappearance at Flint, and were now into a mainly industrial coastline, with views across the wide estuary to the Wirral on the other side.

From Mostyn to Flint there was a succession of junkyards, chemical works, tanks, pipes and soil tips which contrived to be varied without attaining any of the dignity or drama that industrial landscapes can sometimes provide. The man with his shoes off and his eyes closed had evidently been this way before. Flint has a castle, first of the chain of them established by King Edward I in North Wales.

From Flint we crossed an industrial wilderness of factories and works set in drab, flat, featureless country. We stopped at Shotton, the steel town, which has rail connections with Birkenhead and Wrexham, and then we were out of Wales and very soon in Chester, passing a part of the city wall and some interesting canal locks.

Lines from Chester go not only to Holyhead and Crewe, but also to Wrexham, the Wirral and by two different routes to Manchester. Our train was off through Helsby and alongside a motorway to Frodsham and Warrington Bank Quay, where we briefly joined the main line from Euston.

We were now a train full of serious people with work to do making our way through a no-man's-land between Liverpool and Manchester, a workaday landscape where factories alternate with estates of two-storey houses.

At Earlestown we joined the Liverpool-Manchester line and at Newton-le-Willows (no actual willows in sight), we crossed over the main Euston line we had just left, went on to Eccles, of cake fame, and so into Manchester Victoria.

Victoria is a through station and siren voices of station announcers urged us on to Leeds and York, Hull and Newcastle. But Manchester was the end of the day's run for me, a different world from the Welsh mountain town I had left after lunch. I made my way from the remote platform to which our train had been consigned and sought out Manchester's former railway hotel, the Midland.

The ticket collector laughed when I asked if the Midland was attached to Victoria or Piccadilly station. It was a fair walk from either, he explained. It was, I discovered, the hotel just round the corner from the closed Central station. But it was close to Manchester's monstrous and splendid Victorian town hall and the centre of the city's life and it was a comfortable and friendly refuge, its building another monument to the city's capacity for thinking in grand terms.

Manchester to Shrewsbury

Reasonable service, an hour and a half changing at Crewe
Besides being one of the great cities of the north of England, Manchester is also a great railway centre, its two main stations, Victoria and Piccadilly, offering easy connections all over the North with London only two and a half hours away. For those who like to settle in one place and make daily outings instead of constantly changing hotels or bed-and-breakfasts Manchester makes good, hard-headed Northern sense. It has all the big-city amenities in the way of entertainment and cultural life, has a surprising number of places of historic interest to show, is the centre of a regional culture as distinctive as that of the Scots or the Welsh and is well known for its fierce independence of the capital.

Every great city needs escape routes and Manchester has plenty close to hand, the Lancashire and North Wales coasts, the Peak District, the Yorkshire Moors, the Lake District. One of the several ways to get quickly out of the northern industrial belt and into a greener, less crowded environment is to head south-west to Shrewsbury and beyond.

Manchester Piccadilly is a modern station with very good services for the traveller – two competing bookstalls, an off-licence, a kiosk selling picnic food, as well as the more usual buffet. My first train was the 9.00 InterCity for Coventry. It took me swiftly and smoothly out of Manchester and its suburbs, through Stockport, Wilmslow and Alderley Edge and a countryside which just about managed to hold its own against urban encroachments all round. Just when you think the passing scene is fairly familiar stuff it manages to spring a surprise. In this case it was the great radio telescope at Jodrell Bank, close on our left, a huge saucer raised on girders to search out the secrets of outer space.

I had to leave the Coventry train at Crewe. Everyone who travels extensively by train has to change some time or other at Crewe, a series of island platforms in a wild sea of rails and overhead electricity wires lashing about in every direction. In fact, four other lines join the Euston-Scotland main line here – from Manchester, Stoke-on-Trent, Shrewsbury and Chester. However, the whole station has now been reorganized and refurbished, with a better track layout and new passenger amenities. Main-line trains that used to have to creep over the maze can now dash through. Passengers changing here find it a much more agreeable experience than it once was. With 25 minutes between trains I had no problems in joining the 10.03 loco-hauled train to Shrewsbury, Hereford and Cardiff. The 33 miles to Shrewsbury were a non-stop run of 35 minutes.

Once out of Crewe and through Nantwich we were free of industrial entanglements and able to discover that Cheshire does still have some lovely countryside. Wrenbury was a reminder that black and white half-timbered cottages are characteristic of the county and then we were past Whitchurch and into the deep peace of rural Shropshire. County boundaries are not just arbitrary – each county has its own different look, though it's not always easy to say what constitutes it. Shropshire is the picture-book face of traditional English farming: rolling pastures, gentle hills, cows in fields bordered by lush hedgerows and trees everywhere – in the hedgerows, providing shade in fields, forming clumps of woodland. You can almost see life going on at a comfortable, ambling pace.

The Cumbrian Coast line

Carlisle to Barrow infrequent, two and three-quarter hours
An easy two and a quarter hours up the main line from Manchester Victoria, Carlisle is the northern terminus of the Cumbrian Coast line to Grange-over-Sands. At first, the line can seem something of a disappointment. It runs round the Lake District with the impressive Skiddaw or its lesser neighbours a looming presence, yet little of that beauty contributes anything to the coastal scene the railway traveller sees on the first stages of the journey and the northern stretch of the coast has a hard, gravelly look. Iron ore working in the mountains established industry here; spoil tips and big steel works contribute a certain grimness to the scene. When the nineteenth century has done its worst the twentieth century adds the suaver but more menacing shapes of nuclear power. Yet the hopeful traveller who perseveres down this line finds it rewarding.

I set off from Carlisle in a little two-coach diesel that would, if I had wanted, have taken me the full length of the Cumbrian coast and back on to the main line, terminating at Lancaster. It would take nearly four hours and stop at every station. A pleasanter day, I reckoned, would be to go as far as Grange, looking out over Morecambe Bay on the southern side of the bulge of Cumbria, just before the railway goes over the border into Lancashire, and to break that journey at Ravenglass for a trip on the Ravenglass and Eskdale Railway (see page 220).

The run begins unpromisingly across flat mining country, with only the vague shapes of the Cumbrian mountains to the south giving distinction to the scene. The coast is reached at Maryport, with the Scottish shore to be seen across the Solway Firth and the Isle of Man a blue bulk of mountains away to the west. Maryport got its name from Mary Queen of Scots landing here when she fled from Scotland. Less romantically it got its living and its present appearance from exporting coal and iron. It does not look very inviting from the train but it has a good maritime museum and its harbour area is being restored.

The train runs down the coast from here, the beach looking stony and the sea grey and sullen. The Cumbrian mountains, to the east, are lined with mining spoil tips and conceal the beauties of the Lake District.

At Workington, named and looking like the scene of one of the grittier nineteenth century novels of industrial conflict, the once sparkling Derwent has forgotten the glories of Derwent Water and Bassenthwaite Lake and become a grimy, blackened stream. Iron and steel, coal mining and shipbuilding used to be the town's staples, none of which have improved the look of the place.

Whitehaven, though, a few miles down the coast, manages to achieve some distinction with much the same ingredients. As the train approaches on a low embankment at the foot of the cliffs the old-style industrial outline with chimneys on a hill and a small, battered freighter making for the waiting arms of its harbour presents a picture of a bygone industrial age in almost dia-grammatic form. This is a big, busy centre with lines of coal wagons, freight trains of ore waiting on the sidings and an air of purposefulness. The train fills with working people.

After Whitehaven the scene becomes altogether gentler. St Bees Head, which the railway skirts, is the turning point; there is a bird sanctuary here. Then down the coast to Millom the beaches are backed with handsome cliffs, the mountains a benign presence away to the left. We seem to be back in traditional seaside Britain – but for the sinister question mark raised by nuclear pollution of sea and beach at Sellafield. The nuclear industry, one of the biggest employers in the area, stands back and keeps its secrets behind bland screen walls.

At Ravenglass, terminus of the Ravenglass and Eskdale Rail-way, three little rivers, the Irt, the Mite and the Esk, run into an extensive haven, giving a good anchorage for yachts. There's an attractive village consisting of one street of stone houses running down to the haven and a mile away is Muncaster Castle, a Victorian rebuilding in pink granite of a thirteenth-century for-tified home in a magnificent setting beside the Esk, with Scafell in the distance. This is one place along the coast where the beauty of the Lake District reveals itself fully.

King Henry VI, finding asylum in the castle after a beating from the Scots, presented the owner with an enamelled glass bowl, called the Luck of Muncaster. The legend is that so long as the bowl is held intact, the good fortune of the castle's owners will continue. Additional attractions include flamingos and the ghost of a man whose head was cut off.

At Ravenglass station I witnessed a stirring sight, the arrival and departure of a steam excursion train on its way back to Crewe from Sellafield. The locomotive was the streamlined, elegant *Sir Nigel Gresley*, named after its designer. I took the more mundane diesel down the coast round the foot of Bootle Fell and Black Combe and on through Millom, where most of the passengers got off.

Millom stands on the wide Duddon estuary giving the first view of the speciality of this part of the world, the extensive sands exposed for so great a distance when the tide goes out that you can't see the sea that covers them at high tide.

The train now ran over marshland almost on the sands, round both sides of the estuary. From the far side of the estuary there was a better view of Millom, standing out on a little headland, and of Black Combe behind.

We were now in Furness, the peninsula between the Duddon estuary and Morecambe Bay. Beyond Dalton the train ran into Barrow, industrial town and port, stronghold of the Vickers Company, noted for guns and nuclear submarines. Not much to see from the station but a walk revealed a surprisingly gracious Victorian town with side streets, imposing public buildings and statues of town worthies. At the end of a street the bulk of a warship could be seen.

Another train took me on up through the middle of Furness, past the ruins of the once-powerful Furness Abbey and a distant view of Piel Castle away over the sand guarding the entrance to Barrow. Ulverston is a pleasant town and the handiest place for a bus to Haverthwaite to join the steam railway from there to Lakeside and the Windermere steamers.

We came across an arm of the estuary and confronted the huge expanse of sand in Morecambe Bay. The tide was out – and not just out, but out of sight. I could see across to Morecambe and Heysham on the far shore but no sea in between. The train ran round the shore of the bay to Grange-over-Sands, whose name, once puzzling, now became clear. It could hardly call itself 'on sea' for more than an hour or two a day. 'Over' rather than 'on' sands because the resort of grey stone houses and hotels is set in a steep wooded hillside so that almost everybody has extensive views across the bay and over the sands.

This was the end of my day's journey. What began with nineteenth-century industrial grimness had blossomed into de-lightful and unusual country. This sandy bay with its majestic backdrop of mountains had an air of being a world of its own and indeed I was told that its position, and the warmth reflected from the sands, gave it a unique climate.

I stayed at the friendly Grange Hotel, an imposing stone pile on the hillside above the station, giving superb views across the bay. The resort is today valued chiefly as a pleasant base for tours into the Lake District, easily accessible to the north. You have to be a bit wary on the sands – they ring bells and fly flags when the tide's coming in, otherwise those walking too far out could share the fate of poor Mary in Kingsley's poem, calling the cattle home across the sands of Dee and getting fatally trapped by tide and mist. But the place has a well-preserved, individual Victorian charm.

Grange to Carlisle

Approximately hourly to Lancaster, taking an hour, then main line

From Grange-over-Sands all trains starting at Barrow go on to Carnforth and Lancaster; some continue further afield to Preston, Manchester or Euston. My morning train was to take me to Carnforth, two stops down the line, where I planned to visit Steamtown before carrying on to Lancaster, the first main-line station. The sun was shining, some sea was visible across the sands, and little Grange station with its clean gothic stone, its baskets of flowers and its view of the bay looked, like Grange itself, as if the grubbier aspects of the twentieth century hadn't happened and we were still in an era when everything – the railways, the social structure – worked as it was meant to.

The train was on time and the day got off to a good start with a run along the shore of the bay and over an arm of it on a viaduct, stopping at Arnside on the farther shore, a nice-looking little place with a jetty the sea would reach in due course, and then on into Carnforth.

This is a Lancashire town that once had an iron works and still has a railway junction but whose chief claim on our notice today is as the home of Steamtown, just over a fence from the station but a quarter of a mile walk away even so.

Railway or transport museums are springing up all over the country now and nearly all of them are worth a visit, because the history of transport is the history of social development and the history of the railways is the history of the transformation of Britain in less than a century from a predominantly rural to a mainly urban society – one of the most thoroughgoing and far-reaching transformations that any nation has undergone in so short a time.

It was not my intention to spend a lot of time in railway museums that could better be spent on the living railway. To enjoy Britain's present-day railways it is by no means necessary to be the sort of train buff who slavers at the mouth at the sight of an old Great Western Railway guard's cap or the waiting-room coal-shovel from some long-demolished branch line station. However, I decided to make two exceptions; the National Railway Museum at York had been one (see page 108) and the Steamtown Railway Museum was the other.

Steamtown is much more than a museum. It is the place where you stable your locomotive when you have bought one and restored it, the place where old locomotives plucked from scrap-yards are rebuilt lovingly and given new life; and the place helping to make possible the steam-hauled excursions over BR lines which give thousands of holiday-makers and day-outers the time of their lives.

In itself Steamtown is not a pretty sight. It is a set of sidings in the middle of which stands a locomotive running shed built during the war by Italian prisoners. They used defective concrete, some of which has dropped off leaving a mangy effect. There's also a workshop, an ash disposal plant and a concrete tower – the only one left in the country – which lifts coal wagons up and tilts them over to dump their contents into a hopper from which locomotive tenders are filled.

It is nonetheless fascinating not only to lovers of steam but to all who appreciate beauty. For this far from stately home is the residence of *Sir Nigel Gresley*, the streamlined London and North Eastern Railway locomotive of the Thirties which I had seen working at Ravenglass. *Sir Nigel* is an aristocrat if ever I saw one, still capable of speeds of more than 100 mph, though now restricted to 60 mph, and a popular hauler of excursions to the Cumbrian coast and to Scarborough on the Yorkshire coast. The famous *Flying Scotsman*, an earlier LNER aristocrat, is another resident and so are several more engines of great distinction, in working order and able to turn out to haul a train. *Lord Nelson* and *Canadian Pacific* from the Southern and a clutch of powerful but anonymous London, Midland and Scottish engines are here, all in their original livery. Most of these are privately owned, by individuals or societies, and are maintained with the facilities of Steamtown.

Even more impressive in their power, though nothing like so graceful, are the two big Continental engines in the shed, German and French, larger than the British and hung about with writhing pipes connected with devices to increase their efficiency. Unfortunately their size is such that they cannot run on British tracks. But just to look at them standing in the shed is to get an awed impression of their might. There are also cheeky little tank engines from colliery sidings and gasworks, and a selection of special coaches, some of them now hired out to British Rail for use as luxury observation cars.

Steamtown's importance lies not so much in its function as a museum as in its work as a centre for restoring, repairing and maintaining steam locomotives. It is not the only home for steam engines – the Bulmer steam centre at Hereford is another admirable one – but it is the most successful in putting steam locomotives to gainful employment. It is a place full of real enthusiasm and in spite of that forbidding shed a lovely place, even if you're not a steam fanatic.

Incidentally, the knowledgeable Carnforth man who showed me round poured polite cold water on one legend I had long cherished, the one that says there is a secret tunnel somewhere filled with steam locomotives which British Rail are keeping as a reserve in case the oil gives out. Apparently enthusiasts have records of almost every steam locomotive built over the last fifty years and only a handful are unaccounted for. Pity.

From Carnforth local trains join the main line and run the six miles to Lancaster. From here another local goes off down a four-mile branch to Morecambe, the only British seaside resort to have had a comedian named after it. A quick visit here cleared up a misconception I had long had about the place. I had thought of it as just another, less successfully brash Blackpool, reasoning that one Lancashire seaside resort must be very like another. In fact, it's quite different. There's only one Blackpool, as its advertisements say – and Morecambe isn't it.

Morecambe's cheerful, airy station is on the front, where every seaside station should be, and the vista down the promenade is of a fairly quiet, decent-looking, self-respecting resort with no Golden Mile or Tower; right for families and, of course, for aspiring beauty queens.

Lancaster, on the main line, is the station at which the bus waits to whisk you to Heysham for the Isle of Man ferry. Today it was also the station at which announcements were being made that because of some mishap down the line trains to the North were running about half an hour late. So I decided to cut out a planned visit to Windermere, on the branch line from Oxenholme. I regretted missing this but I had previously visited the town that sits on the shore of England's biggest lake. The line to it runs through Kendal, as you can see from the main line train, and then through gentle hills into the town. From Windermere station it's a short bus-ride to Bowness for the lake steamers. For the railway traveller it works much better as a day out from Manchester, or as a holiday centre, than as a stop on a touring trip.

I made my way up the main line to Carlisle, reflecting that if I was minded to break my journey along here a good place to do it would be Penrith, where they have a 15-seater bus called the 'Fellrunner' ranging round the countryside on special-interest day trips.

The Buxton branch

Hourly service from Manchester Piccadilly, taking an hour

The Pennines may be the backbone of England but the railway builders never regarded them as an insuperable barrier. Besides several east-west lines further north, there were at one time four routes across what is now the Peak District National Park. The most northerly of these, the Woodhead tunnel route, has in recent years carried no scheduled passenger services. The Manchester-Sheffield line, with through services to Hull and Harwich, runs through lovely country near Kinder Scout to Edale (where walkers can set out on the Pennine Way). The line continues to Hope, nearest station for Castleton's great caves, Bamford, and Hethersage in Derwent Dale, before tunnelling under the moors to Dore and running on into Sheffield.

The other two lines both ran from Buxton to Derby, one through Bakewell and Matlock, the other a little further south. Both these are now gone but the line to Buxton from Manchester, climbing to the once fashionable spa 100 feet above sea level, still survives, as does the short stretch from Derby up to Matlock at the other end.

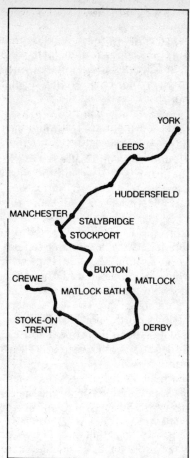

The Sheffield and the Buxton line offer marvellous days out from Manchester, both about an hour's journey.

To take the Buxton line I broke a journey from Shrewsbury to York at Stockport, a useful junction six miles out of Manchester Piccadilly. Lines from Crewe and Stoke on Trent come together here and there's a link to Stalybridge timed to connect with trains from Manchester Victoria to Leeds, York and Newcastle. In this way travellers from south of Manchester can get to Yorkshire and the North-east without having to make a bus trip across Manchester between Piccadilly and Victoria stations.

Stockport is a cotton town and no tourist resort. The station gives a strong impression of belonging to a sensible, good-humoured community. It's lucky perhaps in not being overwhelmed by too many trains and passengers but in the half-hour I had to spend there it seemed a model of how a station should be run. Everything was clean and well kept, the train announcements were made clearly and slowly, the buffet had bright decor, clean tables and willing service. Every time the flow of customers dried up the serving lady briskly cleared and cleaned the tables. Everybody here was taking a pride in running a pleasant station and it showed.

From Stockport the Buxton train was a three-coach diesel, electric trains on this line going only as far as Hazel Grove, the end of the suburbs. By then we could already see the Peaks ahead in the distance. Beyond the suburbs we were into the woods and then began to climb out into the hills.

At New Mills, the first real town out of Stockport, we were on the side of a valley and could see the Manchester-Sheffield line on the opposite hillside to the north. By now we were getting superb views of the Peaks, Kinder Scout away to the north, 2088 feet, and Hab Tor close at hand to the south.

Chapel-en-le-Frith presented itself as a tough little stone town and then there were more glorious views of the moors lifting away to the Peaks as we turned south through Dove Holes to Buxton. This country invites you to get out and walk, or just leave the train, stroll out of the station and enjoy the view and the fresh moorland air. All this wilderness and grandeur was just a step from the railway and considerably less than an hour from the heart of Manchester.

The train terminated at Buxton, the Derbyshire spa and the highest town of any size in Britain. It became fashionable to take the waters here in the eighteenth century and the vogue lasted well into the twentieth. Taking the waters has gone out of fashion but Buxton is a gracious and popular walking and touring centre. The town is trying to establish an annual opera festival, its opera house being reckoned one of the finest in the north of England, and this was in progress. In the pavilion behind the opera house a two-piece ensemble – piano and oboe, both amateur – was dispensing Strauss to the lunch-time crowd.

Buxton is a good town for the railway visitor or weekender. The station is close to the action, a few minutes from the opera house, pavilion and shopping streets. It's a beautiful town spread over several hills, rewarding to walk around. Wherever you look there's something of interest and there is wild, magnificent country all around.

There's an old town at the top of a hill with the spa buildings spread round the foot of it. Best of these is the crescent built by John Carr of York in 1784 after the style of Palladian Bath. The assembly room which forms part of the block has been restored to its original grandeur and is now quite certainly the most beautiful reference library in the country.

In these elegant surroundings the station keeps its end up – literally – by retaining from its original building an end wall with a fine fan-shaped window.

Stockport to York

Hourly service, about two hours, change at Stalybridge

I would have liked to go on to Matlock Bath, but in the absence of a linking line I was now bound for York by way of Stockport and Stalybridge. From Buxton the train swooped quickly down to Stockport and there my luck was in. In the matter of late trains you win some and lose some. This time I gained. Instead of having to wait nearly an hour for a Stalybridge train I found that the previous train, which I should have missed, was running an unusual 15 minutes late. There was just time to board it before it pulled out.

This little train journey of eight miles turned out to be surprisingly scenic for a run through the Manchester suburbs. We left on the big viaduct high above Stockport and then struck off to the north-east at a level which enabled us for much of the time to see beyond Reddish and Denton to the Peaks.

On the way we crossed the two arms of the Manchester-Sheffield line, at Reddish and Guide Bridge, before running past vast square mill buildings, a canal basin and the usual sea of junked cars to reach Stalybridge.

Here the Liverpool-York train had been detained to allow us to make the connection. Our train ran in behind it on the same platform so that we could change with the least possible delay and we were off a minute later.

This time I crossed the Pennines by the shortest, most direct route. At Stalybridge we were on the very edge of Manchester, with the moors rising immediately to our right, the High Peak beyond, a green belt fashioned by nature. Greater Manchester lay behind us with Oldham just over the hill to our left. The great Leeds - Bradford - Halifax - Huddersfield - Dewsbury - Wakefield mass lay ahead. Now we were pulling over the barrier of moorland which keeps the two masses apart and ensures that the two sprawling communities maintain their different characters and develop in their own ways.

The train climbed a high ledge under Saddleworth Moor into a great bowl of hills in which we seemed to have left the industrial world far behind us. We plunged into the Standedge tunnel, fourth longest in England at three miles, and emerged in time in high moorland at Marsden, making straight for our objective, instead of finding a longer but easier way round as the line between Halifax and Rochdale does.

Up here on the high moors we were not in wild country. There were small towns and villages, even mills, but all in a setting of wide, clear views and uncluttered heights. The experience was short but intense and then we were over a viaduct and running down a hillside ledge, passing grey mill towns in the valley below us, from Slaithwaite down into Milnsbridge and Huddersfield. Stalybridge to Huddersfield took only 20 minutes and now we were into a different world. From Huddersfield, solid cloth town famous for its choral singing, through Mirfield, Batley and Morley – the towns now ran together in a continuous mass of houses and mills culminating in the great high spread of Leeds.

There was nothing much to see in the last stretch except dumps of wrecked cars, offered in huge heaps by the side of the line as if laid out as sacrifices to the railway gods.

From Leeds we went on through the coalfields and up across the plain to the beckoning minster at York, just an hour and a half from Stalybridge.

Derby to Matlock

Every two hours in the morning, hourly afternoons, taking 35 minutes

Later, I made the trip to Matlock I would have liked to make from Buxton through the Peak District National Park. Matlock can now only be reached by train rather more prosaically from Derby. The local train has connections from Nottingham and a day trip from London is also quite possible.

Derby station has been refurbished to bring out the Midland Railway griffins in myrtle and turquoise. It is on the Birmingham to Sheffield main line and our train, in smart blue and white livery, turns off it just before Ambergate to run up the Derwent valley, crossing and recrossing the swift river and plunging in and out of tunnels. At Matlock Bath it reaches the deep, narrow gorge which provides the way through to Matlock town.

Once a popular spa, Matlock is now a pleasant town of stone buildings with a pub beside the river and houses climbing a hillside. This is a good starting point for walks up the river to Darley Dale and into the Peak country of crags and caves.

More is provided for visitors at Matlock Bath, the station

before the terminus. A cable car starts from near the station to take visitors up to the Heights of Abraham, a theme park and leisure centre offering spectacular views. On the other side of the gorge the High Tor area offers equally splendid views and walks. The whole area is the nearest England gets to a Swiss landscape and the station building has a fretted, vaguely Swiss look. With amusement parks, lead mines and caves to visit, and walks to take, this is still a popular inland resort, though not now offering to cure you of anything except boredom. Though the resort itself is heavily commercialized, a walk out into the moorland takes you into some of the most beautiful, unspoilt country in England – and all only half an hour from industrial, main-line Derby.

Derby to Crewe

Hourly, about an hour and 20 minutes

Back at Derby, it was time to sample the useful but unglamorous cross-country line that joins Nottingham, and sometimes also Lincoln and Newark, to Crewe with connections for Liverpool and the North Wales coast. From Nottingham the train runs across a mining and industrial area to reverse at Derby. After Derby, however, the landscape cheers up: my local train soon left the main line and took off by the River Dove through rural Derbyshire and Staffordshire. Across the river on the left at Tutbury are the remains of a castle which held Mary Queen of Scots as a prisoner on several occasions.

The river winds in a broad valley between here and the pleasant little Staffordshire town of Uttoxeter, where the train passes the town's beautiful racecourse. In the market place here Dr Johnson once stood bare-headed in the rain as an act of contrition for a youthful refusal to help on his father's bookstall.

The train now ran over the moors and into the Potteries, the distinctive Five Towns made famous by Arnold Bennett – there are in fact six, now amalgamated into the city of Stoke-on-Trent. The old kilns, looking like great brick bottles, can be seen from the train. Stoke, on the main line to Manchester, has shaken off the old smoke, the kilns now being fired by electricity. There is a Wedgwood museum here commemorating the great Josiah, the city's most famous son. A coach link from the station takes visitors to the Alton Towers leisure park, where you can see such attractions as a Chinese pagoda and an imitation Stonehenge from a cable car.

Having joined the main line at Stoke we left it again at Kidsgrove to run through Alsager and across fairly flat country to terminate at Crewe.

Sheffield to St Pancras

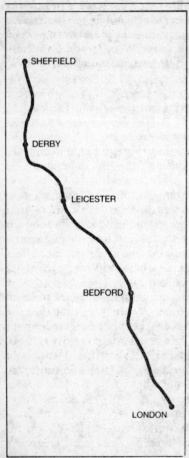

About every hour and a half, two and a half hours

The service from Sheffield to London St Pancras is by 125s. Some go by way of Derby; others turn off to Nottingham and reverse there, taking five minutes longer.

For most of the way from Derby to London the line crosses fairly flat, uninspiring country. If, as I believe, there is no such thing as a totally uninteresting train ride there is no doubt that some lines are more rewarding than others and that this is one of the others. It is the sort of line that reminds you that you can take to a book or visit the buffet when the passing scene flags. Leicester, quite a cheerful city on its day, hasn't much to show the passing traveller on a wet Saturday evening.

Near Kettering I noticed a lorry trailer bearing the legend 'Danger – poison gas – Keep away', certainly the most dramatic sight on this line.

Nothing wrong with Market Harborough and Kettering, I noted as we passed by: solid, sensible-looking small towns both. Bedford was more interesting,

John Bunyan was jailed here for twelve years as 'a common upholder of several unlawful meetings' and produced *Pilgrim's Progress*.

On the left beyond Bedford is the massive bulk of the old airship hangars at Cardington. The R100 and R101 were housed here but development was halted after the R101 crashed in flames in 1930. Now airships are again being built here.

As we got nearer the London area the train seemed to speed up and we raced through Luton in brisk style, neither its airport nor its car factory visible to the train traveller. By Harpenden we were out of the rather nondescript Bedfordshire countryside into Hertfordshire, large parts of which look like a private park.

We ran smoothly into the north London suburbs, running unchecked to West Hampstead and then slowing through Kentish Town to reach the terminus five minutes early. St Pancras is a most satisfying station to arrive at, the train coming in under Barlow's vast single-span canopy, dwarfed by the space the roof encloses. The simplicity of the engineer's clean concept contrasts with the scholarly fussing of Gilbert Scott's gothic pile in the front.

I was off to another railway gothic pile, the Great Eastern Hotel at Liverpool Street station. It is principally a City hotel catering for business functions and for the City's swollen lunch-time and early evening population. It has some magnificent public rooms, including a ballroom for 500 and a beautifully panelled pub with a fine ceiling. Strangest of all, tucked away inside the rambling edifice is a Masonic Egyptian temple built in 1903 with Edwardian opulence, adorned with pillars of rare white virgin marble and practically everything else that money could buy at the time.

Nothing quite so startling is offered to the train traveller but it makes a comfortable stopover if you are setting off early next day from Liverpool Street station or Fenchurch Street, as I was, and is handy for the Tower of London, Petticoat Lane and other City sights.

9
Excursions

Excursions are as old as the railways themselves. When the Stockton and Darlington Railway was opened in 1825 the first train to carry paying passengers was an excursion and people have been travelling by train for pleasure ever since. Thomas Cook organized the first cut-price special train in 1841, when he persuaded the Midland Counties railway company to take 570 people from Leicester to Loughborough and back for a shilling. Cook went on to found his tour company and railways have been offering special deals for days out ever since. Incidentally, 570 is still a good number for a profitable excursion.

Today there is a tremendous range of special trains and special tickets to tempt you to take to the train for a day out with the family. It's still a very cheap day's fun and brings places up to 250 miles away within the scope of an unstrained day's excursion. Train trips are particularly well adapted, too, for round trips which involve travel by boat. From London, for instance, you can have a day out on the river on a round trip from Paddington to Henley by train, boat from Henley to Windsor and back to Paddington by train. A visit to the nearest main-line station or BR-appointed travel agent will reveal an extraordinary variety of imaginative ideas for getting you out and about cheaply, in comfort or even in unashamed luxury.

At its simplest the railway excursion is just a cheap ticket which enables you to make you own outing on a scheduled train. Southern Region, for example, offers many such cheap-rate tickets for days out from London to seaside resorts. Many areas offer cheap, seven-day runabout tickets giving unlimited travel within a particular area – ideal for excursions from a holiday location. There are also round-trip tickets enabling you to make one-day circular tours by specified trains at cheap rates – Euston, Shrewsbury, Swansea, Paddington, for instance, to take in the line through the middle of Wales, or Euston, Carlisle, Leeds, King's Cross for the Settle and Carlisle line.

Rather more elaborate are excursions by special trains. Some of these are simply ways of getting to a popular location like York and back at a bargain price. Others add special amenities or services like the steam-hauled excursions from York to Scarborough or days out by special train to Stratford-upon-Avon, with meals on the train, guided tours and theatre seat included. In some of these, like those using the Orient Express Pullman train, the luxury train itself is a major part of the attraction. Day trips organized by rail enthusiasts' societies usually represent a substantial saving of money as well as the convenience of reserved seats in special trains and sightseeing coach trips. Nearly all such special trains carry buffet cars or a trolley refreshment service.

More elaborate and more expensive are commercially organized guided tours catering largely for visitors to Britain. With these a visitor can spend a day at one of the major sightseeing centres or two or three days on a tour to Scotland. The accent here is on comfort and special amenities rather than saving money.

There is nothing to stop any group of people – rail enthusiasts, sports club, political party, Women's Institute, or whatever – organizing their own train excursion. Even at rock-bottom prices it can be a substantial fund-raiser. The procedure is quite simple: you tell your local British Rail commercial manager what you want, and when you want to travel; he works out what can be offered and how much it will cost you. You pay ten per cent when you confirm the order and the balance a week before the trip takes place. You fix your own ticket price. If you can fill a train of 700, the maximum, your club or association can make a good profit on a low-priced ticket. On a train of 450, about the minimum in practical terms, you might have to charge more and still only break even. The vital part is selling the tickets. If you don't sell enough you can lose money, since the train cost is fixed. It's everybody's chance to try their hand at railway economics.

Yarmouth to Bristol excursion

Typical of the BR special-train excursion was one my wife and I took from Norfolk to Bristol. One secret of a successful train outing is to pick carefully and go somewhere you can reach

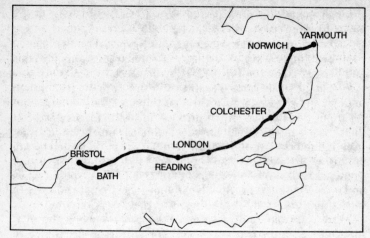

without strain and without having to get up at an absurdly early
hour.

It was the Spring Bank Holiday – no time to be driving – and
rain threatened, so a long train ride with a guaranteed seat seemed
a good option. The price was good value for a 520-mile round trip
to the other side of the country.

The ticket allowed us to take our local train to Norwich to join
the special which had started from Yarmouth. A courier settled us
in our seats, made sure we all knew the times of the return
journey, dealt with any problems cheerfully but made no attempt,
thank goodness, at corporate jollity. We were family parties,
some young couples, a few train-spotters but mostly just unidenti-
fiable day-outers.

We left Norwich soon after 8.00, more or less on time, and ran
up the main London line at normal main-line speed, picking up at
Diss, Stowmarket and Ipswich. It's a familiar run I always enjoy,
through Norfolk and Suffolk farmland and comfortable little
towns, curving round Ipswich with glimpses of shipping in the
port and the great bridge high over the River Orwell (Eric Blair,
the old Etonian, named himself after it to become George Orwell,
the writer). Then across the Stour at Manningtree and on down
through Essex – Roman Colchester on its hill, neat little towns
of commuter houses, Chelmsford with park and public buildings
tidily disposed on either side of the high railway embankment,
and Shenfield where the London suburbs begin.

Our courier didn't feel called upon to draw attention to the sights (there was, in any case, no public-address system) but an elderly railwayman walking up the aisle just after we passed Manningtree pointed out that we were going through Constable country with Flatford Mill and Dedham not far away to the right.

For me interest sharpened at Stratford, four miles from Liverpool Street, a wilderness of carriage sidings, Continental freight yards and lines taking off in sharp curves. Here we left the familiar main line to creep away gingerly across the wasteland of east London, over Stratford marsh, through Hackney and Dalston, edging between tower blocks and factories, looking down into tiny backyards. We surveyed London from the crowded east to genteel Canonbury, through Islington and Barnsbury and over a long viaduct to Camden Road. Away to the south we could see St Paul's hemmed in by the City's tower blocks, the great romantic castle and train shed of St Pancras Station, only properly to be seen from here, the Post Office Tower and a classical church.

At Camden Road we could study urban dereliction and renewal, through Kentish Town admire the great Victorian gin palaces dominating the mean streets and triumphantly surviving slum clearance. We rolled quietly through the north-west suburbs in cuttings rich with wild country growth, with here and there allotments cultivated on the gentler slopes. It's a fascinating view of backyard London in its shirtsleeves.

At Willesden Junction our train crossed the main line out of Euston and passed mountains of scrap iron to join the main line out of Paddington at Acton. We moved down the slow line to Southall, where train-spotters could note steam tank engines of the GWR Preservation Group, then switched to the fast track and picked up speed for the West, through Slough and off towards the gentler delights of Taplow and Pangbourne with glimpses of the Thames and the steep wooded hills of the Chilterns at Goring and Streatley.

We skirted the Berkshire Downs and raced for Swindon and the West, with lovely views over the Avon valley. We battled through dramatic red rock cuttings to beautiful Bath, its tranquil, classical stone terraces spread decorously over the hillside before us. The train stopped here and many of our fellow travellers chose this superb old spa as their day-out destination. At Bristol, reached soon after one o'clock, we took a bus from the splendidly dotty Victorian stone castle of a station into the main square for lunch.

During the afternoon there was time to enjoy the city. An arm
of the floating harbour pushes right up to the central square and it
was from here, as a plaque records, that John Cabot sailed to
discover North America in 1497. Ships no longer come up here to
discharge cargoes from the New World – the warehouse is now a
museum – but the floating harbour still has reminders of Bristol's
heroic merchant adventurer days. Ferries ply from the central
square for a forty-minute trip round the harbour, and on a day out
this is an excellent way to taste Bristol's special flavour. In dock
here is the *Great Britain*, Brunel's iron steamer launched in 1843,
a wonderfully evocative sight with its looming iron hull and black
funnel standing straight up from the deck.

Later, we took a bus to Clifton, most delightful of suburbs, and
walked across the suspension bridge, designed by Brunel and
finished in 1864, after his death. Spanning the Avon Gorge at a
height of 245 feet, it offers magnificent views to those with a head
for heights and is an experience no other city can offer.

Our train began its return journey soon after six. On the way
home we raced back to Southall before switching to the slow line
and climbing on to the cross-London line at Acton. We chose this
more leisurely section of the journey to have a picnic supper.

Regaining the Great Eastern main line we ran down it so fast
that we reached Norwich 45 minutes ahead of schedule. The
outing had been a pleasure from start to finish.

10
Theme Trips

Theme trips and tours are a good way to give extra interest to explorations by train and a very wide variety of interests can be followed in this way. A theme trip is an excursion taken in pursuit of a leisure interest or hobby.

For railway enthusiasts, of course, almost every trip is a theme trip in this sense. There's a lifetime's travelling in visiting places of railway interest – there are dozens of preserved lines, for instance (see Chapter 11), before you get to tracking down stations that have been closed or tracing long-defunct branch lines.

But theme trips are not just for railway buffs. Real-ale enthusiasts (admittedly, they are often the same people – there's a natural affinity between rail and ale) can sample most of the best brews of the country without ever straying far from a railway station. Never mind what they tell you about country pubs with roses round the door – serious ale fancying is an urban pursuit and the train takes you right where the action is – and, of course, back again with no drink-drive problems.

Britain's heritage of great buildings provides obvious scope for many theme trips. Stately-home visiting is not really a railway pastime, except in the form of train-and-coach-tour excursions, but cathedral-spotting certainly is. Only four of England's Anglican cathedrals are not in railway towns: all the others are an easy walk from the station, the majority visible from the train. Similarly, you can notch up a considerable score of castles seen just by keeping your eyes open on train rides. Many of them are either on hilltops, easily seen from miles away, or guarding gaps in the hills through which the railway passes. Most of these are worth special visits.

Theme trips by train, making long-distance excursions easy, are particularly helpful if your interest is architecture. Seeking out Georgian architecture, for instance, you could spend one day immersed in the splendours of Bath, the West Country city of unsurpassed elegance in stone, with its Pump Room, Assembly Rooms, Guildhall and streets of stately colonnaded terraces. And the next, perhaps, on the other side of the country in Bury St Edmunds admiring Georgian shop fronts in a town of mellow brick.

There is tremendous scope for all sorts of Victorian interests. The great Victorian town halls, for instance, a fascinating study in civic pride, can all be reached by train. So can nearly all the Victorian and Edwardian seaside piers, each with its own special character.

History can be happily followed in a series of train trips. In the wars between the English and the Scots and the Civil War, for instance, success depended on capturing important towns and castles; train trips can often follow the routes the advancing or retreating armies took and you can visit buildings that still bear the scars of battle.

Roman Britain offers great possibilities for a theme tour. The Romans were unerring judges of strategic locations and their settlements are mostly key points on the railway network today – York, Newcastle, Carlisle, Chester, Lincoln, Exeter and many more.

For art-lovers there are a great number of galleries outside London, some of them housing important collections. Nearly all of them can be visited on day trips from most major cities. Most cities also have museums, too, with local collections of great interest. In addition to municipal museums of local and natural history a large number of specialist museums have recently grown up. Industrial archaeology is particularly well served: you can visit mills and mines and watch all sorts of machines at work.

Britain's natural beauties could make very suitable subjects for train-trip themes. You could, for instance, concentrate on mountains and moorland – trains run through, into or very close to most of the mountain, hill and moorland areas in Scotland, Wales, the Lake District, the Pennines, Exmoor and Dartmoor. You can even go to the top of Snowdon by train. In many cases you can find an excursion combining a train trip with a coach tour of the area.

These and many other areas offer possibilities for walking or cycling trips by train. With the aid of a map you can often plan a walking or cycling outing in which you start out on one line and come back on another. Kent and Sussex are particularly rich in possibilities of this sort – Lenham to Headcorn, Charing to Pluckley or Selling to Chilham, for instance.

Waterways suggest many theme trips. The railways originally competed with the canals and served the same places, so it's easy to reach most of Britain's canals and navigable waterways by train, in many cases by excursions which include a boat trip. Thames boat trips start from Oxford, Reading, Windsor, Hampton Court and other places. The Broads can be reached at Norwich, Wroxham and Oulton Broad, the Fenland waterways from Cambridge or Ely and the canal system at many towns in the Midlands, Merseyside and elsewhere.

Estuaries are an interest of their own and offer satisfying trips for those who like to watch ships and yachts. The Thames at Gravesend, Southend or Erith, Harwich town, the Severn at Severn Beach, the Mersey at Liverpool or New Brighton, the Humber at Hull, the Tyne, the Firth of Forth and the Clyde are all good locations for ship-spotters.

Literary pilgrimages could provide a series of outings to some very pleasnt places. Shakespeare at Stratford-upon-Avon and Dr Johnson at Lichfield are easy runs from Birmingham. Dickens' birthplace is an hour and a half down the line from Waterloo at Portsmouth. You can reach the Brontës' home at Haworth by steam train on a preserved line from Keighley.

Dickens, who loved railways, would provide a theme on his own, taking in not only Portsmouth but Sudbury (the model for Eatanswill) on the branch from Marks Tey, Ipswich (a Pickwickian stop), Great Yarmouth for its *David Copperfield* connections, Broadstairs and Chatham where Dickens lived, and many more.

Sports fans need no telling about theme trips. Soccer supporters following their teams all over the country, often by special trains, already have the most extensive programme of theme trips in the country. Cricket, tennis and rugby followers take day trips to watch their sports and even chess enthusiasts can have a day out at the Hastings tournament.

There are an astonishing number of arts festivals of different kinds throughout the year, of which the Edinburgh Festival is the most celebrated. They provide chances to enjoy rich offerings of opera, music, drama or poetry concentrated into a few days in one place. The idea that London is the only place to go for first-rate drama is quite mistaken. Plays put on in the great provincial cities are often more adventurous than those to be seen in London. An overnight trip to see a play and explore a strange city makes a very satisfying weekend outing.

Information to help in planning any theme trips, and maybe to suggest others, can be obtained from national and regional tourist boards (addresses on page 231), from books about your special subject in the local library and from magazines covering your particular interest (there's a magazine devoted to almost any subject you can think of, and your local reference library can give details).

Train travel lends itself well to many sorts of collecting. Visiting different towns to browse in unfamiliar secondhand bookshops or to seek out pottery or print bargains in markets can be great fun. A variation that can provide an absorbing long-term hobby is to make the trips themselves the collectors' items. Arm yourself with a camera, for example, and see how many railway termini you can collect – a quick count gives something over 130, so you won't run out too quickly. The charm of this is that it will take you down some intriguing branch lines to interesting places you might not otherwise have thought of visiting – Pembroke Dock, Sudbury, Colne, Sheerness or Bishop Auckland.

Best of all is to plan tours or day trips to follow your own individual interest, the quirkier and more offbeat the better – photographing all the municipal statues of Queen Victoria, for instance, or having a drink at all the pubs in the country called Marquis of Granby. Whatever turns you on could be a fascinating train-trip theme.

11
Preserved Lines

By no means the least of the pleasures of train travel is to ride on one of the small railways run by groups of enthusiasts who have saved them from extinction when branch lines have been closed or when quarries have ceased to operate. Many lines which are no longer a commercial proposition can be kept going by people prepared to give their services for the fun of taking part in the running of a railway. Railway preservation groups now represent an important leisure activity, drawing on apparently inexhaustible funds of dedication by enthusiasts of all ages and classes. The timetables of more than twenty-five preserved lines are included in the BR Passenger Timetable.

One of the most spectacular of all steam railways is BR's own Vale of Rheidol, its only narrow-gauge passenger line, which climbs up the Rheidol Valley from Aberystwyth to Devil's Bridge 12 miles away and attains a height of 680 feet above sea level.

The line has a gauge of 60 cm (1 ft 11½ in) and was opened in 1902, mainly to serve the lead and other mines at the head of the valley. These have long been closed but the old workings can still be seen.

From Aberystwyth main railway station, trains hauled by veteran steam engines *Prince of Wales*, *Owain Glyndwr* and *Llewelyn* take an hour to move steadily up the south side of the valley to Aberffrwd, 200 feet above sea level, then struggle up another four miles of twisting track, sometimes on a ledge overhanging a precipitous drop, to gain another 480 feet to the top of the valley. There are breathtaking views over the tree-clad hills and tumbling river from the upper stretches of the line.

Devil's Bridge, three minutes walk from the terminus, is actually three bridges, one above the other. According to legend, the lowest was built by the devil, who claimed as payment the first soul to cross the bridge. The villagers sent a dog over.

A nature trail round the area takes in the Mynach Falls, with a 400 ft drop into a gorge, and many other superb views.

Preserved lines vary from the picturesque narrow-gauge railways of Wales to standard-gauge branch lines recently part of the BR network. Many such lines run through beautiful country. Some serve as useful public transport links. Others are notable for their rare and exotic locomotives and coaches. Many provide the excitement of steam-railway travel. Together they form a rich field of railway enjoyment spread all over the country. A selected list is given on pages 232–4.

From the riches available I chose three that happened to fit into my travels. Their charms and attractions and the enthusiasm of their operators are typical of many other preserved lines.

The Ravenglass and Eskdale

The signal clicked into the down position, the 2-8-2 steam locomotive *River Esk* gave a raucous whistle and the 12.50 Ravenglass to Dalegarth train was off on time with a satisfying series of chuffs and chunters. Soon she settled into a purposeful rhythmic chuff-a-chuff and began a steady climb into the hills leaving a wreath of white smoke behind her.

We were on the Ravenglass and Eskdale Railway and I was living once again one of the satisfying experiences of childhood, a ride on a steam train. All these years later, I discovered, it was as thrilling as ever. After the bland smoothness of the InterCity expresses there was a feeling here of a living thing putting forth its strength triumphantly, of an effort being made, a battle against inertia being won. It felt more akin to riding a horse.

No wonder parents who remember steam trains will travel many miles to renew the experience for themselves and give their children this thrill. But among the 200 passengers of all ages on our train (eight wooden coaches, some covered, some open) there were also many who had come because this seven-mile train journey into the hills was the most enjoyable possible way of seeing some wonderful country.

From Ravenglass, on the Cumbrian coast, the train moves steadily up into the Cumbrian mountains, first up the valley of the little River Mite, then over Muncaster Fell into the Esk Valley. At each turn in the line there are new views of this wild and rugged country and ahead loom the distant heights of Whin Rigg and

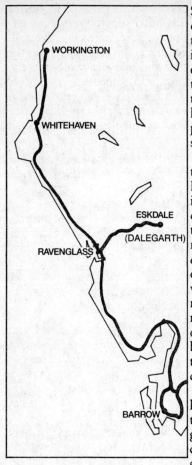

Scafell. A ride on an open coach through this landscape is the best way, other than walking, to get the feel of it and enjoy the sounds and sights of the mountains. Even when the train is hauled by a diesel locomotive, as sometimes happens, it is still an experience to savour.

I was enjoying the ultimate treat of a ride on the footplate. In front of me was a bewildering array of brasswork and copper pipes. Beside me Peter, the engine-driver, moved the regulator which governed *River Esk*'s performance. Every so often he reached behind him with a hand shovel and put more coal into the glowing furnace in front of us, spreading it deftly where it was wanted. We both sat on the front of the tender with our feet in a low compartment close to the rails.

The Ravenglass and Eskdale, known to its many friends as the T'laal Ratty, is a narrow-gauge line with a mere 15 inches between the rails, the same gauge as the Romney, Hythe and Dymchurch miniature railway. The *River Esk* and some of the other locomotives are scaled-down versions of standard-gauge steam locomotives. One or two, however, are original designs. *Northern Rock*, built in the Ratty's own workshops, looks slightly Victorian with her tall chimney and large gleaming dome but is highly practical and is claimed to be the most powerful 15-inch gauge locomotive in the world.

The Ratty began life as a working railway of three-foot gauge, bringing iron ore from the mines in the mountains down to the coast. When the mining company failed the line was bought in 1915 by W. J. Bassett-Lowke, the well-known model railway engineer, who converted it to the narrow gauge. It began a new lease of life carrying mail and goods as well as passengers, but in recent years has concentrated on holiday traffic. It carries up to 300,000 passengers a year and pays its own way with the aid of a large number of volunteers who help with track maintenance and railway operation.

In many ways the Ratty is surprisingly modern and businesslike. Its signalling system, involving radio control of all trains from the signal box at Ravenglass, is an efficient and economical method BR is adopting for some of its branch lines.

The Ratty has a keen nose for fund-raising enterprises. One building taken over from Ravenglass BR station is now a pub, the Ratty Arms. Another is a museum setting out the line's industrial history. Catering in the station buffets at Ravenglass and Dalegarth is let out to a concessionaire. The line has even got a productive relationship with its nuclear neighbours at Sellafield: apprentices from the nuclear establishment get practical experience by helping to build the Ratty's locomotives.

Although the Ratty has taken to building its own locomotives its stable includes locomotives from a number of different builders, including the 4-4-2 *Synolda*, built by Bassett-Lowke in 1912. *River Esk*, though looking like a miniature main-line express engine, was actually built in 1923 to haul quarry trains.

The line makes a splendid day out and the steam-hauled excursion from Crewe, with connections from as far away as London, gives passengers time to ride up and down the Ratty. It is also very popular with walkers. Some fine, wild country in Eskdale can be reached by the Ratty's trains from Dalegarth and the intermediate stations.

The North Yorkshire Moors

Often the very reason that caused a railway line to be closed is a good reason for reopening it. So it has been with the North Yorkshire Moors Railway from Grosmont, on the Middlesbrough-Whitby line, to Pickering 18 miles to the south. The reason was that the line has very little ordinary passenger potential. Few people live within reach of the railway and there

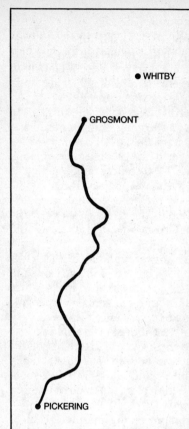

are no industries along the way to generate freight. It therefore made excellent sense for Dr Beeching, the celebrated railway butcher of the 1960s, to axe this unprofitable line.

It made excellent sense to reopen it later for exactly the same reason – it runs through the beautiful North York Moors National Park in an area where there are few roads, and so could carry holiday-makers through or into the National Park without the provision of new roads and car parks in places where they would be intrusive. Add steam locomotives and a band of enthusiastic volunteers and you have a formula for a reopened railway that pays its way.

The North Yorkshire Moors Railway is part of a line originally built by George Stephenson to provide a horse-drawn service between Whitby and Pickering. George Hudson, the railway king of the 1840s, bought the line, extended it from Pickering to Malton on the York-Scarborough line, and made it possible to run through trains from London to Whitby. Stephenson's horses were replaced by steam engines and a deviation was built to avoid a stretch of line where Stephenson had provided a one-in-ten incline up which carriages were pulled by rope. The new line had an incline of one in 49, still one of the steepest on any standard-gauge passenger route.

Today the line connects at Grosmont, its northern terminus, with the pretty Esk Valley line from Middlesbrough to Whitby. It is possible to travel by rail from Whitby or Middlesbrough down the North Yorkshire Moors line to Pickering on a combined BR-NYMR ticket.

The railway is operated by a permanent staff of twenty-five, augmented by volunteer labour, with the enthusiasm and panache common to most preserved railways. I travelled from Grosmont on one of the steam services – there are also diesel trains – and found it an exhilarating experience even on a misty day.

Grosmont has a small but cheerful buffet on the platform and a cup of coffee got the journey off to a warming start. Our train was made up of old BR centre-aisle coaches of about mid-1950s vintage reupholstered in what looked like old cinema carpeting. The steam locomotive was a black 0-8-0 colliery tank engine, one of a stable of twenty steam and five diesel engines owned by the railway. Not all of these are in running order but only three are needed at any one time to maintain the summer service. The railway has its own workshops at Grosmont and also restores old coaching stock.

The journey of about an hour runs through forest, rock cliffs and moorland and over a peat bog. To cross this Stephenson sank timber piles and sheep fleeces filled with heather to make a firm foundation. When the rails buckled one hot summer an engine and two carriages sank in the bog but were later recovered.

The line rises to a summit of 550 feet above sea level and shortly before this point is reached the three outsize golf balls of the Fylingdales early-warning system can be seen. They are actually fibreglass covers for radar scanners and stand 150 feet high, adding an eerie touch of science fiction to a landscape of timeless beauty and grandeur.

There are three intermediate stations on the line and at each of these, Goathland, Newtondale Halt and Levisham, passengers are encouraged to get off and walk through the forests. Leaflets setting out routes and likely times taken for various walks are available. You can walk through forests and over moorland which cannot be reached by any other form of public transport or by car. Walkers can expect to see kestrels, woodpeckers, curlew and heron; even passengers who do not leave the train may see roe deer and foxes. This great area of peaceful country beauty and sparkling air can be reached from industrial Middlesbrough in a little more than an hour.

To make ends meet the North Yorkshire Moors Railway has introduced some enterprising special services. Once a week the railway runs a train of Pullman coaches built in 1960, *Opal* and *Garnet* parlour cars with kitchen car *Robin*. A five-course meal is served while the train makes the return journey.

Pickering, the end of the line and headquarters of the railway trust, is a little town of some character with a ruined castle which until recently belonged, oddly, to the Duchy of Lancaster. It was built in the twelfth century and English monarchs used to enjoy visiting it to hunt wild boar and deer. The town of attractive hilly streets of stone houses is a popular centre for touring the North York Moors.

The Festiniog

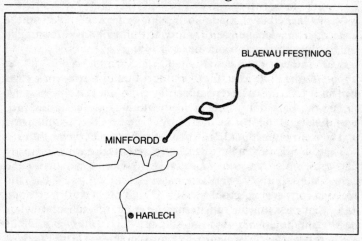

Waiting on Minffordd station I heard a series of raucous steam whistles, then puffs of white smoke. Moments later the train which had been climbing a gradient in a curved cutting rounded the bend briskly and clanked into the station with impressive hisses. It was hauled by a strange green and black steam locomotive with gleaming brasswork. It had a chimney and brass dome at either end with the driving cab in the middle, like two tank engines welded together end to end. Smoke was coming from both tall chimneys. This was the redoubtable Double Fairlie locomotive *Merddin Emrys*. Following was a train of eight brown passenger coaches, all well filled: third-class, buffet and first-class observation coach.

This was the 10.44 Porthmadog to Blaenau train of the Festiniog Railway. I joined it at Minffordd from the British Rail station, to which the FR one is connected by a short path, for one of the most impressive and enjoyable train rides of my tour.

The Festiniog is a narrow gauge (60 cm – 1 ft 11½ in) line built originally as a horse-drawn railway to bring slate down from the quarries at Blaenau Ffestiniog in the mountains to the little port of Porthmadog 13½ miles away. Steam engines were introduced and passenger services started in the 1860s and in its day the Festiniog was profitable, efficient and enterprising. Its double-ended steam locomotives are unique and it was the first railway in Britain to introduce bogie coaches, with pivoted groups of wheels to give flexibility on curves.

When bigger ships made Porthmadog uncompetitive and the slate quarries declined the railway fell on evil days. It stopped operations when war broke out in 1939.

After the war enthusiasts bought the abandoned line and set about restoring it. The track – in part built afresh – now joins British Rail at a new interchange station in Blaenau.

Today it is a flourishing concern, running eleven trains each way during a long season, and enjoys a well-deserved popularity.

The train I joined had come from the Porthmadog terminus, a solid stone building in the town, with cafeteria, information office and museum. It had run first across the Cob, an embankment across the mouth of the River Glaslyn forming part of a land reclamation scheme. From here there are fine views of Snowdon and other peaks in the range. After coming off the Cob the line had begun the climb into the mountains which continues until the summit is reached just before Tanygrisiau, a mile from Blaenau. The steam engine pulled the long, well-filled train briskly into Minffordd station with no hint of strain and continued to the summit with no loss of speed except for station stops.

When the train stopped at Minffordd train staff sprang into action. The collector jumped down and opened doors – these are kept locked when the train is in motion as a safety precaution – and we were settled and away in a matter of seconds.

The observation car with individual chairs at the rear of the train represents the railway's de luxe travel. Third class (the Festiniog, like the pre-war railway companies, doesn't have second class) consists of coaches with wooden seats, mostly with cushions.

I had no sooner settled in my seat than the buffet car steward appeared to take orders for refreshments; coffee was served to us shortly after. I could have had draught beer, I learned; the Festiniog claims to be the only railway that serves it on the trains.

At every station there was the same eager enjoyment of the procedures of railway travel, whether giving information to passengers, working the signals or, at the end of the run, detaching the engine for water and running it round the train for the return trip. Although the railway has a paid permanent staff to do the skilled jobs, many of the others are done by volunteers for the sheer fun of taking part in running a railway. Even if you aren't a train buff yourself, their enthusiasm enhances the trip.

Just what can be achieved by railway enthusiasm was demonstrated at Dduallt, near the top end of the line. During the time the line was abandoned the original route had been submerged in a new lake created in connection with an electricity pumped storage scheme. Festiniog Railway enthusiasts had to create two and a half miles of new track, including a short length of tunnel, in order to overcome this obstacle. On a mountainside this was a tremendous undertaking and involved the creation of the only railway spiral loop in Britain. From Dduallt station the line circles round on an embankment to gain height, crosses on a bridge over itself and continues to climb up the hillside.

The sheer fun of making a steam railway work is only part of the pleasure of the Festiniog. As the train climbs smoothly and steadily up the hillside in the Vale of Ffestiniog the views over mountain and valley open up providing panoramas of Snowdonia that are lost to those driving up the road in the valley below. The line runs through rhododendrons and oak forests, sometimes almost in a tunnel of trees. To be carried through this remote country in such intimate contact with nature, and yet in perfect comfort, has a dreamy, magical quality that lifts the spirit.

Just beyond the halfway mark the line goes through a series of sharp curves and the train arrives at Tan-y-Bwlch, in a bowl in the mountains, the principal intermediate stop. There is a station buffet, a view over a lake towards a range of tree-covered hills and a nature trail – the station is inside Snowdonia National Park. Here, 424 feet above sea level, is a good place to break the journey and go on by the next train.

Further on, the views become more open. At Ddaullt there is a picnic site and at Tanygrisiau there are views of peak after peak stretching away in the Snowdon range.

At first sight, Blaenau looks rather grim, a small stone town under a huge overhanging rock, with a mountain of grey slate filling the immediate view. On the map it might not suggest itself as a place worth visiting. It turned out to be a delightful little town with a couple of friendly pubs, two or three cafés in a miniature market square and a shopping street curving up a hill under the overhanging rock.

Blaenau was once the centre of a busy slate trade and the Llechwedd slate caverns, a mile from the town and accessible by bus, offer a fascinating insight into how the slate was mined a century ago. The caverns have their own electric railway which takes visitors down into the caves from which the slate was quarried. One of them, the Cathedral cave, is 200 feet high and in another the ambience of Victorian slate mining has been recreated and you can try your hand at splitting a slate.

Another slate mine houses a Narrow Gauge Railway Centre, which displays many examples of the locomotives and trucks used on the railways laid down to get the slate out of the mines.

12

This is Where I Get Off

Well, here's my station. This is where I get off. There are very nearly 9000 British Rail route miles to travel, without counting London Transport and the private lines, and all of them are worth a look. I have travelled over most of them but I would still like to see the ones I have missed – perhaps another time.

The fact is that train travel is addictive. The more you have, the more you want. It's very agreeable to arrive, particularly in a strange town with someone to meet you. But train travellers very soon want to be on the move again, to feel the gentle swaying, to hear the clack of wheels over points and have the ever-changing British scene paraded past their seats in all its endless fascination.

Today it is possible to rush up and down between London and Glasgow or Edinburgh at speeds up to 125 mph. This is an impressive technological triumph, of course, and a shrewd bid to compete with the airlines. I prefer to travel at half that speed and get a better look at the country through which I am passing. Fortunately, many BR trains will allow us all to continue to do this while the high speed trains cater for those in a tearing hurry.

Train trips round the country have given me some surprises. Not the Highlands and Wales; I expected these parts of Britain to be as wild and beautiful as I found them. But I had not previously known that you could get anywhere quite so remote and ravishing by train as some of the stations on the Settle and Carlisle line. That doesn't mean getting off the train and then going on by some other form of transport, mark you, but just stepping down and finding it all there for you to walk straight into.

It is these most beautiful stretches of line that are now most threatened. It's not just that traffic is light because the lines do not serve big centres of population. The more wild and beautiful the country the more viaducts, bridges and tunnels are needed to carry a railway line through it. It is these graceful examples of

Victorian civil engineering skill, all at least a century old, that now require expensive maintenance work or rebuilding. Barmouth bridge is one example. It had to be closed for some months and now cannot take big excursion trains. At least one viaduct on the Settle and Carlisle line needs rebuilding. And there are already speed and weight limits on the use of other scenic lines. If we want to save them we must make full use of them.

Again, it was scarcely a surprise to find delight in the beauties of Oxford, Bath or York. Their charms are well-known and for that reason I have not dwelt on them at length. But I was pleasantly surprised to find how rewarding it could be to visit such places as Hartlepool, Hull, Bradford and Liverpool – not perhaps the first places to spring to mind when contemplating an excursion, but making up in character what they lack in conventional appeal.

Britain's railway network is not only a means of shifting vast quantities of people and freight where they need to go. It is also a marvellous leisure playground we can all enjoy, offering trips of almost endless variety and yet wonderfully compact, so that you can get from end to end of it – from Penzance to Wick – in less than 24 hours (and complete the return trip comfortably in a weekend).

In the end what my train rides taught me was this: Britain has some of the most wonderful, varied and beautiful country in the world and some of the most serene and lovely cathedrals set in tranquil cities. But even the most forbidding-looking industrial town the train passes through has something to offer that is worth exploring. It's people that matter; they are different wherever you go and they stamp their character on their towns. This great variety and the ease with which you can sample it are what make train travel in Britain so enduring a pleasure.

Useful Addresses

Tourist Boards

British Tourist Authority, Thames Tower, Black's Road, London W6 9EL

English Tourist Board, 4 Grosvenor Gardens, London SW1W 0DU

Scottish Tourist Board, 23 Ravelston Terrace, Edinburgh EH4 3EU and 19 Cockspur Street, London SW1Y 5BL

Wales Tourist Board, Brunel House, 2 Fitzalan Road, Cardiff CF2 1UY and 2–4 Maddox Street, London W1R 9PN

Cumbria Tourist Board, Ashleigh, Holly Road, Windermere, Cumbria LA23 2AQ

East Anglia Tourist Board, 14 Museum Street, Ipswich IP1 1HU

East Midlands Tourist Board, Exchequergate, Lincoln LN2 1PZ

Heart of England Tourist Board, PO Box 15, Worcester WR1 2JT

Isle of Wight Tourist Board, 21 High Street, Newport, IOW, PO30 IJI

London Tourist Board, 26 Grosvenor Gardens, London SW1W 0DU

Northumbria Tourist Board, 9 Osborne Terrace, Jesmond, Newcastle upon Tyne NE2 1NT

North West Tourist Board, Last Drop Village, Bromley Cross, Bolton, Lancs BL7 9PZ

South East England Tourist Board, 1 Warwick Park, Tunbridge Wells, Kent TN2 5TA

Southern Tourist Board, The Old Town Hall, Leigh Road, Eastleigh, Hants SO5 4DE

Thames and Chilterns Tourist Board, 8 The Market Place, Abingdon, Oxon OX14 3UD

West Country Tourist Board, PO Box 73, Exeter EX1 1RJ

Yorkshire and Humberside Tourist Board, 312 Tadcaster Road, York YO2 2HF

Railway Societies

The following societies and other organizations are among those that organize tours. See also the classified columns of *Railway Magazine*.

Chiltern Trains, 13 Golden Hills, Chinnor, Oxford OX9 4PT
F and W Railtours, 13–15 Stroud Road, Gloucester GL1 5AA
Hertfordshire Railtours, 28 Chestnut Walk, Welwyn, Herts AL6 0SD
Lea Valley Railway Club, 61 Vicarage Road, Ware, Herts SG12 7BE
Linkwise Tours, Bacton Road, Edingthorpe, North Walsham, Norfolk NR28 9SP
Locomotive Club of Great Britain, 69 Burnt Ash Lane, Bromley BR1 4DJ
Metro Railtours, 6 Shay Grove, Heaton, Bradford BD9 6SP
Midland Railfans, 25 Bridlewood, Streetly, Sutton Coldfield B74 3HD
Monmouthshire Railway Society, 105 Lavernock Road, Penarth, S. Glamorgan CF6 2QG
National Railway Enthusiasts Association, 26 Elm Green Close, Worcester WR5 3HD
Railway Correspondence and Travel Society, 28 Maidavale Crescent, Coventry CV3 6FZ
Railway Development Society, 15 Clapham Road, Lowestoft, Suffolk NR32 1RQ
Railway Enthusiasts Society, 7 Ollderdale Close, Allerton, Bradford, BD15 9BT
Sherwood Railtours, 39 Kilton Glade, Worksop, Notts S81 0PX
Southern Electric Group, 6 Cliveden Close, Chelmsford CM1 2NP
South Tynedale Travel, 26 Springwell Avenue, Durham DH1 4LY
Sunway Travel, 50 Pennhouse Avenue, Wolverhampton WV4 4BE

Preserved Lines

Here is a selected list of steam railways operated by preservation societies.

Standard Gauge

Kent and East Sussex Railway	Tenterden Town Station Tenterden, Kent	*Tenterden Town to Hexden Bridge (5 miles)*
Bluebell Railway	Sheffield Park Station nr Uckfield, East Sussex	*Sheffield Park to Horsted Keynes (5 miles)*

Dart Valley Railway	Buckfastleigh Station Buckfastleigh, Devon	*Buckfastleigh to Totnes Riverside (7 miles)*
Torbay and Dartmouth Railway	Queens Park Station Paignton, Devon	*Paignton to Kingswear (7 miles)*
Mid-Hants Railway	Alresford Station Alresford, Hants	*Alresford to Medstead (6 miles)*
West Somerset Railway	Minehead Station Minehead, Somerset	*Minehead to Bishop's Lydeard (20 miles)*
Great Central Railway	Great Central Station PO Box 33 Loughborough, Leics	*Loughborough to Rothley (5 miles)*
Nene Valley Railway	Wansford Station Old North Road, Stibbington, Peterborough, Northants	*Wansford to Orton Mere (Peterborough) (5 miles)*
North Norfolk Railway	Sheringham Station Sheringham, Norfolk	*Sheringham to Weybourne (3 miles)*
Severn Valley Railway	The Railway Station Bewdley, Worcs	*Bridgnorth to Kidderminster (16½ miles)*
Keighley and Worth Valley Railway	Haworth Station Keighley, West Yorkshire	*Keighley to Oxenhope (5 miles)*

North Yorkshire Moors Railway	Pickering Station Pickering, North Yorkshire	*Grosmont to Pickering (18 miles)*
Strathspey Railway	The Station, Boat of Garten, Inverness-shire, Scotland	*Boat of Garten to Aviemore (Speyside) (5 miles)*
Narrow Gauge **Sittingbourne and Kemsley Light Railway**	48 Taverners Road, Rainham, Kent	*Sittingbourne to Kemsley Down (2 miles)*
Festiniog Railway	Harbour Station Porthmadog, Gwynedd, Wales	*Porthmadog to Blaenau (12¼ miles)*
Snowdon Mountain Railway	Llanberis, Gwynedd, Wales	*Llanberis to Snowdon Summit (4 miles)*
Talyllyn Railway	Wharf Station Tywyn, Gwynedd, Wales	*Tywyn to Nant Gwernol (7¼ miles)*
Welshpool and Llanfair Light Railway	Llanfair Station Llanfair, Llanfair Caereinion, Wales	*Llanfair Caereinion to Sylfaen (5¼ miles)*
Ravenglass and Eskdale Railway	Ravenglass, Cumbria	*Ravenglass to Dalegarth (7 miles)*

Museums

National Railway Museum, Leeman Road, York
Steamtown Railway Museum, Warton Road, Carnforth, Lancs

BTA Overseas Offices

AUSTRALIA

British Tourist Authority
Associated Midland House
171 Clarence Street
Sydney N.S.W. 2000
T: (02) 29-8627

BELGIUM

British Tourist Authority
Rue de la Montagne
52 Bergstraat, B2
1000 Brussels
T: 02/511.43.90

BRAZIL

British Tourist Authority
Avenida Ipiranga 318A, 12° Andar,
conj. 1201
Edifício Vila Normanda
01046 São Paulo = SP
T: 257-1834

CANADA

British Tourist Authority
94 Cumberland Street, Suite 600
Toronto, Ontario
M5R 3N3
T: (416) 925-6326

DENMARK

British Tourist Authority
Møntergade 3
DK-1116 København
T: (01) 12 07 93

FRANCE

British Tourist Authority
6 Place Vendôme
75001 Paris
T: (1) 42 96 47 60

GERMANY

British Tourist Authority
Neue Mainzer Str. 22
6000 Frankfurt am Main 1
T: (069) 2380750

HONG KONG

British Tourist Authority
Suite 903
1 Hysan Avenue
Hong Kong

IRELAND

British Tourist Authority
Clerys
O'Connell Street
Dublin 1

ITALY

British Tourist Authority
Via S. Eufemia 5
00187 Rome
T: 678 4998 or 678 5548

JAPAN

British Tourist Authority
Tokyo Club Building
3-2-6 Kasumigaseki, Chiyoda-ku
Tokyo 100
T: (03) 581-3603

MEXICO

British Tourist Authority
Edificio Alber
Paseo de la Reforma 332–5 Piso
06600 Mexico DF
T: 533 6375

NETHERLANDS

British Tourist Authority
Leidseplein 5
1017 PR Amsterdam
T: (020) 23.46.67

NEW ZEALAND

British Tourist Authority
c/o Box 2402
Auckland

NORWAY

British Tourist Authority
Mariboes gt 11
0183 Oslo 1
T: (02) 41 18 49

SINGAPORE

British Tourist Authority
14 Collyer Quay 05-03
Singapore Rubber House
Singapore 0104
T: Singapore 2242966/7
Tlx: 28493 BTA SIN

SOUTH AFRICA

British Tourist Authority
7th Floor JBS Building
107 Commissioner Street
Johannesburg 2001
PO Box 6256
Johannesburg 2000
T: (011) 29 6770

SPAIN

British Tourist Authority
Torre de Madrid 6/4
Plaza de España
Madrid 28008
T: (91) 241 13 96

SWEDEN

British Tourist Authority
For visitors: Malmskillnadsg 42 1st Floor
For mail: Box 7293
S-103 90 Stockholm
T: 08-21 24 44

SWITZERLAND

British Tourist Authority
Limmatquai 78
8001 Zurich
T: 01/47 42 77 or 47 42 97

USA CHICAGO

British Tourist Authority
John Hancock Center Suite 3320
875 N. Michigan Avenue
Chicago
Illinois 60611
T: (312) 787 0490

USA DALLAS

British Tourist Authority
Plaza of the Americas
North Tower Suite 750
Dallas
Texas 75201
T: (214) 720 4040

USA LOS ANGELES

British Tourist Authority
612 South Flower Street
Los Angeles
California 90017
T: (213) 623-8196

USA NEW YORK

British Tourist Authority
40 West 57th Street
New York
N.Y. 10019
T: (212) 581-4700
Tlx: 237798

Index